# CLAW, FANG AND BLADE

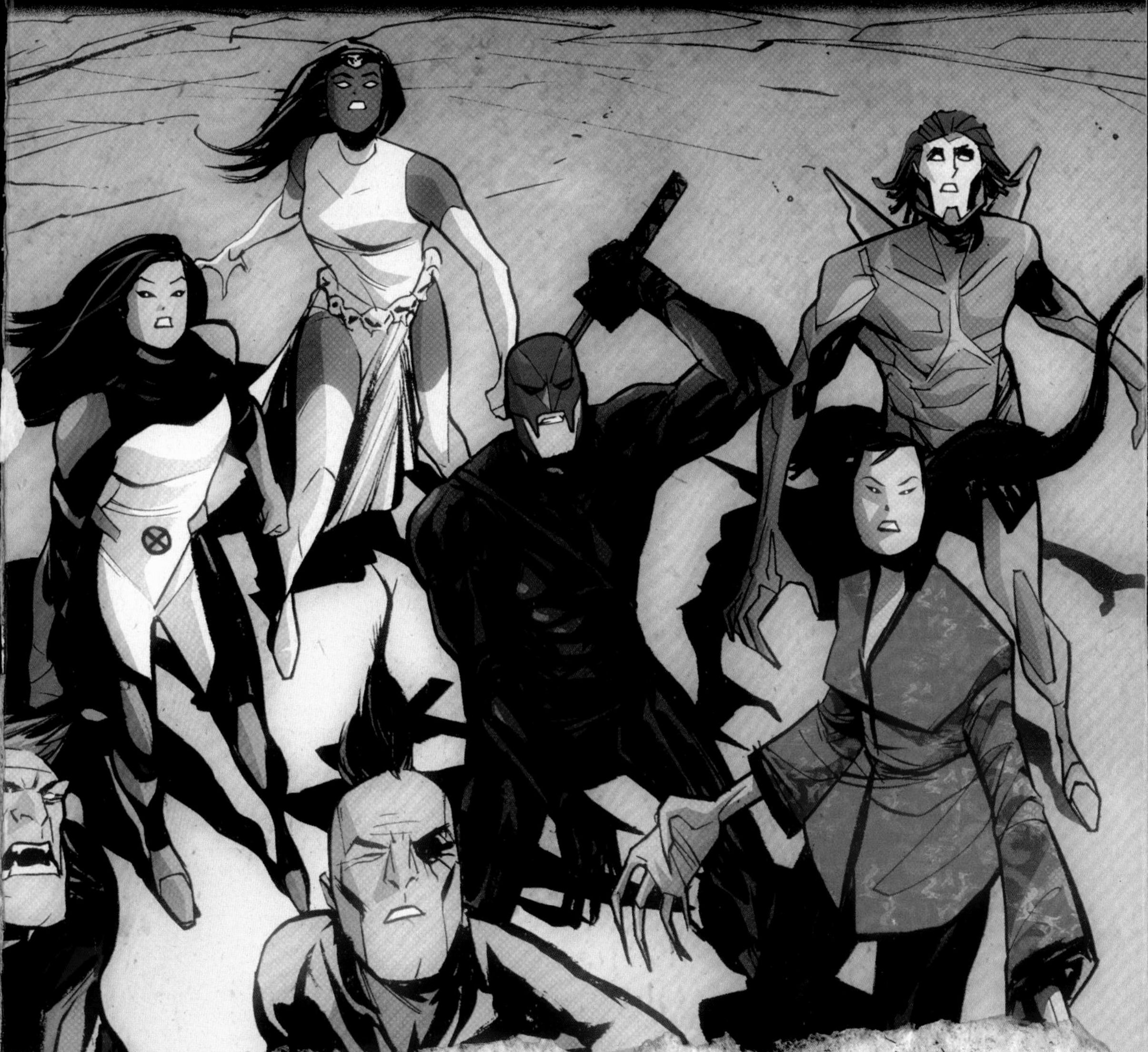

# WOLVERINES

## PARADISE

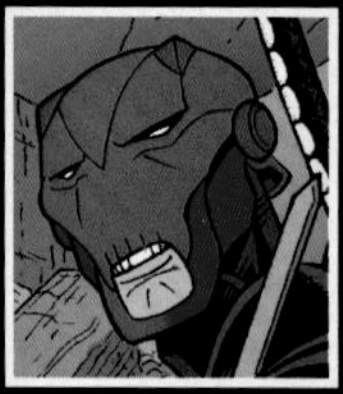

SHOGUN

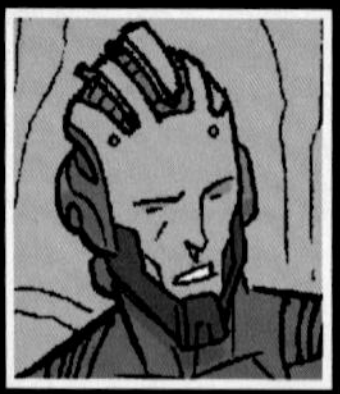

NEURO

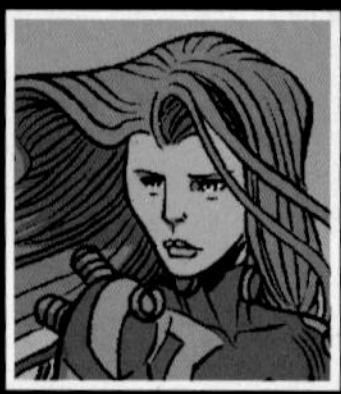

ENDO

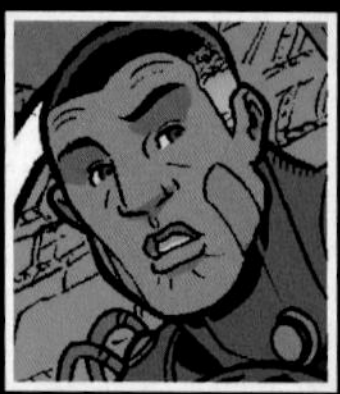

SKEL

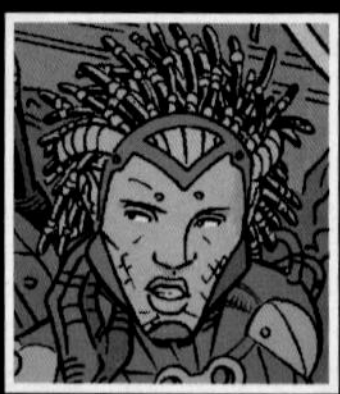

JUNK

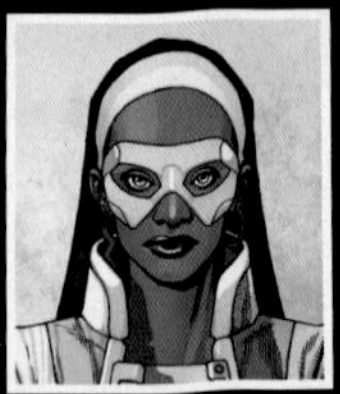

FANTOMELLE

## THE WOLVERINES

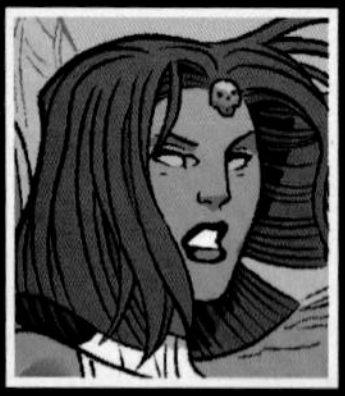

MYSTIQUE

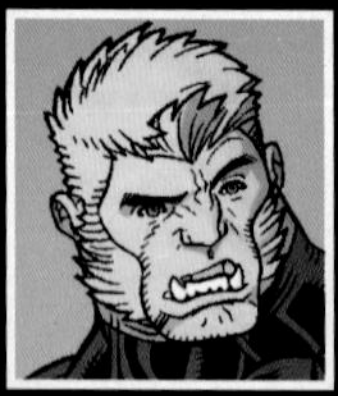

SABRETOOTH

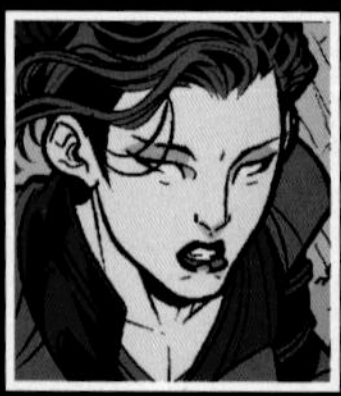

LADY DEATHSTRIKE

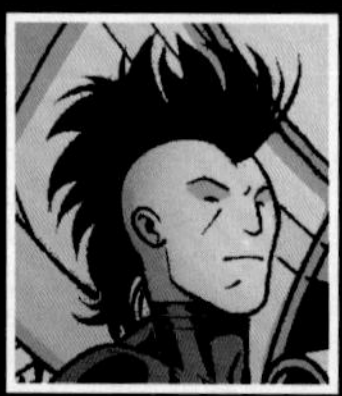

DAKEN

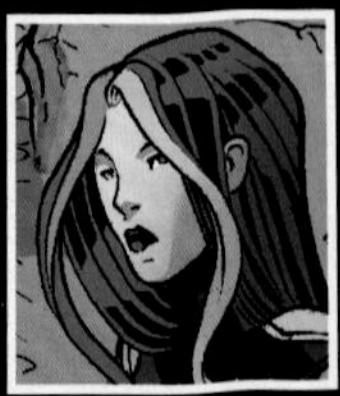

X-23

# the wolverine is dead. His legacy remains.

Logan met his end while destroying a revamped version of the Weapon X Project located in a facility known as Paradise.

Logan could not escape, but others did — five test subjects, all granted strange new powers. None were ever intended to survive outside the program, and all have been infused with a ticking clock in their DNA that will kill them unless it can be deactivated.

These lost weapons kidnapped a group of five of Wolverine's deadliest associates in the hope that their healing factors might hold the answer to saving the test subjects' lives. The refugees from Paradise hold significant leverage over the five killers — secret "control words" that can manipulate, sedate or even kill each of them.

Having now teamed up with another Paradise survivor, Fantomelle, and her psychic-linked fox Culpepper, the two teams infiltrated Mister Sinister's secret fortress intending to retrieve the potential key to their salvation — the remains of Wolverine! But the untimely arrival of the X-Men may put a quick end to their efforts...

COLLECTION EDITOR: **JENNIFER GRÜNWALD**
ASSISTANT EDITOR: **SARAH BRUNSTAD**
ASSOCIATE MANAGING EDITOR: **ALEX STARBUCK**
EDITORS, SPECIAL PROJECT: **MARK D. BEAZLEY**
SENIOR EDITOR, SPECIAL PROJECTS: **JEFF YOUNGQUIST**
SVP PRINT, SALES & MARKETING: **DAVID GABRIEL**

EDITOR IN CHIEF: **AXEL ALONSO**
CHIEF CREATIVE OFFICER: **JOE QUESADA**
PUBLISHER: **DAN BUCKLEY**
EXECUTIVE PRODUCER: **ALAN FINE**

**WOLVERINES VOL. 2: CLAW, BLADE AND FANG.** Contains material originally published in magazine form as WOLVERINES #6-10. First printing 2015. ISBN# 978-0-7851-9287-9. Published by MARVEL WORLDWIDE, INC., a subsidiary of MARVEL ENTERTAINMENT, LLC. OFFICE OF PUBLICATION: 135 West 50th Street, New York, NY 10020.  **Printed in Canada.** ALAN FINE, President, Marvel Entertainment; DAN BUCKLEY, President, TV, Publishing and Brand Management; JOE QUESADA, Chief Creative Officer; TOM BREVOORT, SVP of Publishing; DAVID BOGART, SVP of Operations & Procurement, Publishing; C.B. CEBULSKI, VP of International Development & Brand Management; DAVID GABRIEL, SVP Print, Sales & Marketing; JIM O'KEEFE, VP of Operations & Logistics; DAN CARR, Executive Director of Publishing Technology; SUSAN CRESPI, Editorial Operations Manager; ALEX MORALES, Publishing Operations Manager; STAN LEE, Chairman Emeritus. For information regarding advertising in Marvel Comics or on Marvel.com, please contact Jonathan Rheingold, VP of Custom Solutions & Ad Sales, at jrheingold@marvel.com. For Marvel subscription inquiries, please call 800-217-9158. **Manufactured between 4/3/2015 and 5/11/2015 by SOLISCO PRINTERS, SCOTT, QC, CANADA.**

10 9 8 7 6 5 4 3 2 1

RAY FAWKES (#6, #8, #10) & CHARLES SOULE (#7, #9)

ARTISTS
JASON MASTERS (#6), KRIS ANKA (#7), JUAN DOE (#8),
PETER NGUYEN & DEREK FRIDOLFS (#9)
AND JONATHAN MARKS (#10)

COLORISTS
GUY MAJOR (#6), MATTHEW WILSON (#7), JUAN DOE (#8),
JOHN KALISZ (#9) AND LEE LOUGHRIDGE (#10)

# WOLVERINES

## CLAW, FANG AND BLADE

COVER ART
SIMONE BIANCHI (#6), ALEX GARNER (#7), SIMONE BIANCHI &
ADRIANO DALL'ALPI (#8), NICK BRADSHAW & FCO PLASCENCIA (#9)
AND KRIS ANKA (#10)

LETTERER
VC'S CORY PETIT

ASSISTANT EDITOR
CHRISTINA HARRINGTON

EDITORS
KATIE KUBERT
& MIKE MARTS

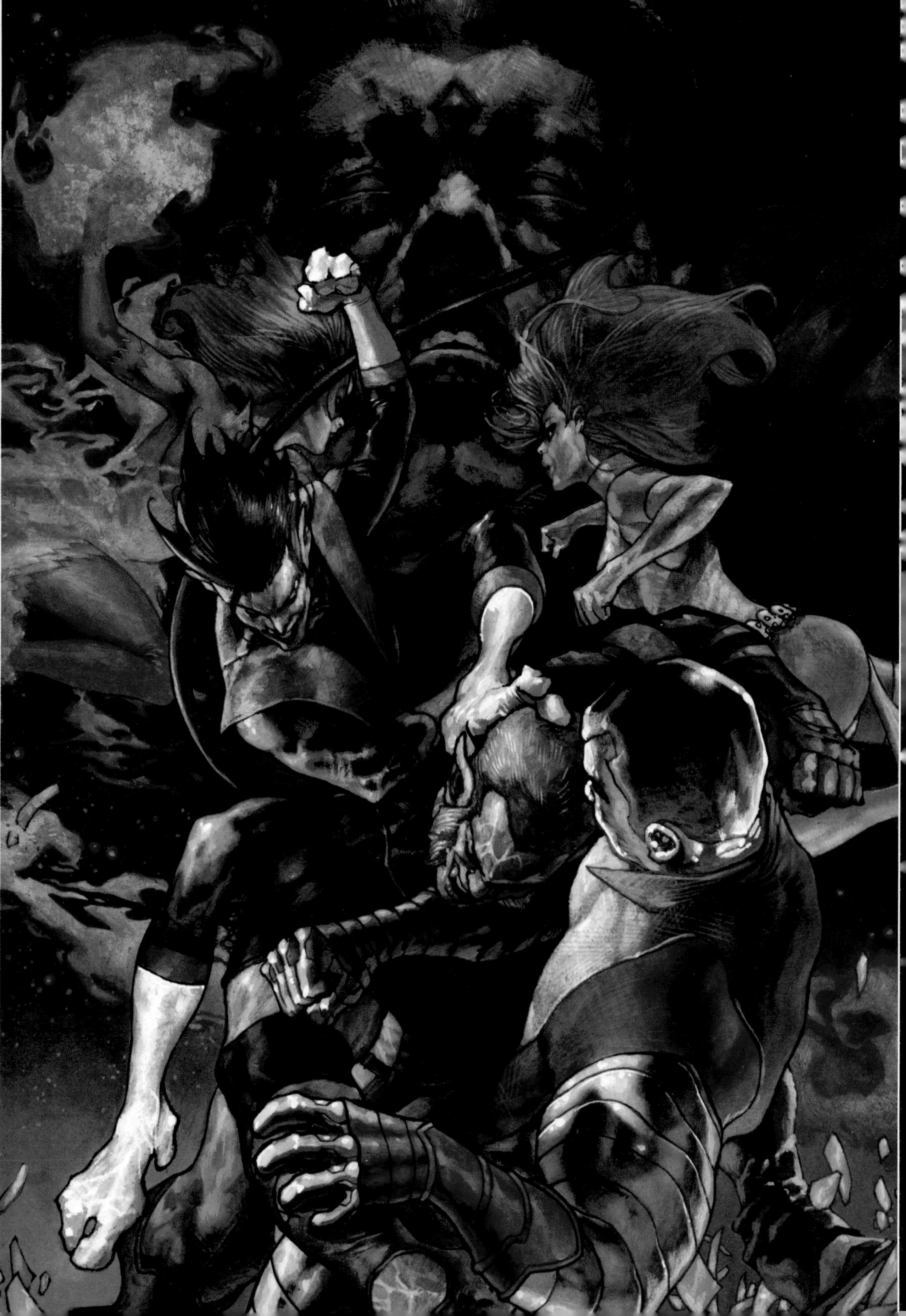

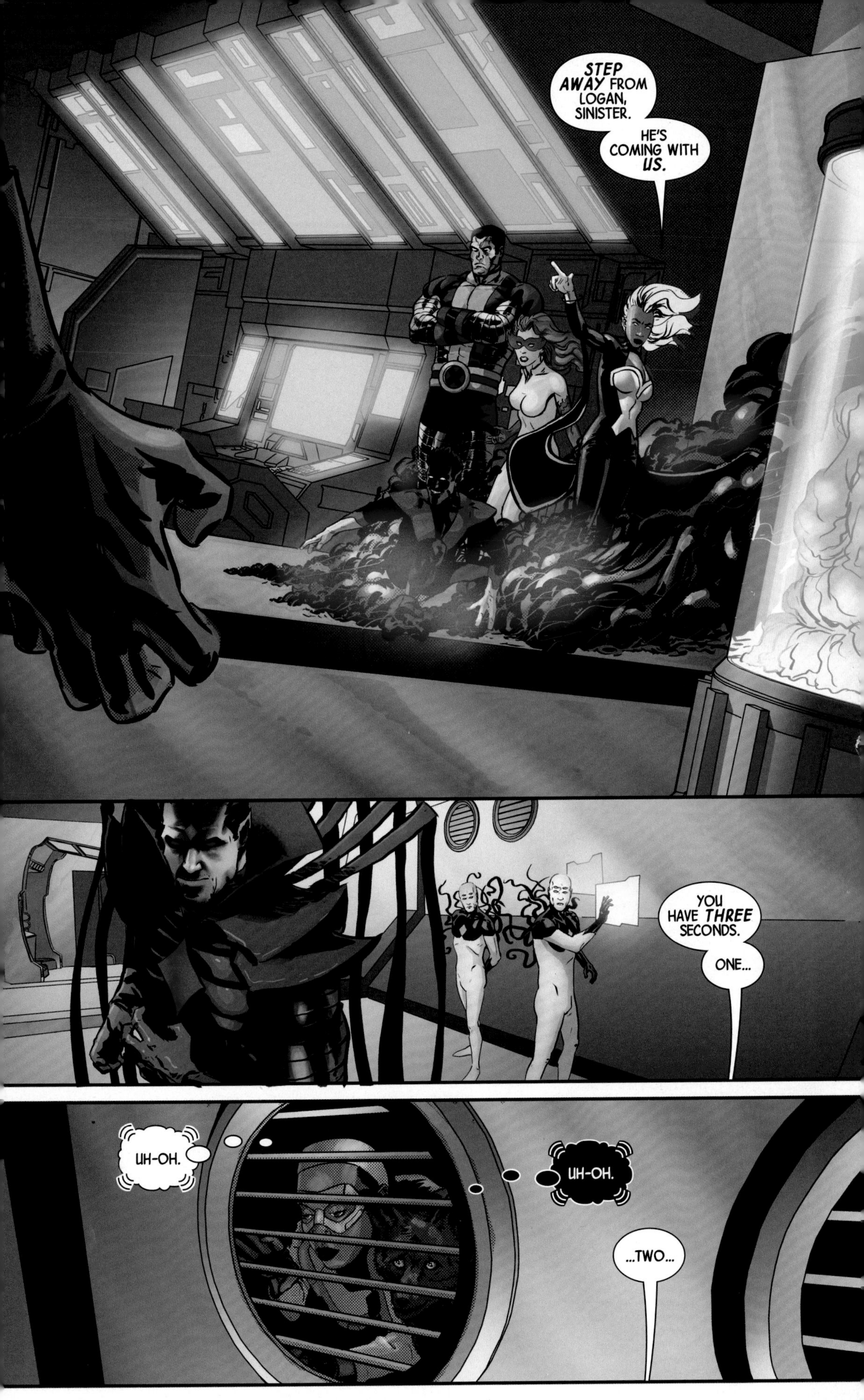
STEP AWAY FROM LOGAN, SINISTER.
HE'S COMING WITH US.
YOU HAVE THREE SECONDS.
ONE...
UH-OH.
UH-OH.
...TWO...

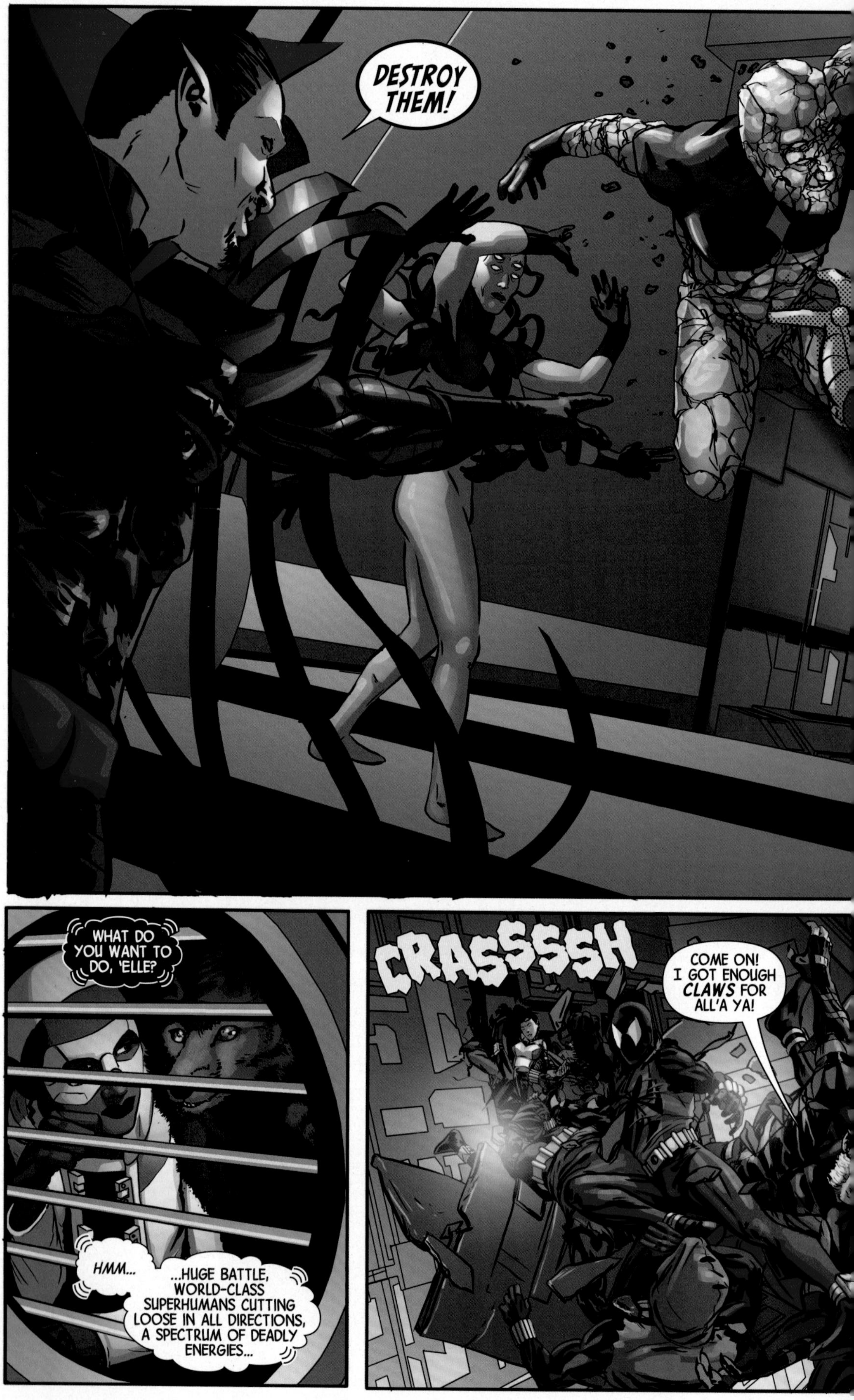
DESTROY THEM!
WHAT DO YOU WANT TO DO, 'ELLE?
HMM...
...HUGE BATTLE, WORLD-CLASS SUPERHUMANS CUTTING LOOSE IN ALL DIRECTIONS, A SPECTRUM OF DEADLY ENERGIES...
CRASSSSH
COME ON! I GOT ENOUGH CLAWS FOR ALL'A YA!

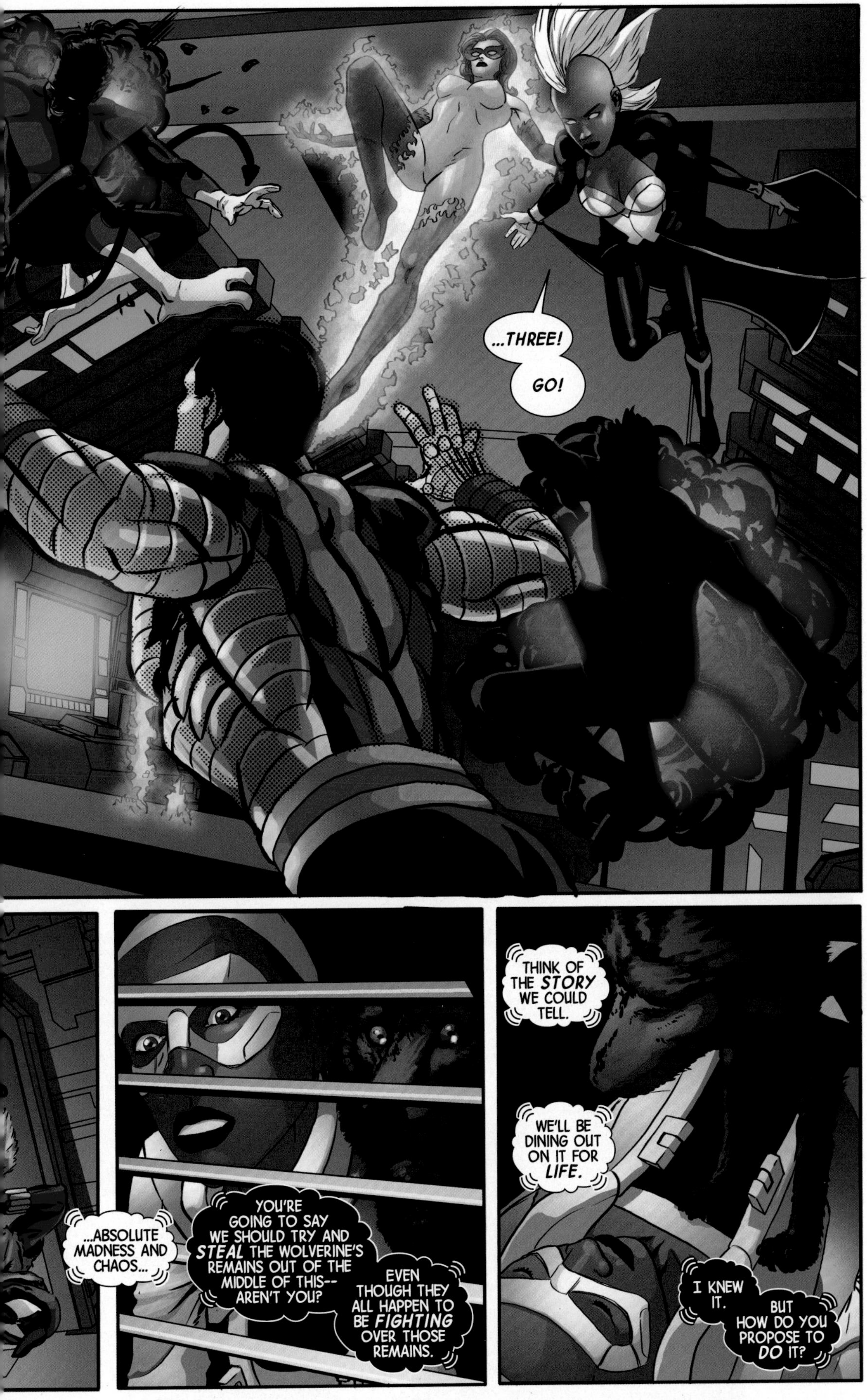
...THREE!
GO!
...ABSOLUTE MADNESS AND CHAOS...
YOU'RE GOING TO SAY WE SHOULD TRY AND STEAL THE WOLVERINE'S REMAINS OUT OF THE MIDDLE OF THIS-- AREN'T YOU?
EVEN THOUGH THEY ALL HAPPEN TO BE FIGHTING OVER THOSE REMAINS.
THINK OF THE STORY WE COULD TELL.
WE'LL BE DINING OUT ON IT FOR LIFE.
I KNEW IT.
BUT HOW DO YOU PROPOSE TO DO IT?

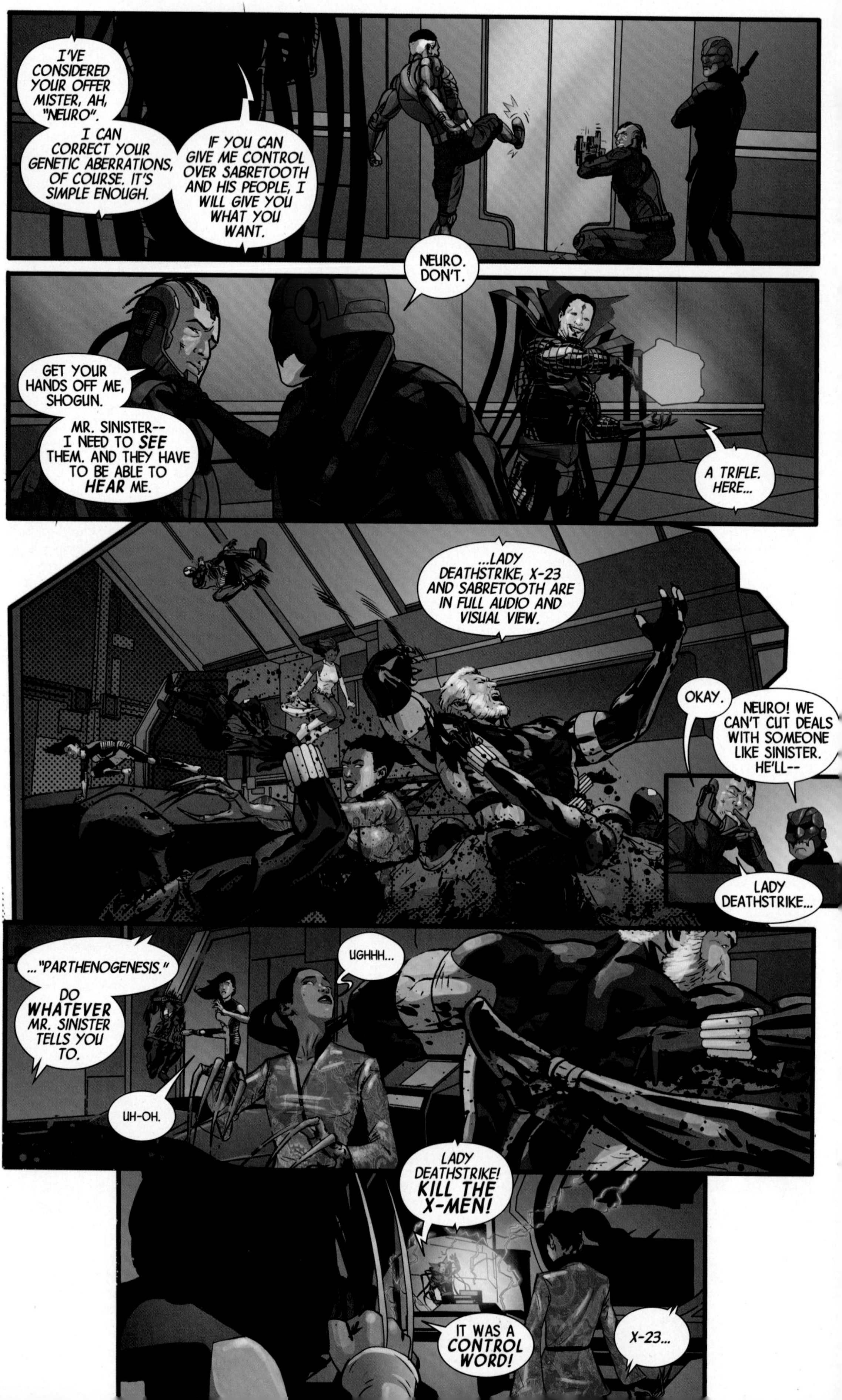
I'VE CONSIDERED YOUR OFFER MISTER, AH, "NEURO".
I CAN CORRECT YOUR GENETIC ABERRATIONS, OF COURSE. IT'S SIMPLE ENOUGH.
IF YOU CAN GIVE ME CONTROL OVER SABRETOOTH AND HIS PEOPLE, I WILL GIVE YOU WHAT YOU WANT.
NEURO. DON'T.
GET YOUR HANDS OFF ME, SHOGUN.
MR. SINISTER-- I NEED TO SEE THEM. AND THEY HAVE TO BE ABLE TO HEAR ME.
A TRIFLE. HERE...
...LADY DEATHSTRIKE, X-23 AND SABRETOOTH ARE IN FULL AUDIO AND VISUAL VIEW.
OKAY.
NEURO! WE CAN'T CUT DEALS WITH SOMEONE LIKE SINISTER. HE'LL--
LADY DEATHSTRIKE...
..."PARTHENOGENESIS."
DO WHATEVER MR. SINISTER TELLS YOU TO.
UGHHH...
UH-OH.
LADY DEATHSTRIKE! KILL THE X-MEN!
IT WAS A CONTROL WORD!
X-23...

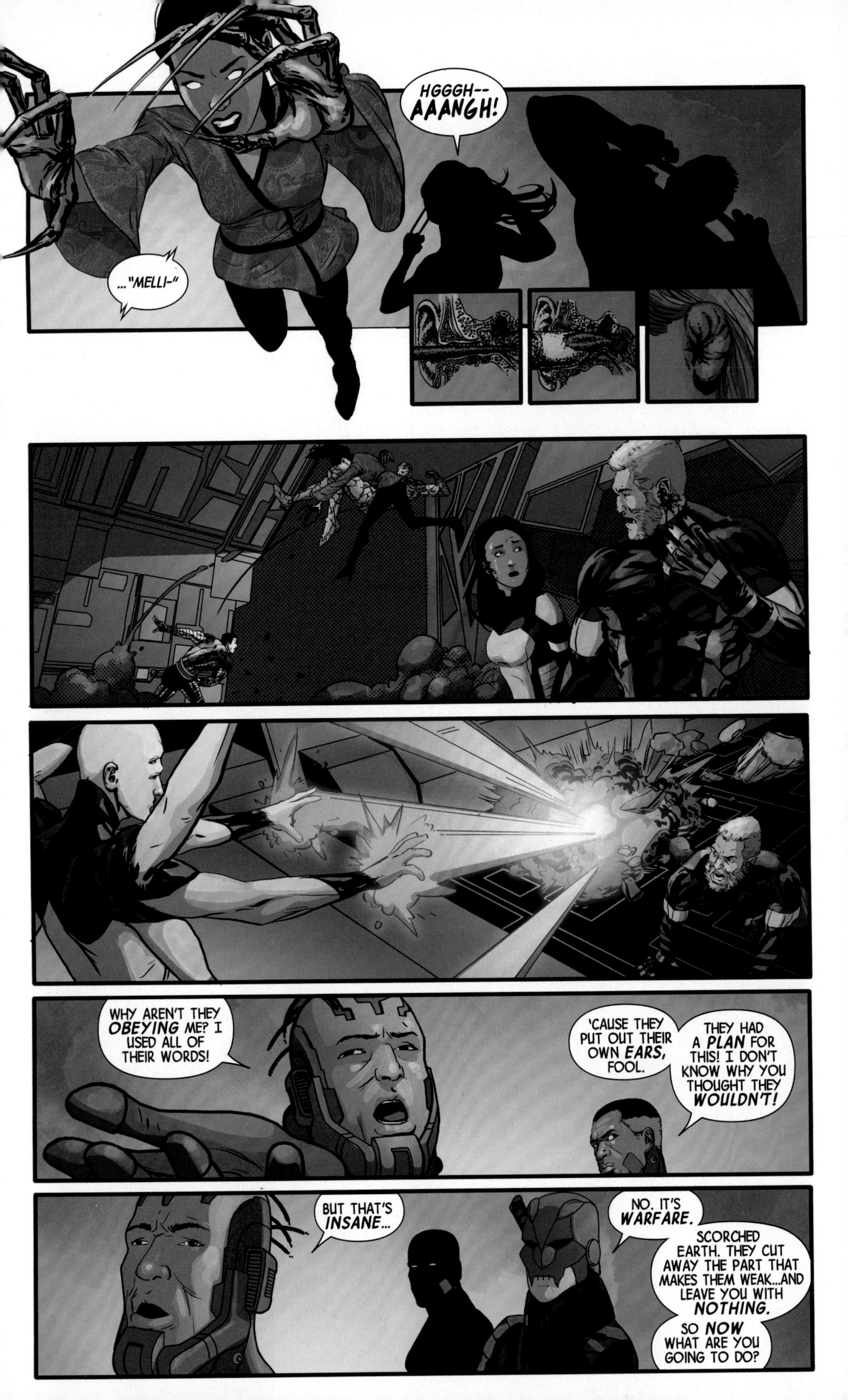
HGGGH--AAANGH!
..."MELLI-"
WHY AREN'T THEY OBEYING ME? I USED ALL OF THEIR WORDS!
'CAUSE THEY PUT OUT THEIR OWN EARS, FOOL.
THEY HAD A PLAN FOR THIS! I DON'T KNOW WHY YOU THOUGHT THEY WOULDN'T!
BUT THAT'S INSANE...
NO. IT'S WARFARE.
SCORCHED EARTH. THEY CUT AWAY THE PART THAT MAKES THEM WEAK...AND LEAVE YOU WITH NOTHING.
SO NOW WHAT ARE YOU GOING TO DO?

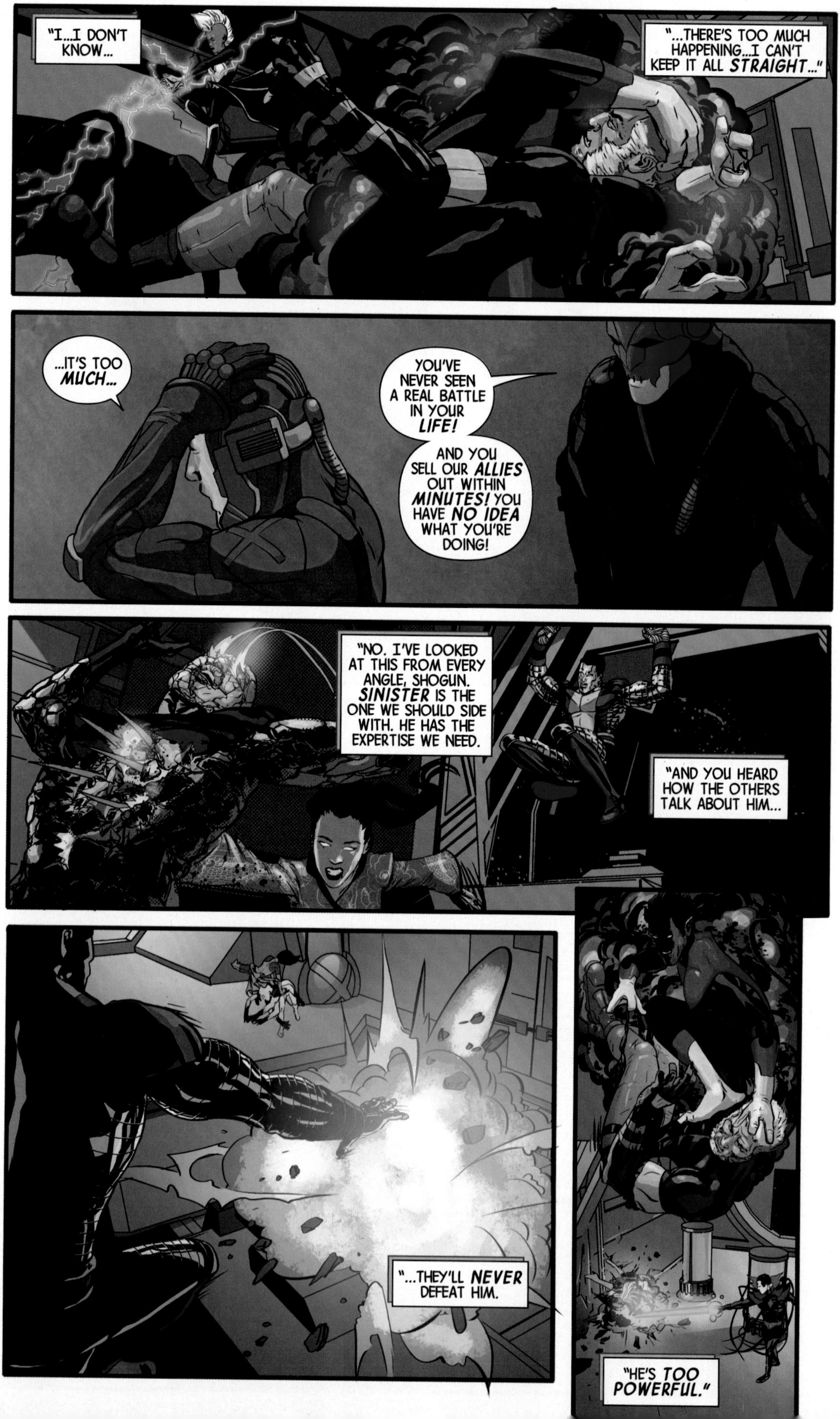
"I...I DON'T KNOW...
"...THERE'S TOO MUCH HAPPENING...I CAN'T KEEP IT ALL STRAIGHT..."
...IT'S TOO MUCH...
YOU'VE NEVER SEEN A REAL BATTLE IN YOUR LIFE!
AND YOU SELL OUR ALLIES OUT WITHIN MINUTES! YOU HAVE NO IDEA WHAT YOU'RE DOING!
"NO. I'VE LOOKED AT THIS FROM EVERY ANGLE, SHOGUN. SINISTER IS THE ONE WE SHOULD SIDE WITH. HE HAS THE EXPERTISE WE NEED.
"AND YOU HEARD HOW THE OTHERS TALK ABOUT HIM...
"...THEY'LL NEVER DEFEAT HIM.
"HE'S TOO POWERFUL."

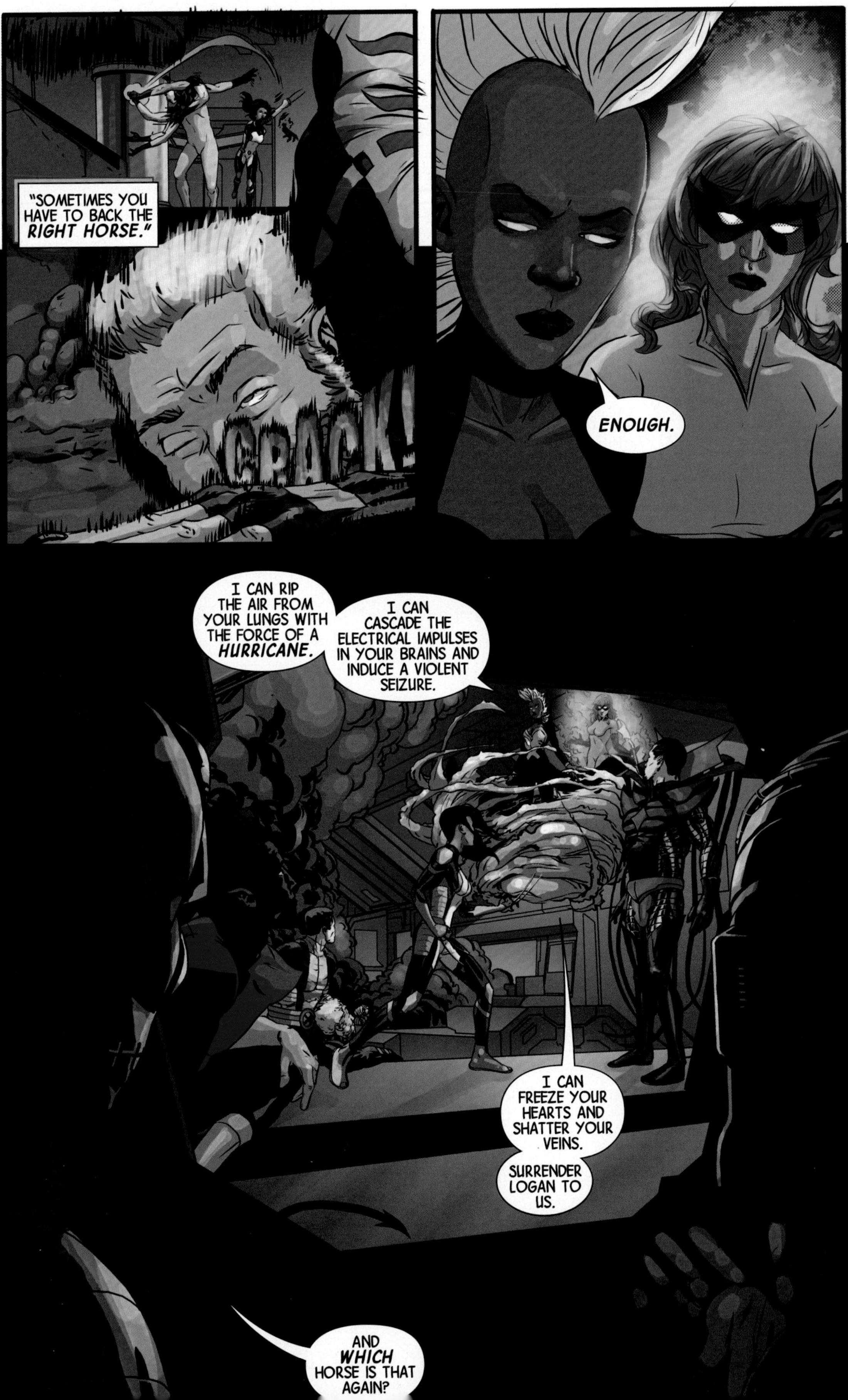
"SOMETIMES YOU HAVE TO BACK THE RIGHT HORSE."
CRACK!
ENOUGH.
I CAN RIP THE AIR FROM YOUR LUNGS WITH THE FORCE OF A HURRICANE.
I CAN CASCADE THE ELECTRICAL IMPULSES IN YOUR BRAINS AND INDUCE A VIOLENT SEIZURE.
I CAN FREEZE YOUR HEARTS AND SHATTER YOUR VEINS.
SURRENDER LOGAN TO US.
AND WHICH HORSE IS THAT AGAIN?

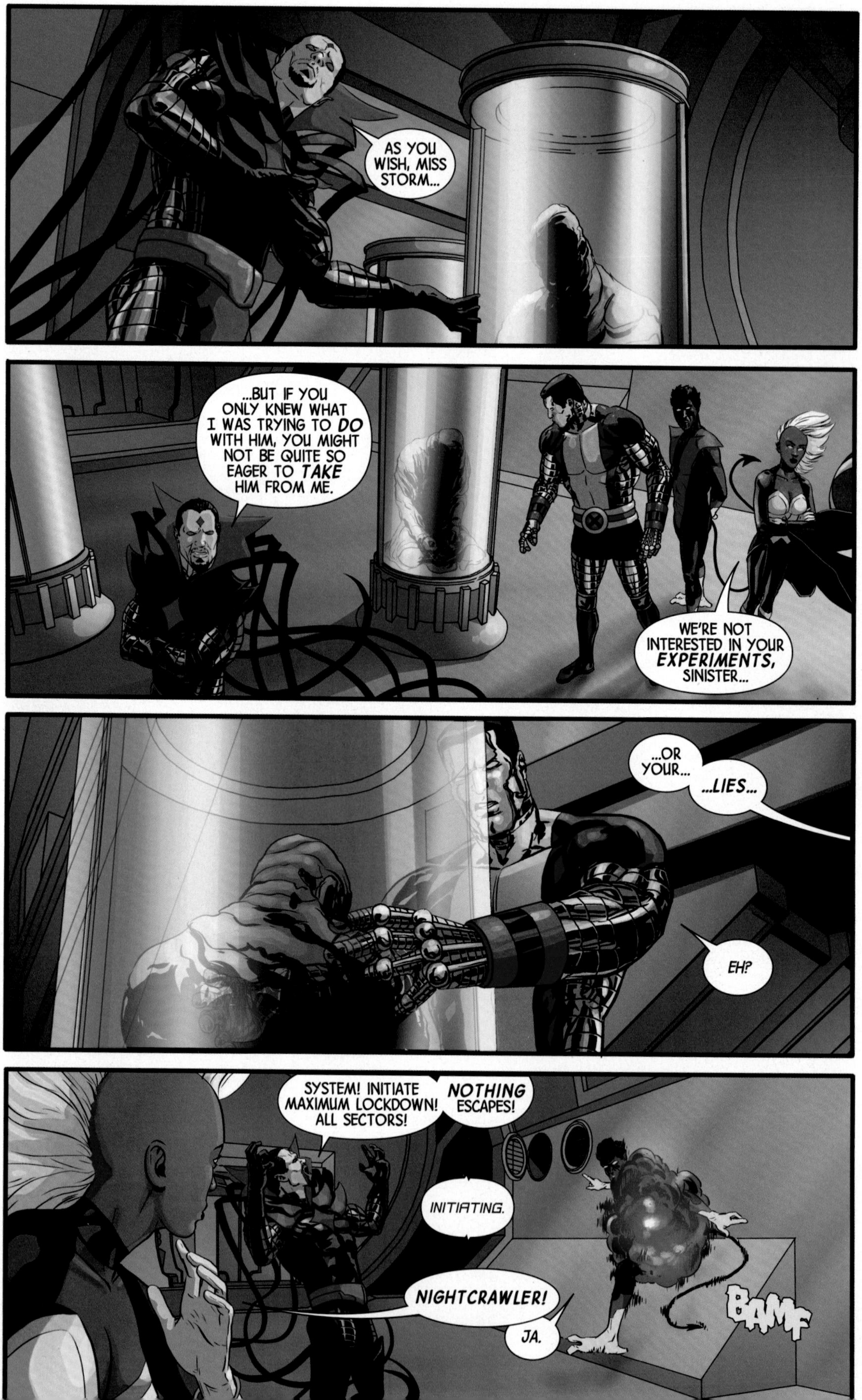
AS YOU WISH, MISS STORM...
...BUT IF YOU ONLY KNEW WHAT I WAS TRYING TO DO WITH HIM, YOU MIGHT NOT BE QUITE SO EAGER TO TAKE HIM FROM ME.
WE'RE NOT INTERESTED IN YOUR EXPERIMENTS, SINISTER...
...OR YOUR...
...LIES...
EH?
SYSTEM! INITIATE MAXIMUM LOCKDOWN! ALL SECTORS!
NOTHING ESCAPES!
INITIATING.
NIGHTCRAWLER!
JA.
BAMF

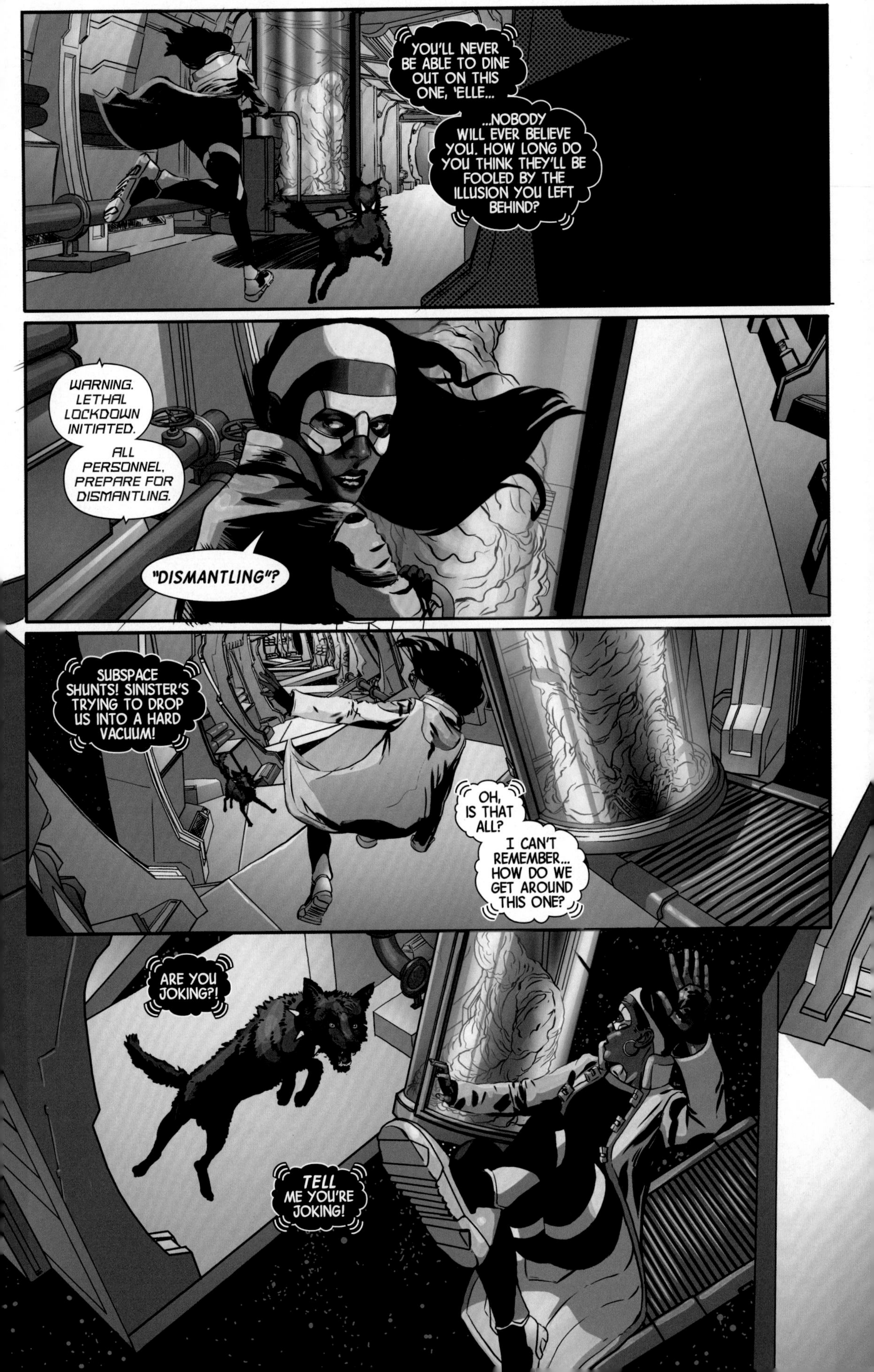
YOU'LL NEVER BE ABLE TO DINE OUT ON THIS ONE, 'ELLE...
...NOBODY WILL EVER BELIEVE YOU. HOW LONG DO YOU THINK THEY'LL BE FOOLED BY THE ILLUSION YOU LEFT BEHIND?
WARNING. LETHAL LOCKDOWN INITIATED.
ALL PERSONNEL, PREPARE FOR DISMANTLING.
"DISMANTLING"?
SUBSPACE SHUNTS! SINISTER'S TRYING TO DROP US INTO A HARD VACUUM!
OH, IS THAT ALL?
I CAN'T REMEMBER... HOW DO WE GET AROUND THIS ONE?
ARE YOU JOKING?!
TELL ME YOU'RE JOKING!

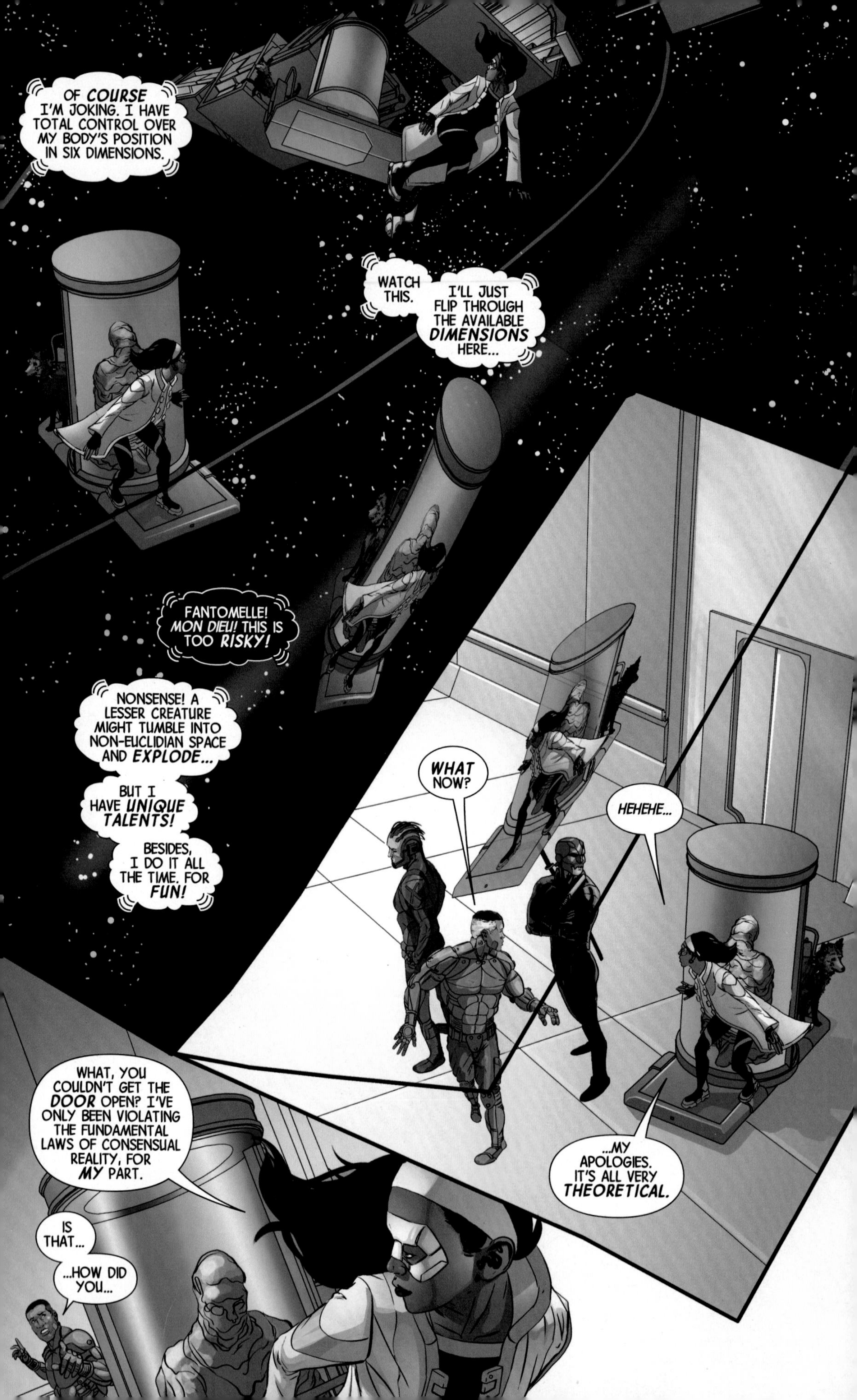

OF COURSE I'M JOKING. I HAVE TOTAL CONTROL OVER MY BODY'S POSITION IN SIX DIMENSIONS.
WATCH THIS.
I'LL JUST FLIP THROUGH THE AVAILABLE DIMENSIONS HERE...
FANTOMELLE! MON DIEU! THIS IS TOO RISKY!
NONSENSE! A LESSER CREATURE MIGHT TUMBLE INTO NON-EUCLIDIAN SPACE AND EXPLODE...
BUT I HAVE UNIQUE TALENTS!
BESIDES, I DO IT ALL THE TIME. FOR FUN!
WHAT NOW?
HEHEHE...
WHAT, YOU COULDN'T GET THE DOOR OPEN? I'VE ONLY BEEN VIOLATING THE FUNDAMENTAL LAWS OF CONSENSUAL REALITY, FOR MY PART.
...MY APOLOGIES. IT'S ALL VERY THEORETICAL.
IS THAT...
...HOW DID YOU...

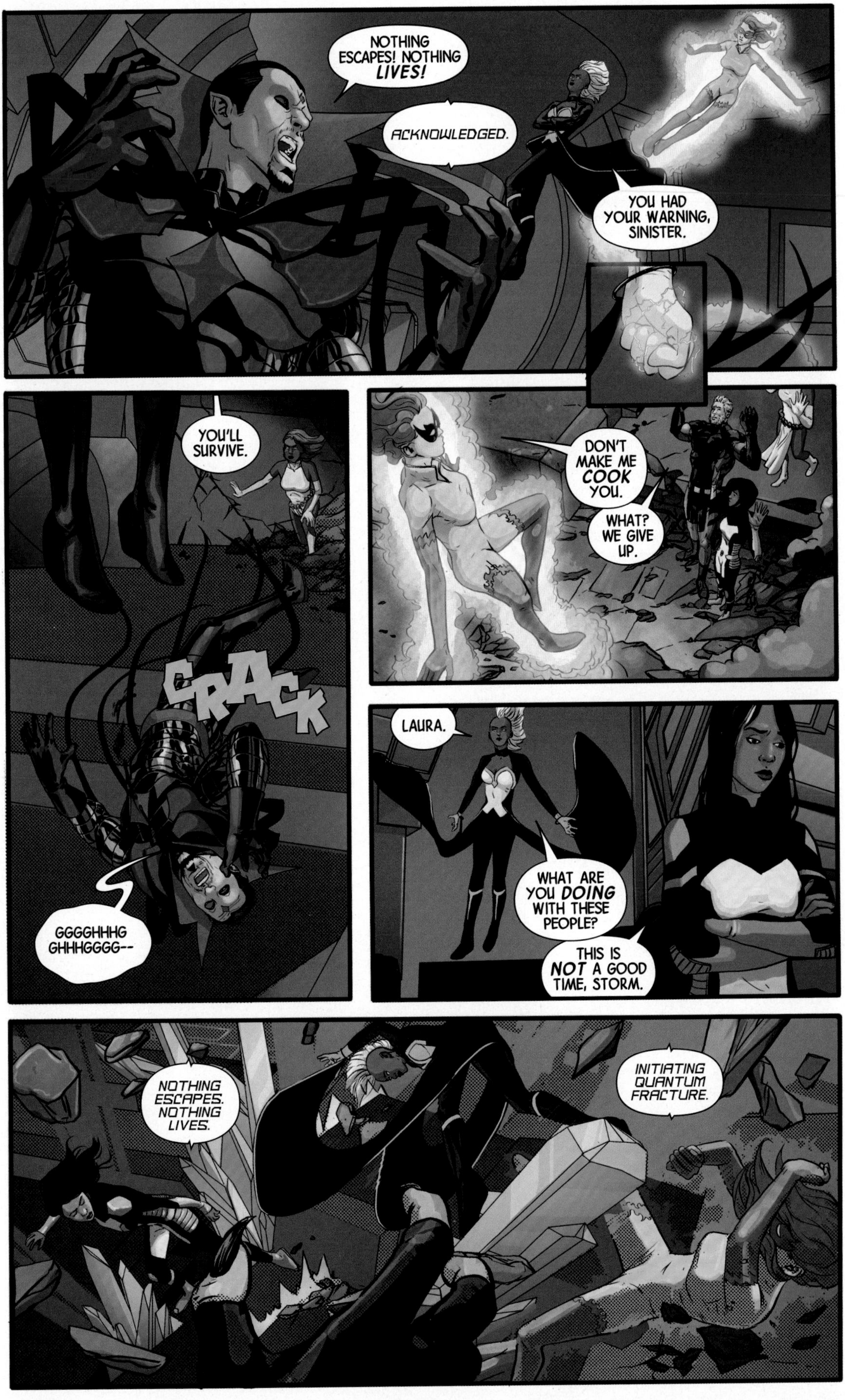
NOTHING ESCAPES! NOTHING LIVES!
ACKNOWLEDGED.
YOU HAD YOUR WARNING, SINISTER.
YOU'LL SURVIVE.
CRACK
GGGGHHHG GHHHGGGG--
DON'T MAKE ME COOK YOU.
WHAT? WE GIVE UP.
LAURA.
WHAT ARE YOU DOING WITH THESE PEOPLE?
THIS IS NOT A GOOD TIME, STORM.
NOTHING ESCAPES. NOTHING LIVES.
INITIATING QUANTUM FRACTURE.

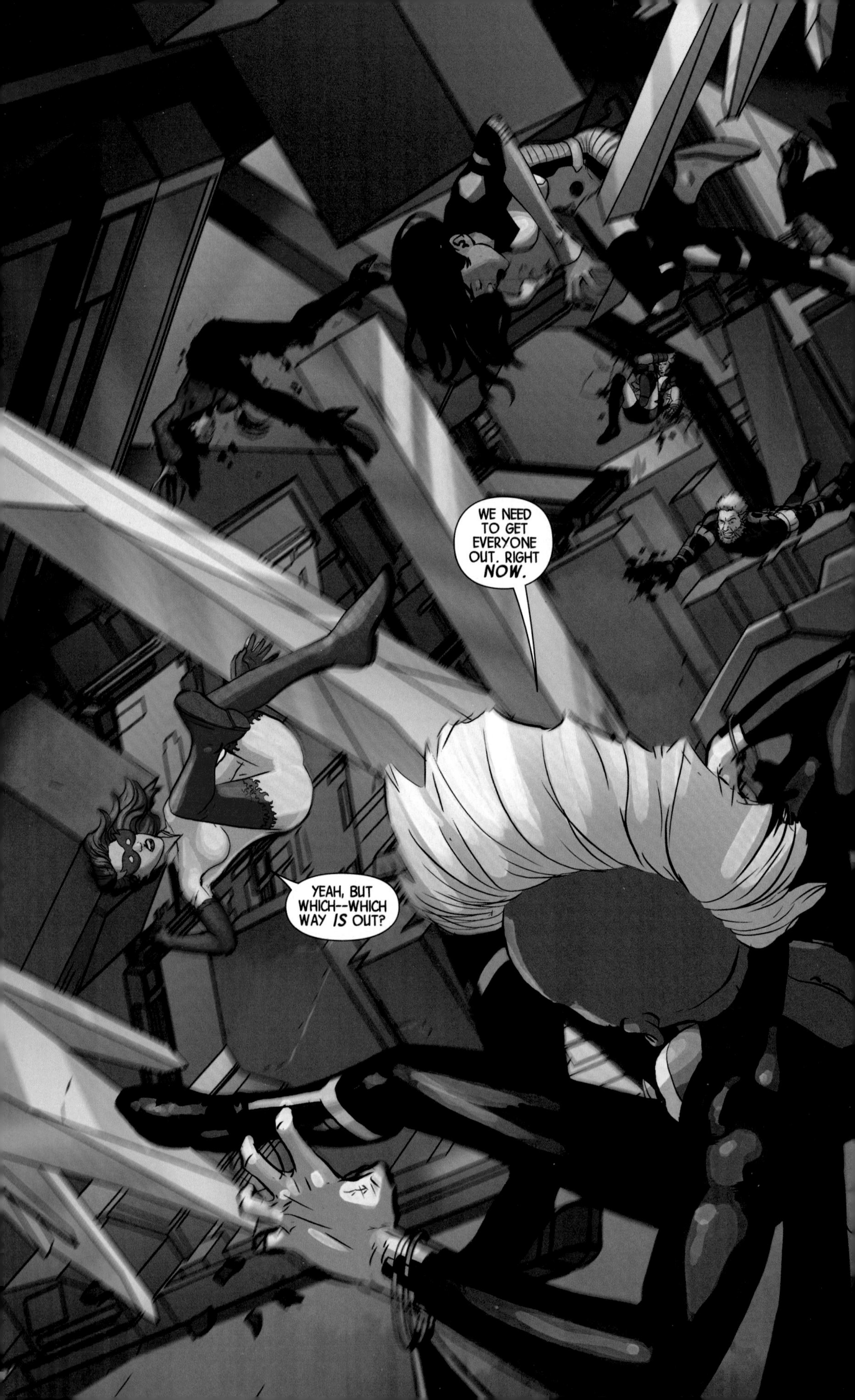
WE NEED TO GET EVERYONE OUT. RIGHT NOW.
YEAH, BUT WHICH--WHICH WAY IS OUT?

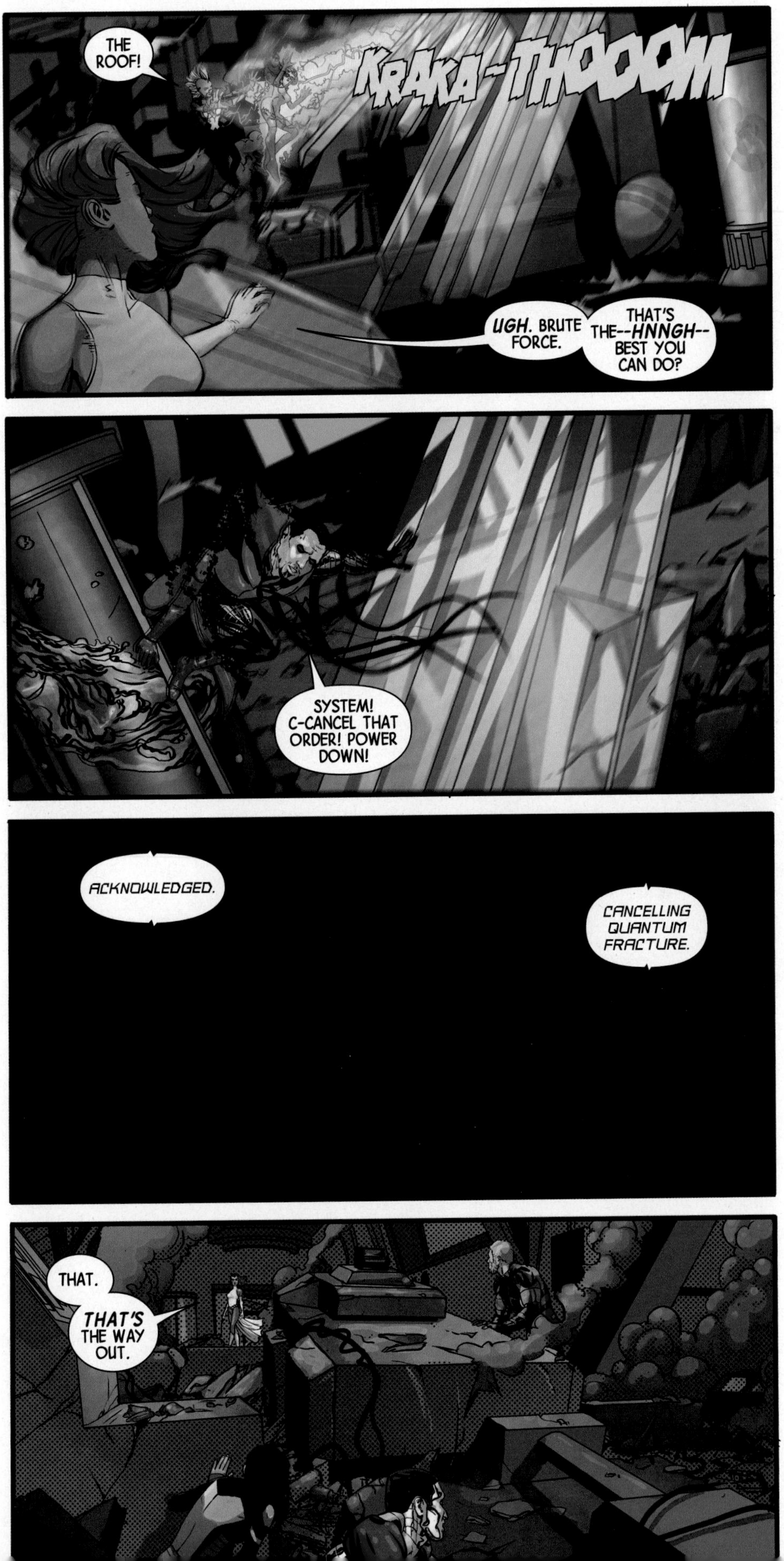
THE ROOF!
KRAKA-THOOOM
UGH. BRUTE FORCE.
THAT'S THE--HNNGH-- BEST YOU CAN DO?
SYSTEM! C-CANCEL THAT ORDER! POWER DOWN!
ACKNOWLEDGED.
CANCELLING QUANTUM FRACTURE.
THAT.
THAT'S THE WAY OUT.

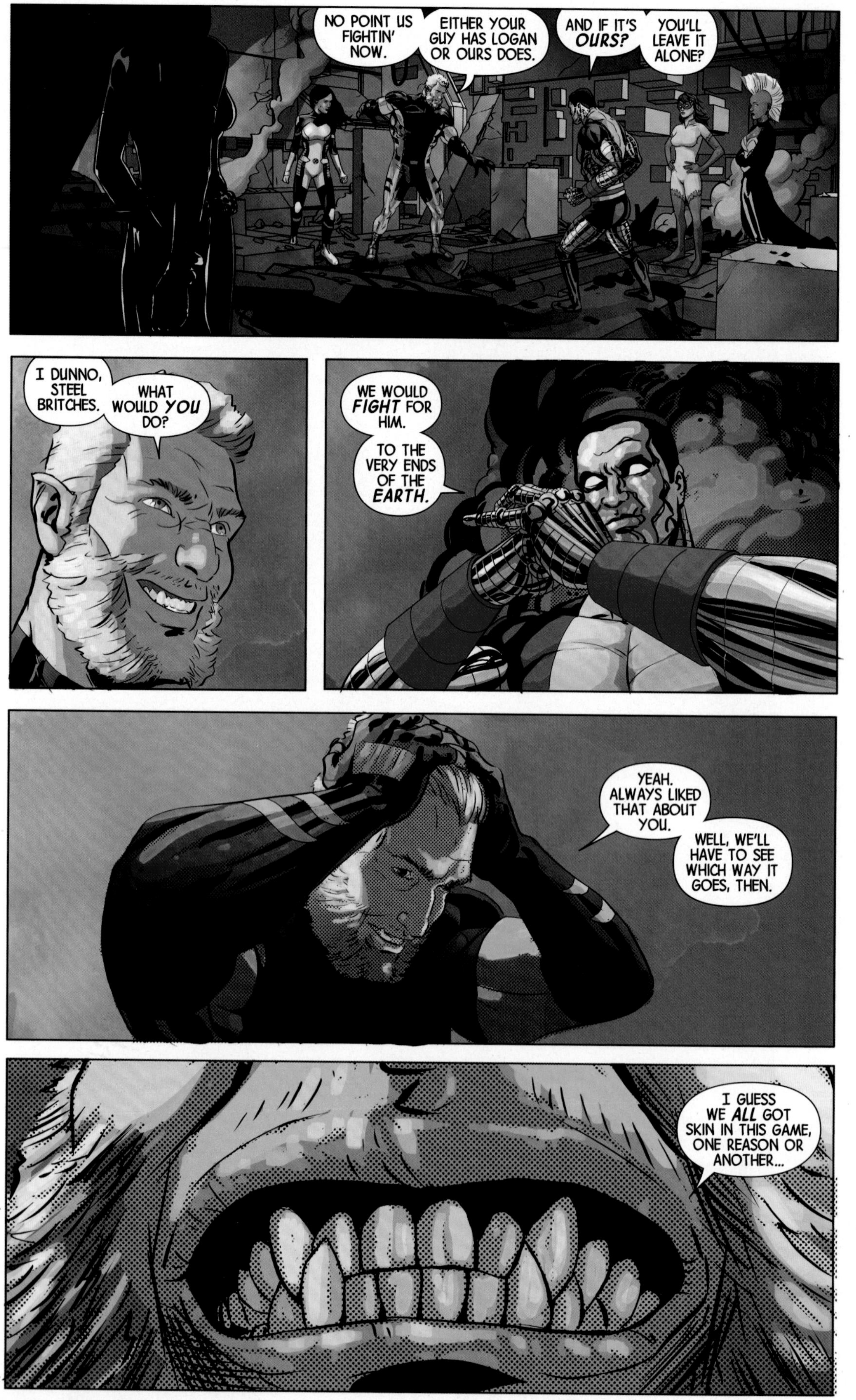
NO POINT US FIGHTIN' NOW.
EITHER YOUR GUY HAS LOGAN OR OURS DOES.
AND IF IT'S OURS?
YOU'LL LEAVE IT ALONE?
I DUNNO, STEEL BRITCHES.
WHAT WOULD YOU DO?
WE WOULD FIGHT FOR HIM.
TO THE VERY ENDS OF THE EARTH.
YEAH. ALWAYS LIKED THAT ABOUT YOU.
WELL, WE'LL HAVE TO SEE WHICH WAY IT GOES, THEN.
I GUESS WE ALL GOT SKIN IN THIS GAME, ONE REASON OR ANOTHER...

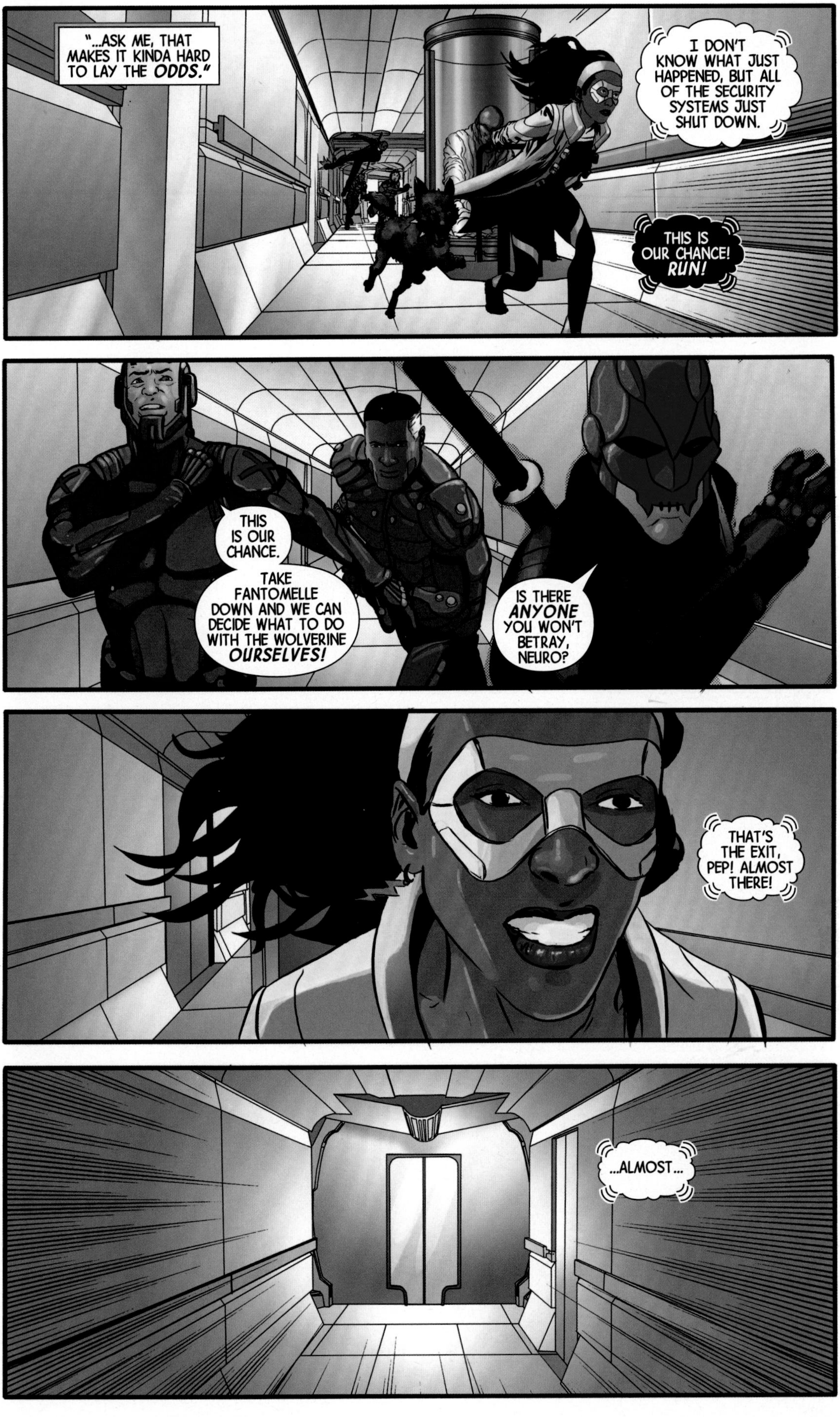

"...ASK ME, THAT MAKES IT KINDA HARD TO LAY THE ODDS."
I DON'T KNOW WHAT JUST HAPPENED, BUT ALL OF THE SECURITY SYSTEMS JUST SHUT DOWN.
THIS IS OUR CHANCE! RUN!
THIS IS OUR CHANCE.
TAKE FANTOMELLE DOWN AND WE CAN DECIDE WHAT TO DO WITH THE WOLVERINE OURSELVES!
IS THERE ANYONE YOU WON'T BETRAY, NEURO?
THAT'S THE EXIT, PEP! ALMOST THERE!
...ALMOST...

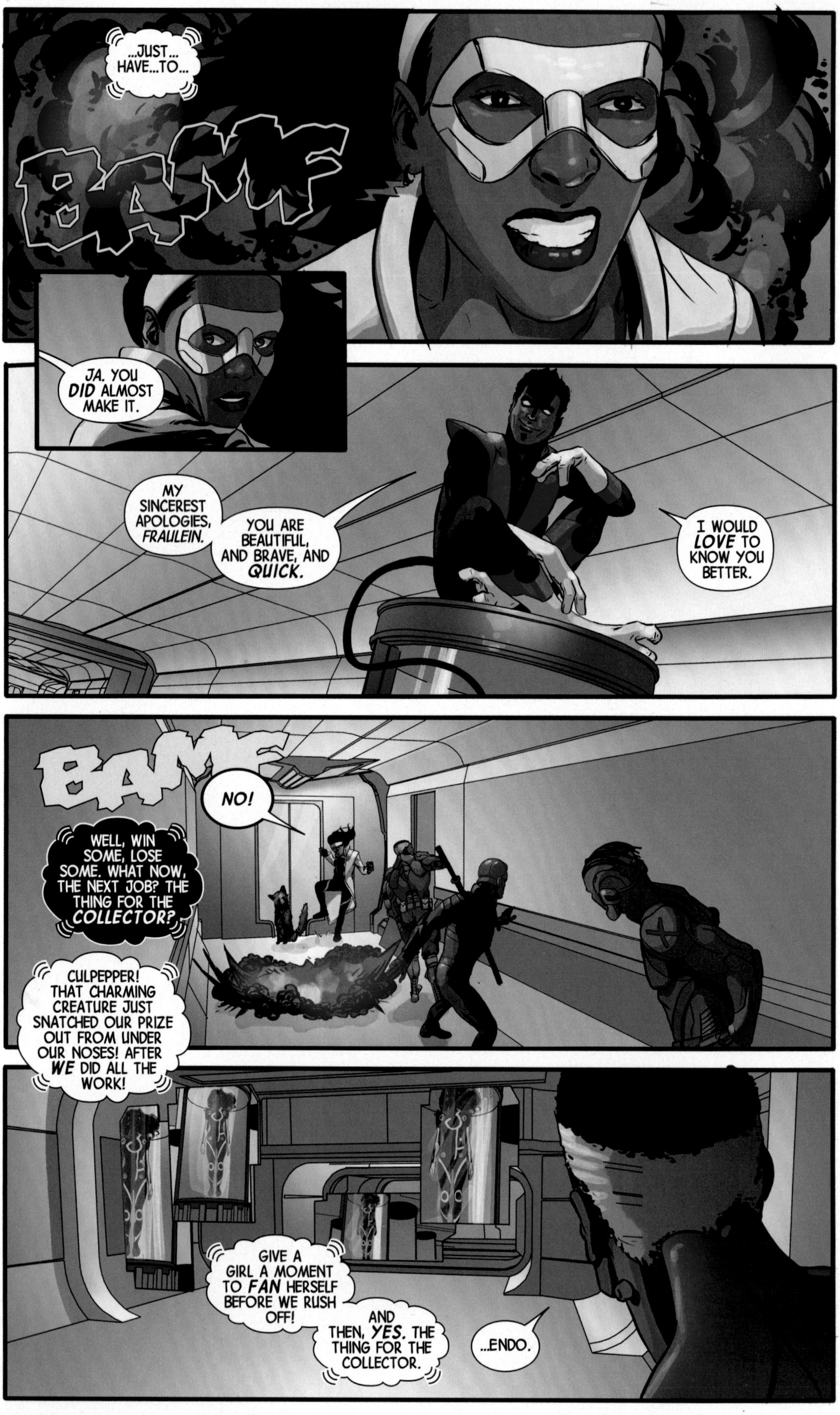
...JUST... HAVE...TO...
BAMF
JA. YOU DID ALMOST MAKE IT.
MY SINCEREST APOLOGIES, FRAULEIN.
YOU ARE BEAUTIFUL, AND BRAVE, AND QUICK.
I WOULD LOVE TO KNOW YOU BETTER.
BAMF
NO!
WELL, WIN SOME, LOSE SOME. WHAT NOW, THE NEXT JOB? THE THING FOR THE COLLECTOR?
CULPEPPER! THAT CHARMING CREATURE JUST SNATCHED OUR PRIZE OUT FROM UNDER OUR NOSES! AFTER WE DID ALL THE WORK!
GIVE A GIRL A MOMENT TO FAN HERSELF BEFORE WE RUSH OFF!
AND THEN, YES. THE THING FOR THE COLLECTOR.
...ENDO.

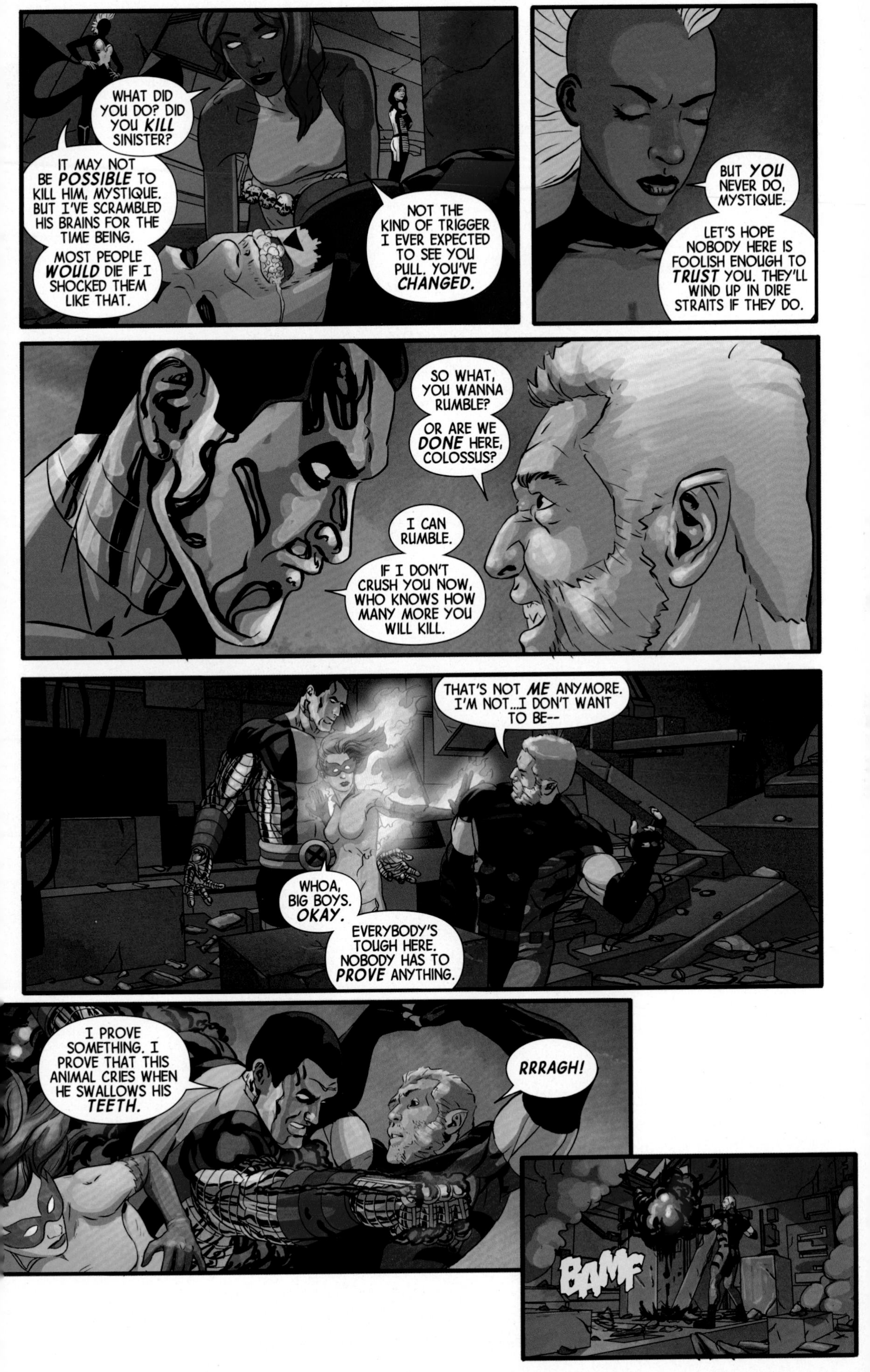
WHAT DID YOU DO? DID YOU KILL SINISTER?
IT MAY NOT BE POSSIBLE TO KILL HIM, MYSTIQUE. BUT I'VE SCRAMBLED HIS BRAINS FOR THE TIME BEING.
MOST PEOPLE WOULD DIE IF I SHOCKED THEM LIKE THAT.
NOT THE KIND OF TRIGGER I EVER EXPECTED TO SEE YOU PULL. YOU'VE CHANGED.
BUT YOU NEVER DO, MYSTIQUE.
LET'S HOPE NOBODY HERE IS FOOLISH ENOUGH TO TRUST YOU. THEY'LL WIND UP IN DIRE STRAITS IF THEY DO.
SO WHAT, YOU WANNA RUMBLE?
OR ARE WE DONE HERE, COLOSSUS?
I CAN RUMBLE.
IF I DON'T CRUSH YOU NOW, WHO KNOWS HOW MANY MORE YOU WILL KILL.
THAT'S NOT ME ANYMORE. I'M NOT...I DON'T WANT TO BE--
WHOA, BIG BOYS. OKAY.
EVERYBODY'S TOUGH HERE. NOBODY HAS TO PROVE ANYTHING.
I PROVE SOMETHING. I PROVE THAT THIS ANIMAL CRIES WHEN HE SWALLOWS HIS TEETH.
RRRAGH!
BAMF

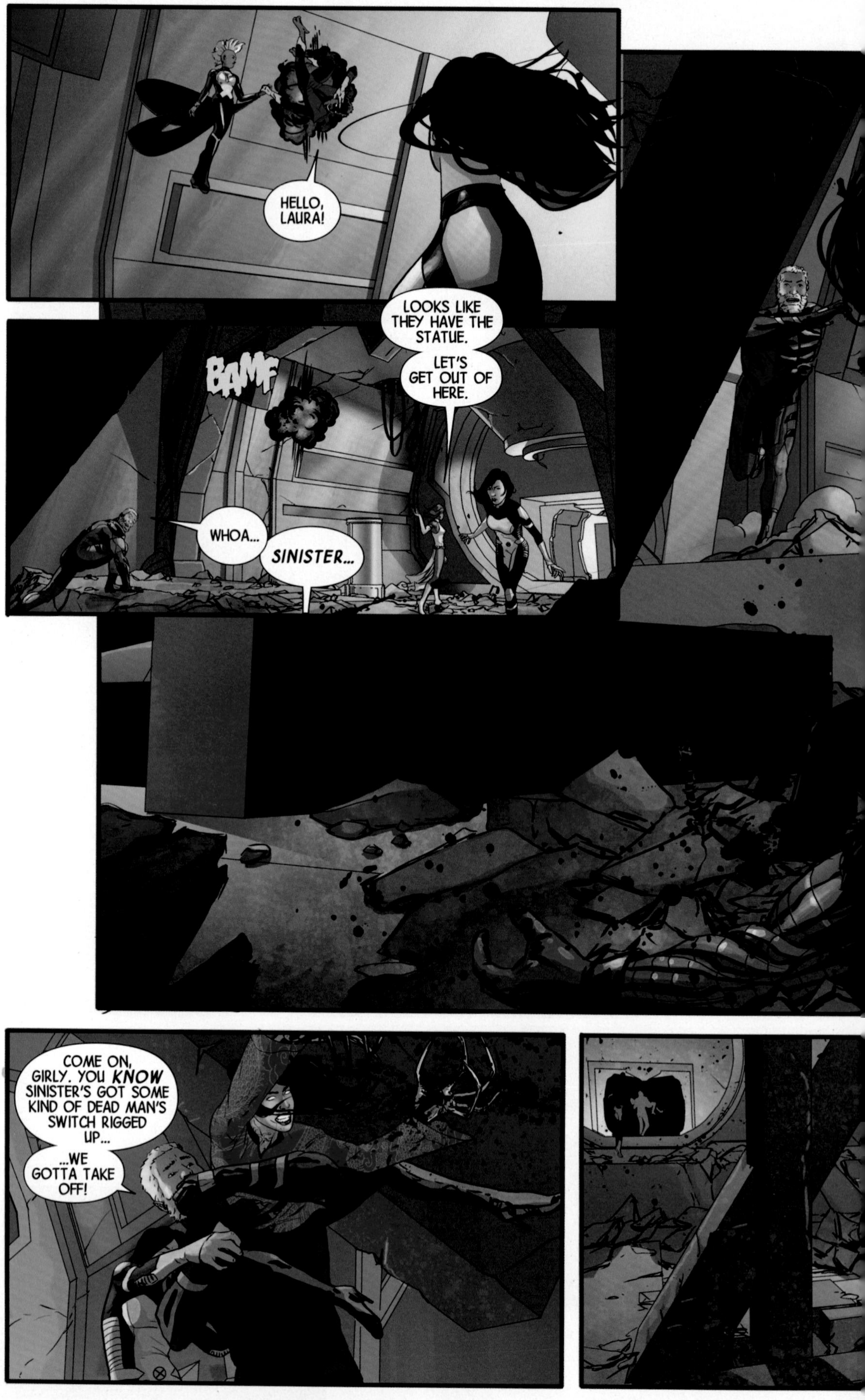
HELLO, LAURA!
LOOKS LIKE THEY HAVE THE STATUE.
LET'S GET OUT OF HERE.
BAMF
WHOA...
SINISTER...
COME ON, GIRLY. YOU KNOW SINISTER'S GOT SOME KIND OF DEAD MAN'S SWITCH RIGGED UP...
...WE GOTTA TAKE OFF!

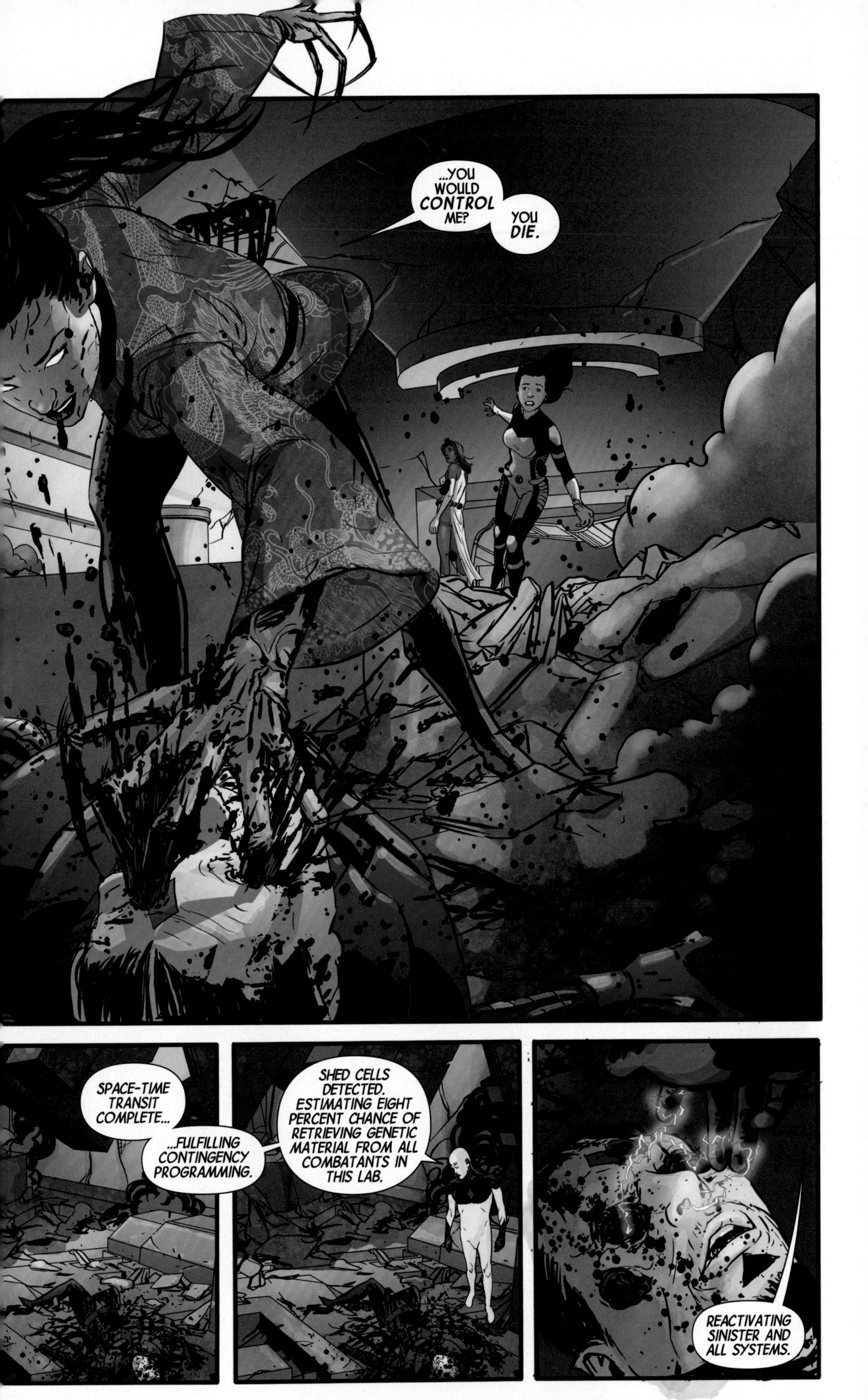
...YOU WOULD CONTROL ME?
YOU DIE.
SPACE-TIME TRANSIT COMPLETE...
...FULFILLING CONTINGENCY PROGRAMMING.
SHED CELLS DETECTED. ESTIMATING EIGHT PERCENT CHANCE OF RETRIEVING GENETIC MATERIAL FROM ALL COMBATANTS IN THIS LAB.
REACTIVATING SINISTER AND ALL SYSTEMS.

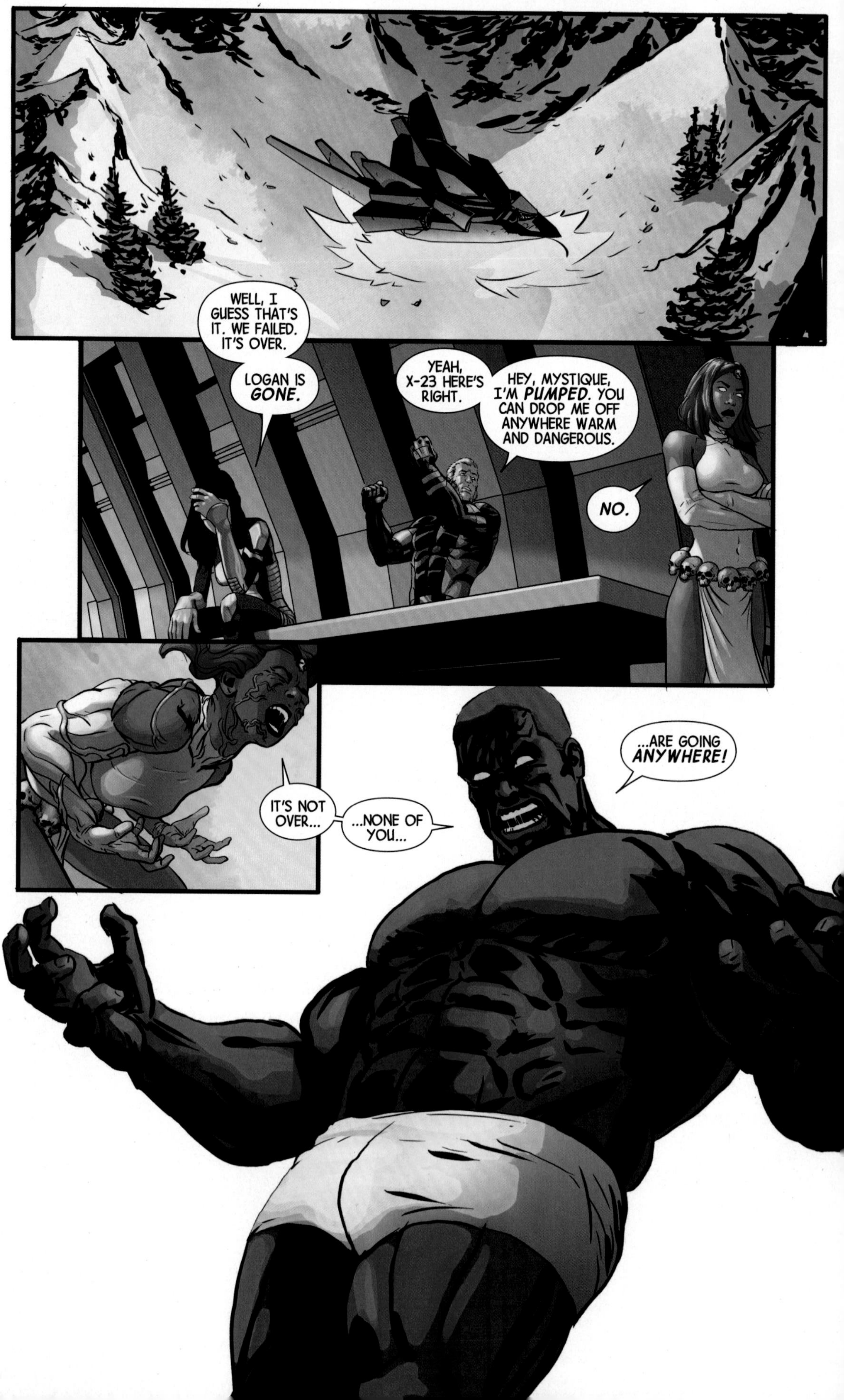
WELL, I GUESS THAT'S IT. WE FAILED. IT'S OVER.
LOGAN IS *GONE.*
YEAH, X-23 HERE'S RIGHT.
HEY, MYSTIQUE, I'M *PUMPED.* YOU CAN DROP ME OFF ANYWHERE WARM AND DANGEROUS.
NO.
IT'S NOT OVER...
...NONE OF YOU...
...ARE GOING *ANYWHERE!*

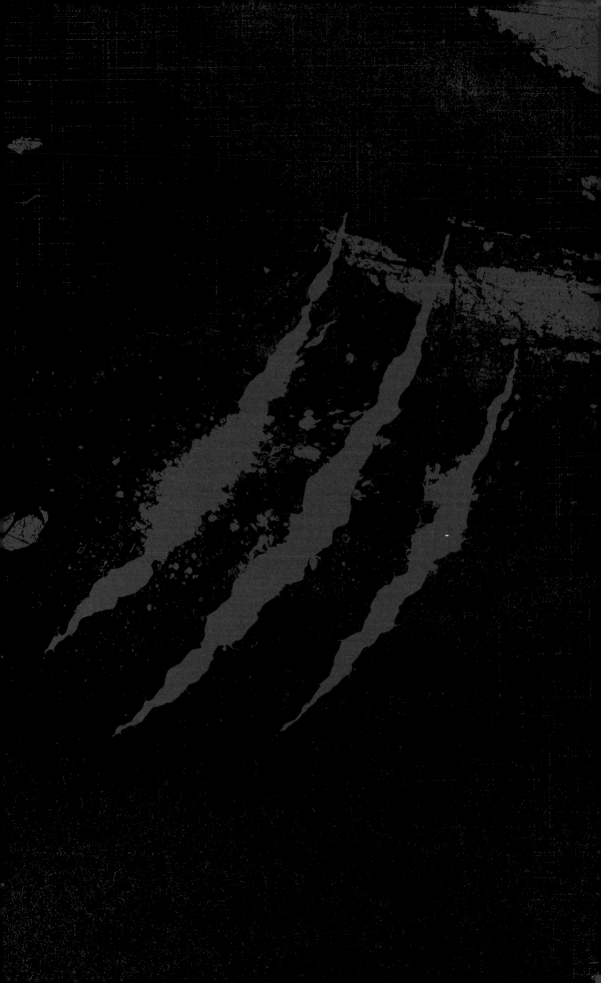

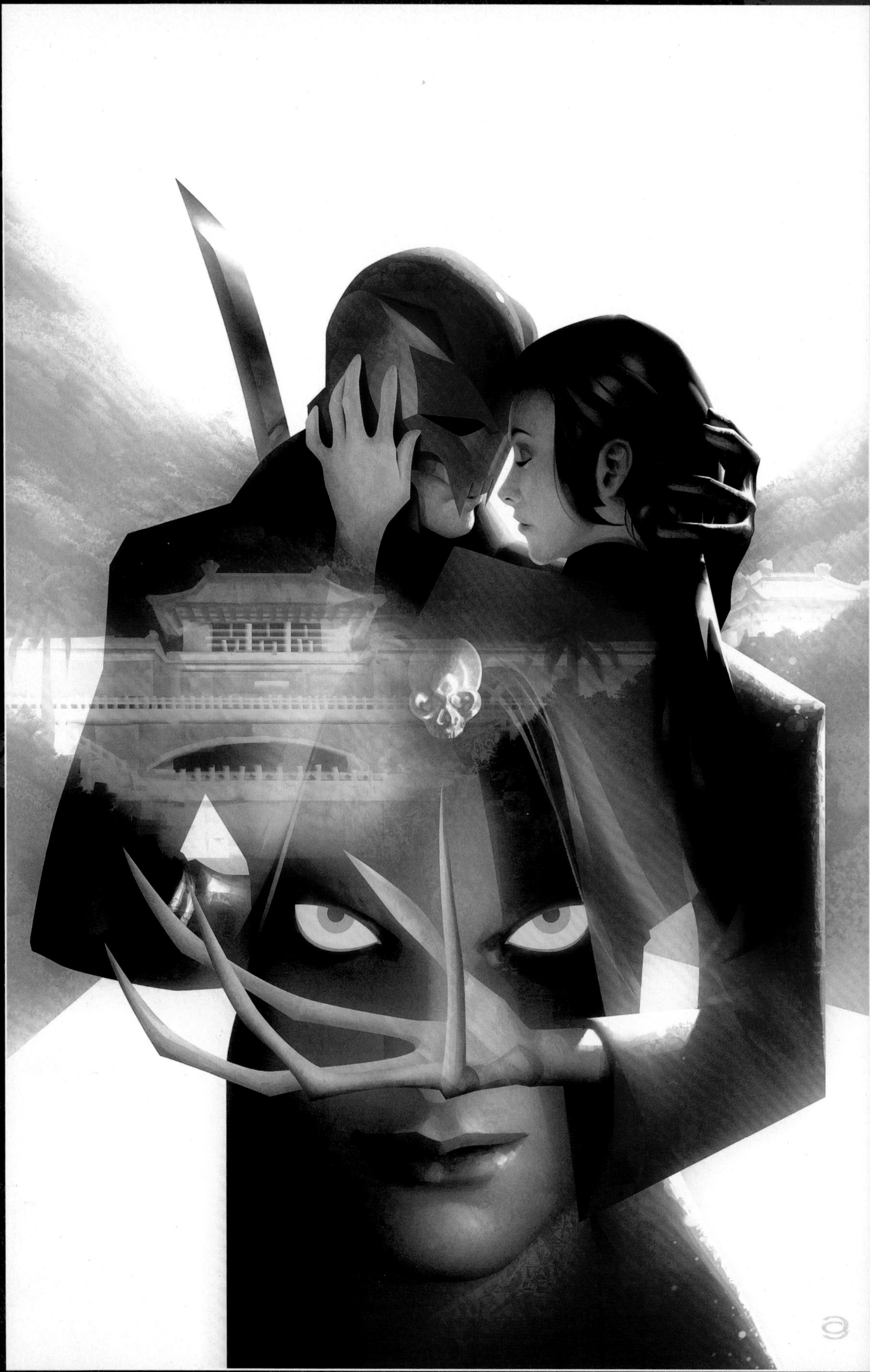

#7

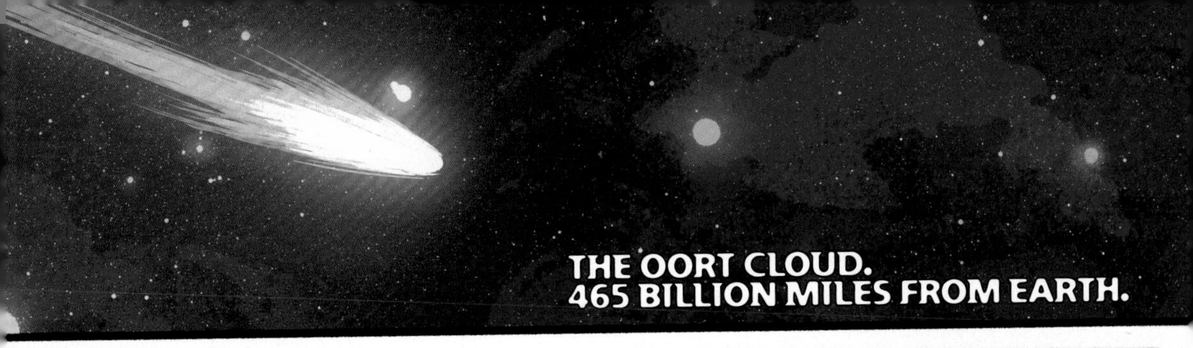
THE OORT CLOUD.
465 BILLION MILES FROM EARTH.

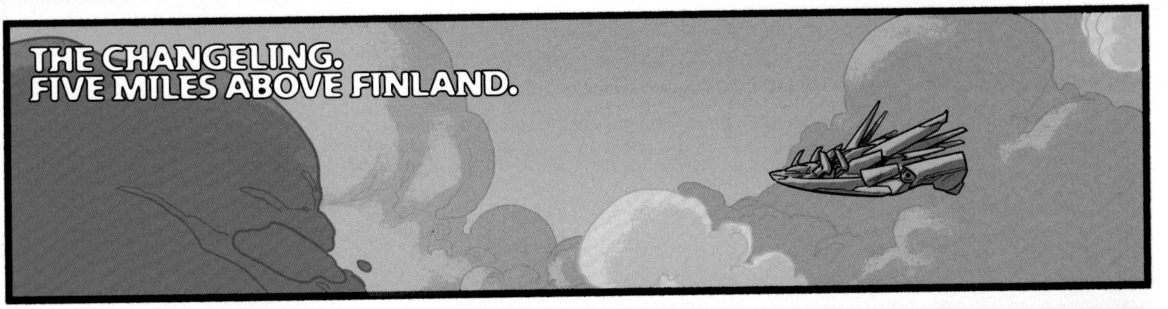
THE CHANGELING.
FIVE MILES ABOVE FINLAND.

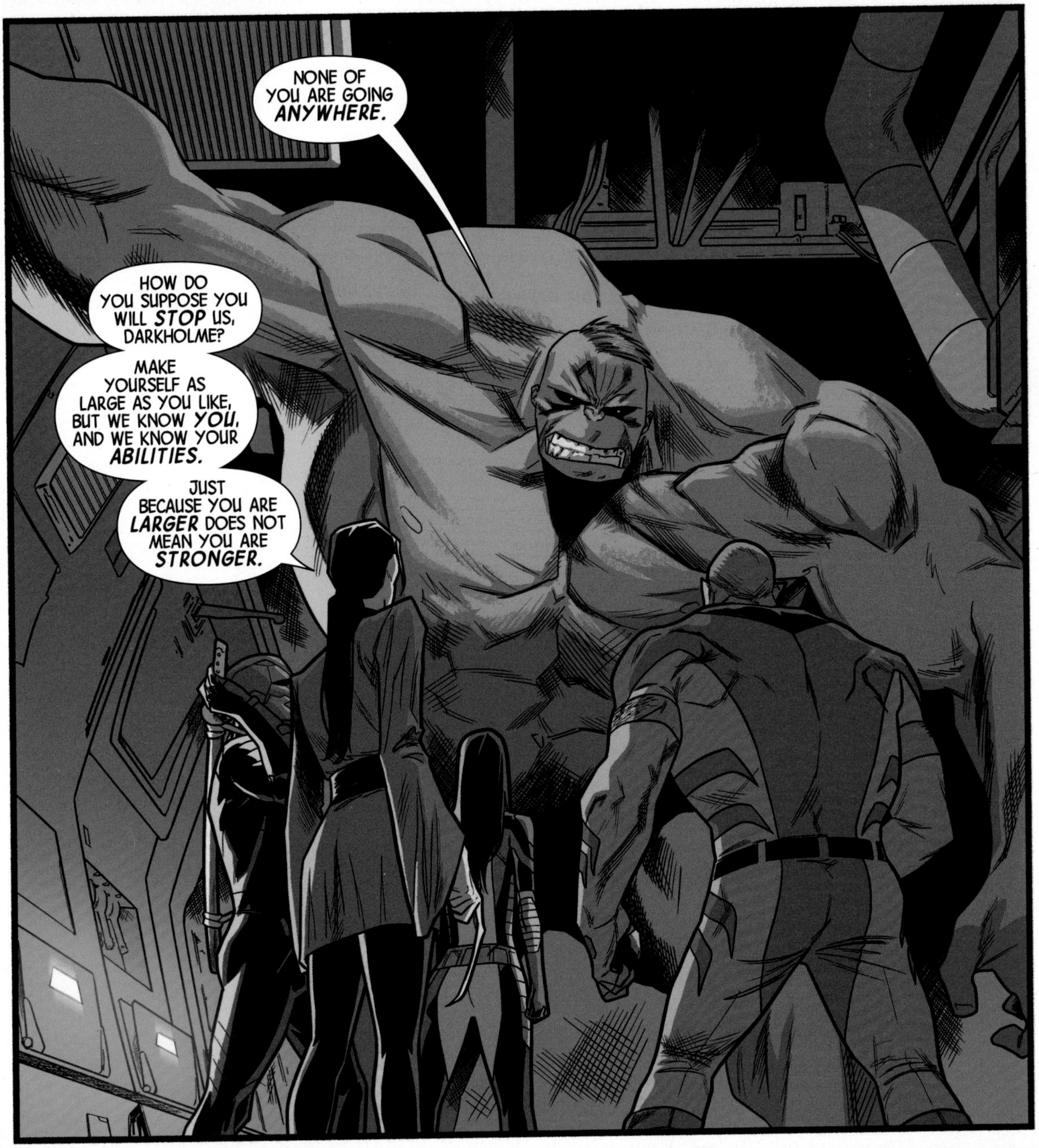
NONE OF YOU ARE GOING ANYWHERE.
HOW DO YOU SUPPOSE YOU WILL STOP US, DARKHOLME?
MAKE YOURSELF AS LARGE AS YOU LIKE, BUT WE KNOW YOU, AND WE KNOW YOUR ABILITIES.
JUST BECAUSE YOU ARE LARGER DOES NOT MEAN YOU ARE STRONGER.

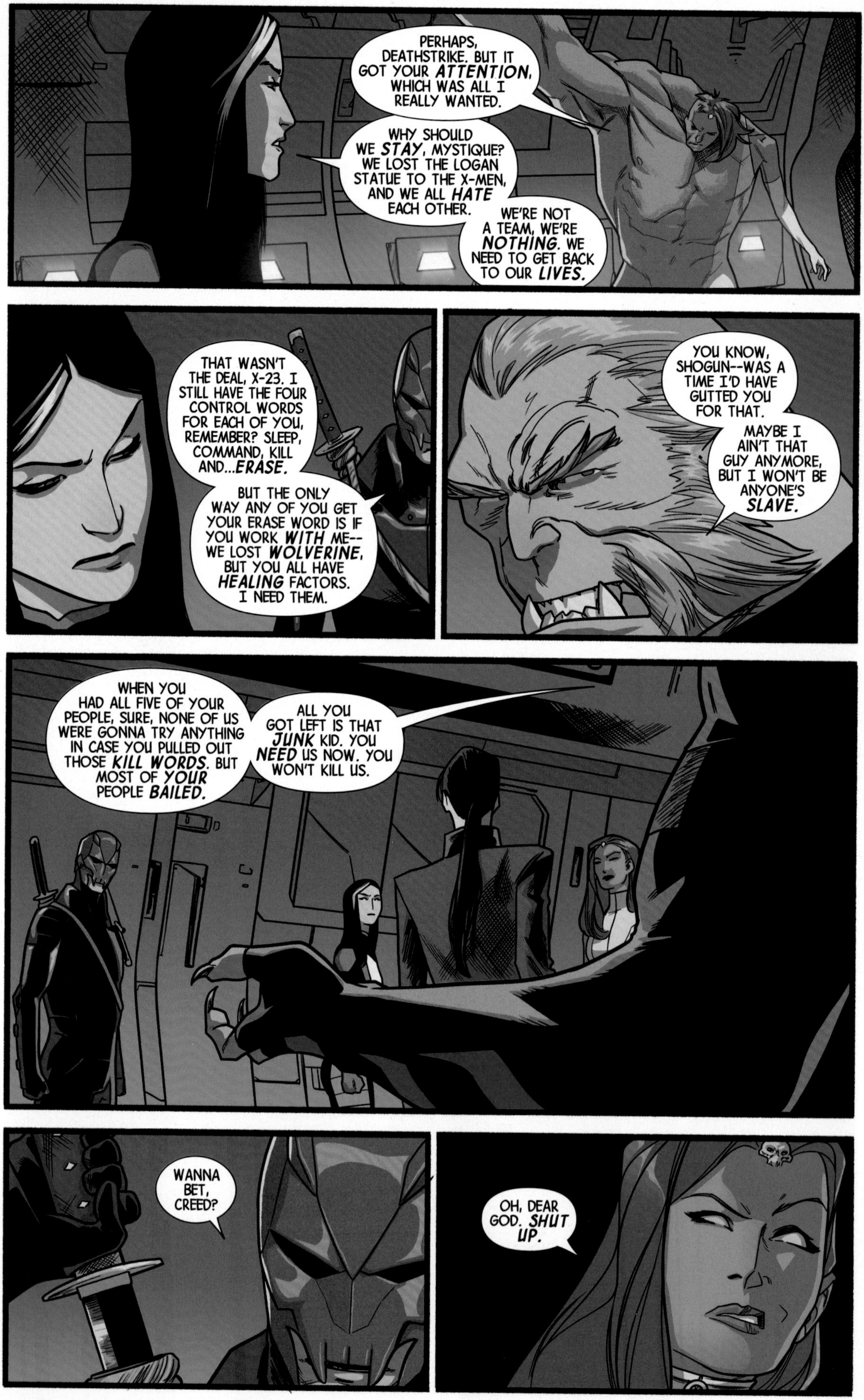
PERHAPS, DEATHSTRIKE. BUT IT GOT YOUR ATTENTION, WHICH WAS ALL I REALLY WANTED.
WHY SHOULD WE STAY, MYSTIQUE? WE LOST THE LOGAN STATUE TO THE X-MEN, AND WE ALL HATE EACH OTHER.
WE'RE NOT A TEAM, WE'RE NOTHING. WE NEED TO GET BACK TO OUR LIVES.
THAT WASN'T THE DEAL, X-23. I STILL HAVE THE FOUR CONTROL WORDS FOR EACH OF YOU, REMEMBER? SLEEP, COMMAND, KILL AND...ERASE.
BUT THE ONLY WAY ANY OF YOU GET YOUR ERASE WORD IS IF YOU WORK WITH ME-- WE LOST WOLVERINE, BUT YOU ALL HAVE HEALING FACTORS. I NEED THEM.
YOU KNOW, SHOGUN--WAS A TIME I'D HAVE GUTTED YOU FOR THAT.
MAYBE I AIN'T THAT GUY ANYMORE, BUT I WON'T BE ANYONE'S SLAVE.
WHEN YOU HAD ALL FIVE OF YOUR PEOPLE, SURE, NONE OF US WERE GONNA TRY ANYTHING IN CASE YOU PULLED OUT THOSE KILL WORDS. BUT MOST OF YOUR PEOPLE BAILED.
ALL YOU GOT LEFT IS THAT JUNK KID. YOU NEED US NOW. YOU WON'T KILL US.
WANNA BET, CREED?
OH, DEAR GOD. SHUT UP.

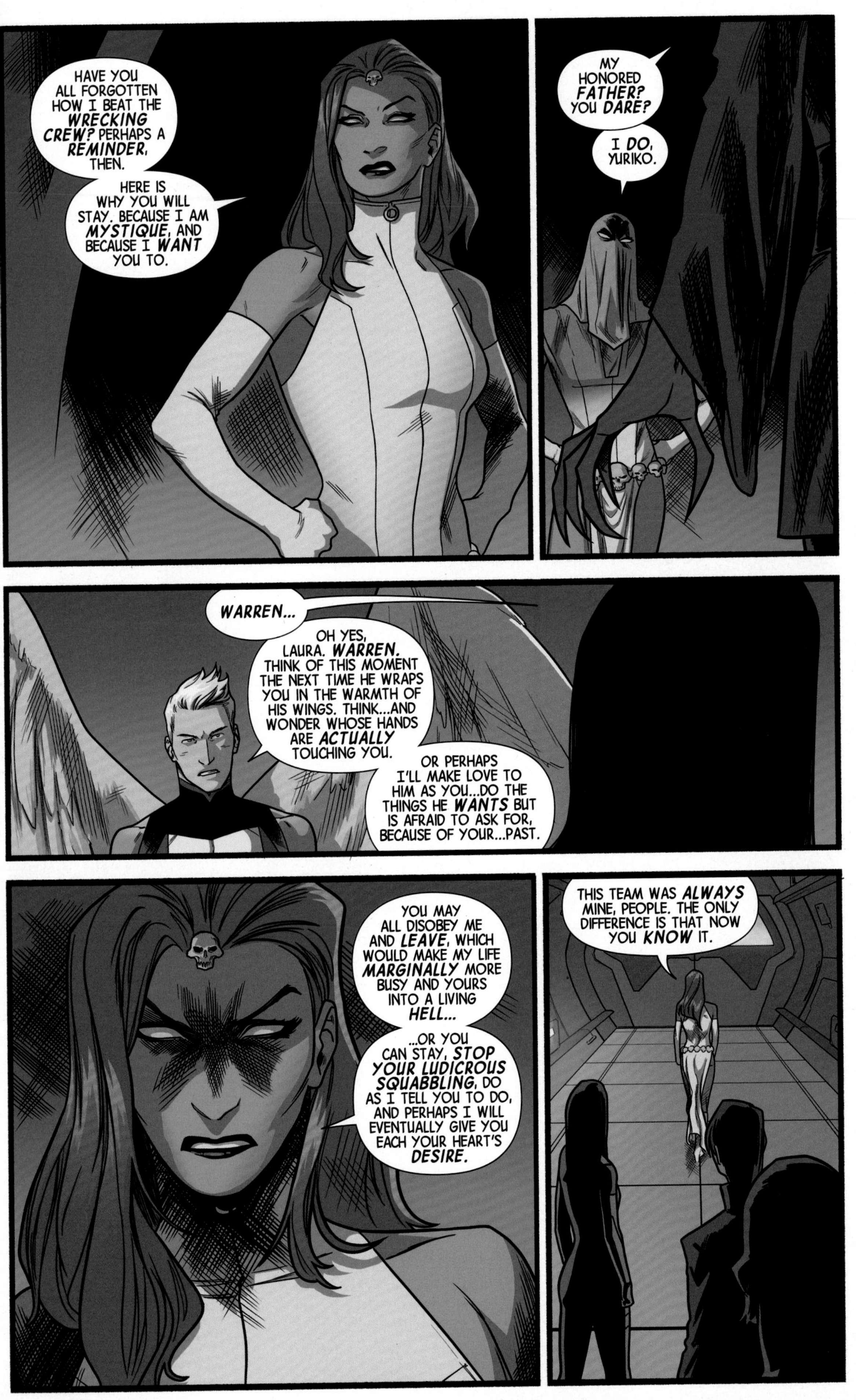
HAVE YOU ALL FORGOTTEN HOW I BEAT THE WRECKING CREW? PERHAPS A REMINDER, THEN.
HERE IS WHY YOU WILL STAY. BECAUSE I AM MYSTIQUE, AND BECAUSE I WANT YOU TO.
MY HONORED FATHER? YOU DARE?
I DO, YURIKO.
WARREN...
OH YES, LAURA. WARREN. THINK OF THIS MOMENT THE NEXT TIME HE WRAPS YOU IN THE WARMTH OF HIS WINGS. THINK...AND WONDER WHOSE HANDS ARE ACTUALLY TOUCHING YOU.
OR PERHAPS I'LL MAKE LOVE TO HIM AS YOU...DO THE THINGS HE WANTS BUT IS AFRAID TO ASK FOR, BECAUSE OF YOUR...PAST.
YOU MAY ALL DISOBEY ME AND LEAVE, WHICH WOULD MAKE MY LIFE MARGINALLY MORE BUSY AND YOURS INTO A LIVING HELL...
...OR YOU CAN STAY, STOP YOUR LUDICROUS SQUABBLING, DO AS I TELL YOU TO DO, AND PERHAPS I WILL EVENTUALLY GIVE YOU EACH YOUR HEART'S DESIRE.
THIS TEAM WAS ALWAYS MINE, PEOPLE. THE ONLY DIFFERENCE IS THAT NOW YOU KNOW IT.

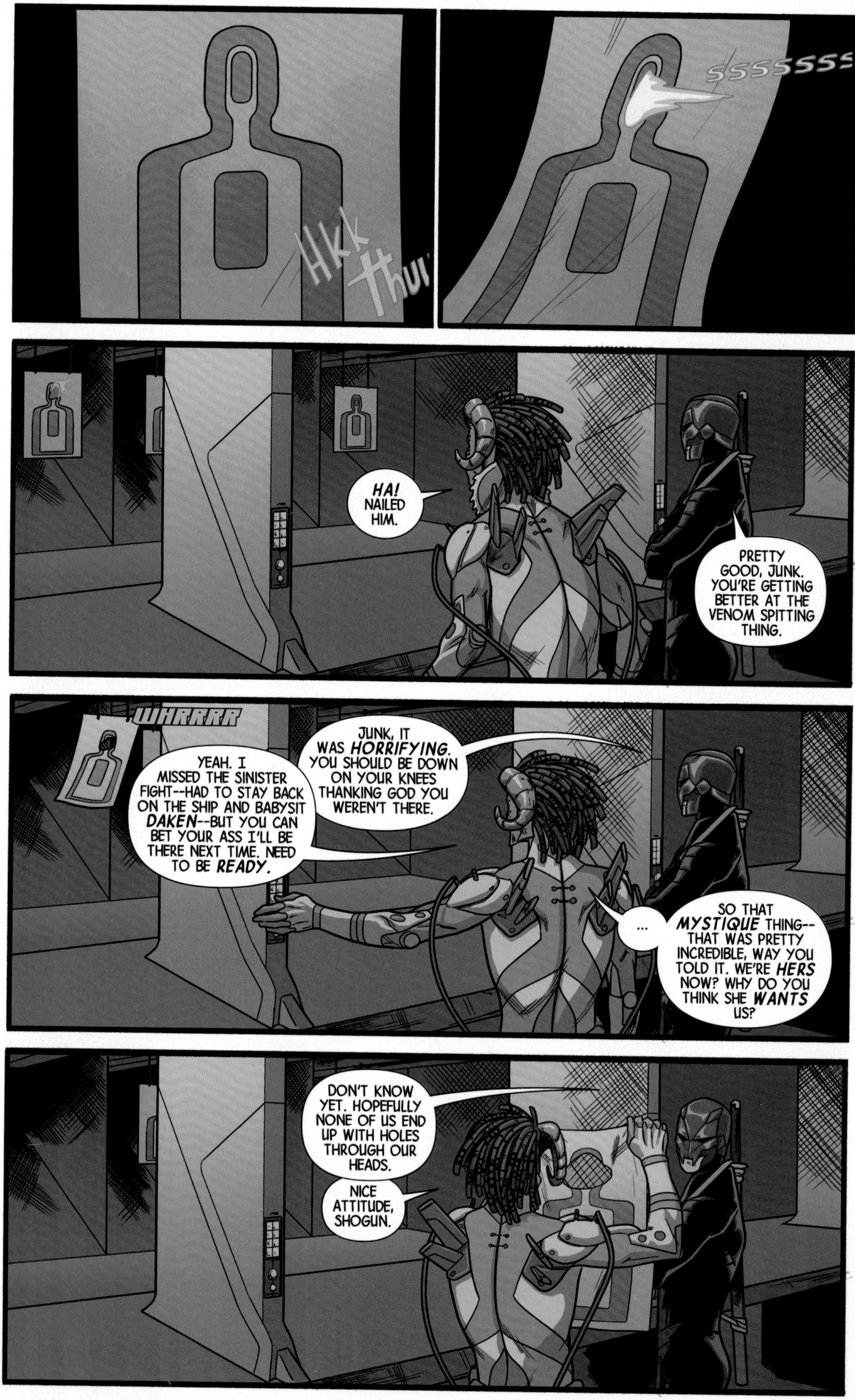
HKK
THUI
SSSSSSS
HA! NAILED HIM.
PRETTY GOOD, JUNK. YOU'RE GETTING BETTER AT THE VENOM SPITTING THING.
WHRRRR
YEAH. I MISSED THE SINISTER FIGHT--HAD TO STAY BACK ON THE SHIP AND BABYSIT DAKEN--BUT YOU CAN BET YOUR ASS I'LL BE THERE NEXT TIME. NEED TO BE READY.
JUNK, IT WAS HORRIFYING. YOU SHOULD BE DOWN ON YOUR KNEES THANKING GOD YOU WEREN'T THERE.
...
SO THAT MYSTIQUE THING--THAT WAS PRETTY INCREDIBLE, WAY YOU TOLD IT. WE'RE HERS NOW? WHY DO YOU THINK SHE WANTS US?
DON'T KNOW YET. HOPEFULLY NONE OF US END UP WITH HOLES THROUGH OUR HEADS.
NICE ATTITUDE, SHOGUN.

SHOGUN. MYSTIQUE WANTS YOU. SHE'S ON THE BRIDGE.

DID SHE SAY WHAT SHE WANTS ME *FOR,* DAKEN?

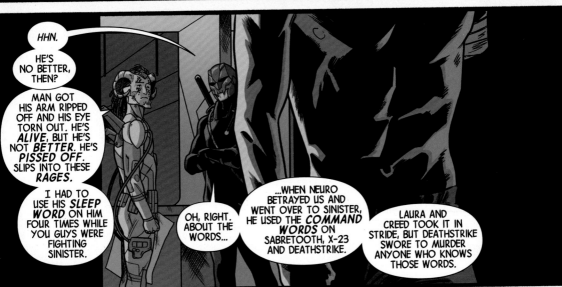

HHN.

HE'S NO BETTER, THEN?

MAN GOT HIS ARM RIPPED OFF AND HIS EYE TORN OUT. HE'S *ALIVE,* BUT HE'S NOT *BETTER.* HE'S *PISSED OFF.* SLIPS INTO THESE *RAGES.*

I HAD TO USE HIS *SLEEP WORD* ON HIM FOUR TIMES WHILE YOU GUYS WERE FIGHTING SINISTER.

OH, RIGHT. ABOUT THE WORDS...

...WHEN NEURO BETRAYED US AND WENT OVER TO SINISTER, HE USED THE *COMMAND WORDS* ON SABRETOOTH, X-23 AND DEATHSTRIKE.

LAURA AND CREED TOOK IT IN STRIDE, BUT DEATHSTRIKE SWORE TO MURDER ANYONE WHO KNOWS THOSE WORDS.

WAIT... *WHAT?*

HERE'S WHAT I'M GETTING AT, JUNK.

KEEP PRACTICING.

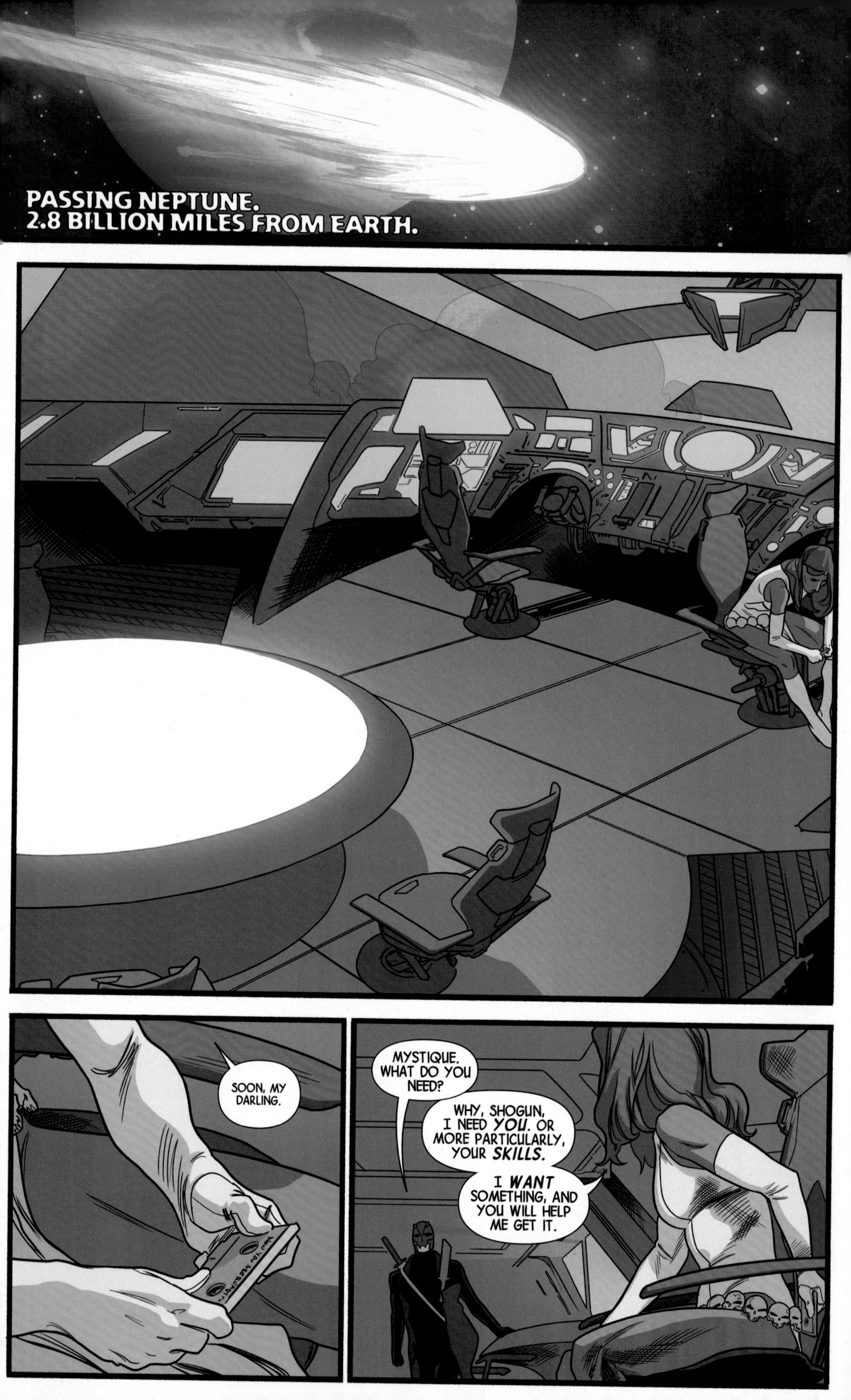
PASSING NEPTUNE.
2.8 BILLION MILES FROM EARTH.
SOON, MY DARLING.
MYSTIQUE. WHAT DO YOU NEED?
WHY, SHOGUN, I NEED YOU. OR MORE PARTICULARLY, YOUR SKILLS.
I WANT SOMETHING, AND YOU WILL HELP ME GET IT.

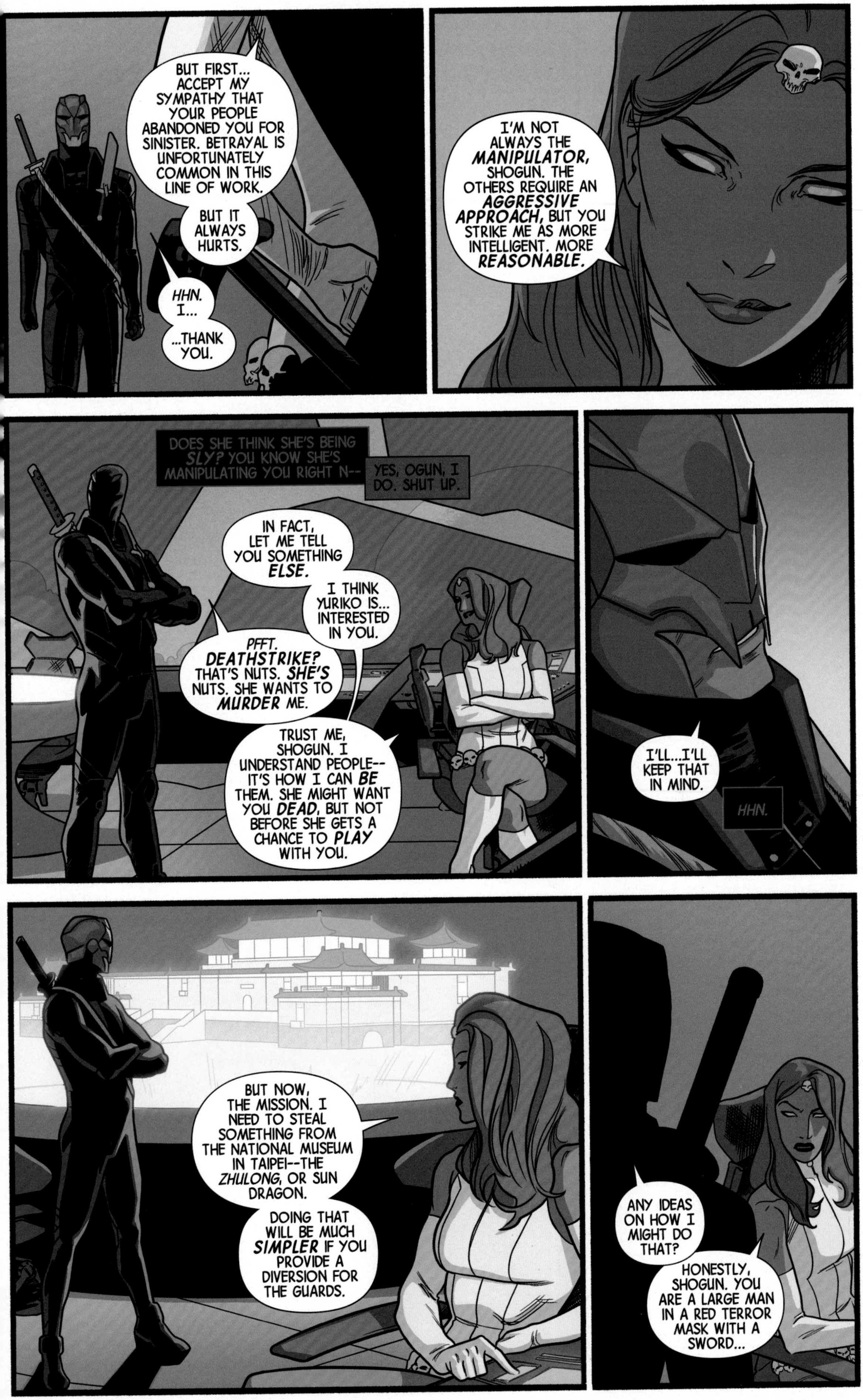
BUT FIRST... ACCEPT MY SYMPATHY THAT YOUR PEOPLE ABANDONED YOU FOR SINISTER. BETRAYAL IS UNFORTUNATELY COMMON IN THIS LINE OF WORK.
BUT IT ALWAYS HURTS.
HHN. I...
...THANK YOU.
I'M NOT ALWAYS THE MANIPULATOR, SHOGUN. THE OTHERS REQUIRE AN AGGRESSIVE APPROACH, BUT YOU STRIKE ME AS MORE INTELLIGENT. MORE REASONABLE.
DOES SHE THINK SHE'S BEING SLY? YOU KNOW SHE'S MANIPULATING YOU RIGHT N--
YES, OGUN, I DO. SHUT UP.
IN FACT, LET ME TELL YOU SOMETHING ELSE.
I THINK YURIKO IS... INTERESTED IN YOU.
PFFT. DEATHSTRIKE? THAT'S NUTS. SHE'S NUTS. SHE WANTS TO MURDER ME.
TRUST ME, SHOGUN. I UNDERSTAND PEOPLE-- IT'S HOW I CAN BE THEM. SHE MIGHT WANT YOU DEAD, BUT NOT BEFORE SHE GETS A CHANCE TO PLAY WITH YOU.
I'LL...I'LL KEEP THAT IN MIND.
HHN.
BUT NOW, THE MISSION. I NEED TO STEAL SOMETHING FROM THE NATIONAL MUSEUM IN TAIPEI--THE ZHULONG, OR SUN DRAGON.
DOING THAT WILL BE MUCH SIMPLER IF YOU PROVIDE A DIVERSION FOR THE GUARDS.
ANY IDEAS ON HOW I MIGHT DO THAT?
HONESTLY, SHOGUN. YOU ARE A LARGE MAN IN A RED TERROR MASK WITH A SWORD...

TAIPEI.

"...I CAN'T IMAGINE IT WILL BE ALL THAT DIFFICULT."

HEY!

NOTHING ABOUT HOW I'M A FOOL FOR DOING THIS, OGUN? NORMALLY YOU'D BE CALLING ME AN IDIOT RIGHT ABOUT NOW.

<WHO IN THE WORLD IS THA-->*

<WHO CARES? DO YOU NOT SEE THE SWORD!>

*TRANSLATED FROM MANDARIN.

KLCK

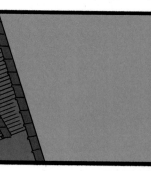

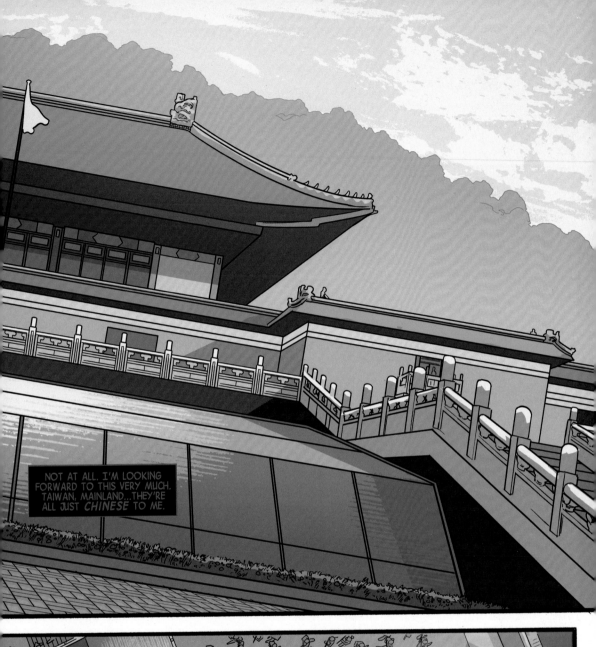

NOT AT ALL. I'M LOOKING FORWARD TO THIS VERY MUCH. TAIWAN, MAINLAND...THEY'RE ALL JUST *CHINESE* TO ME.

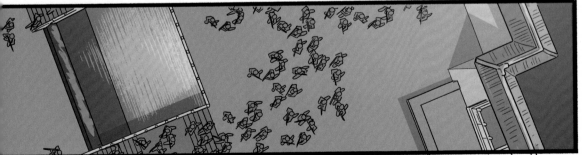

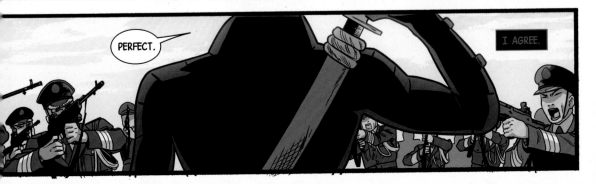

PERFECT.

I AGREE.

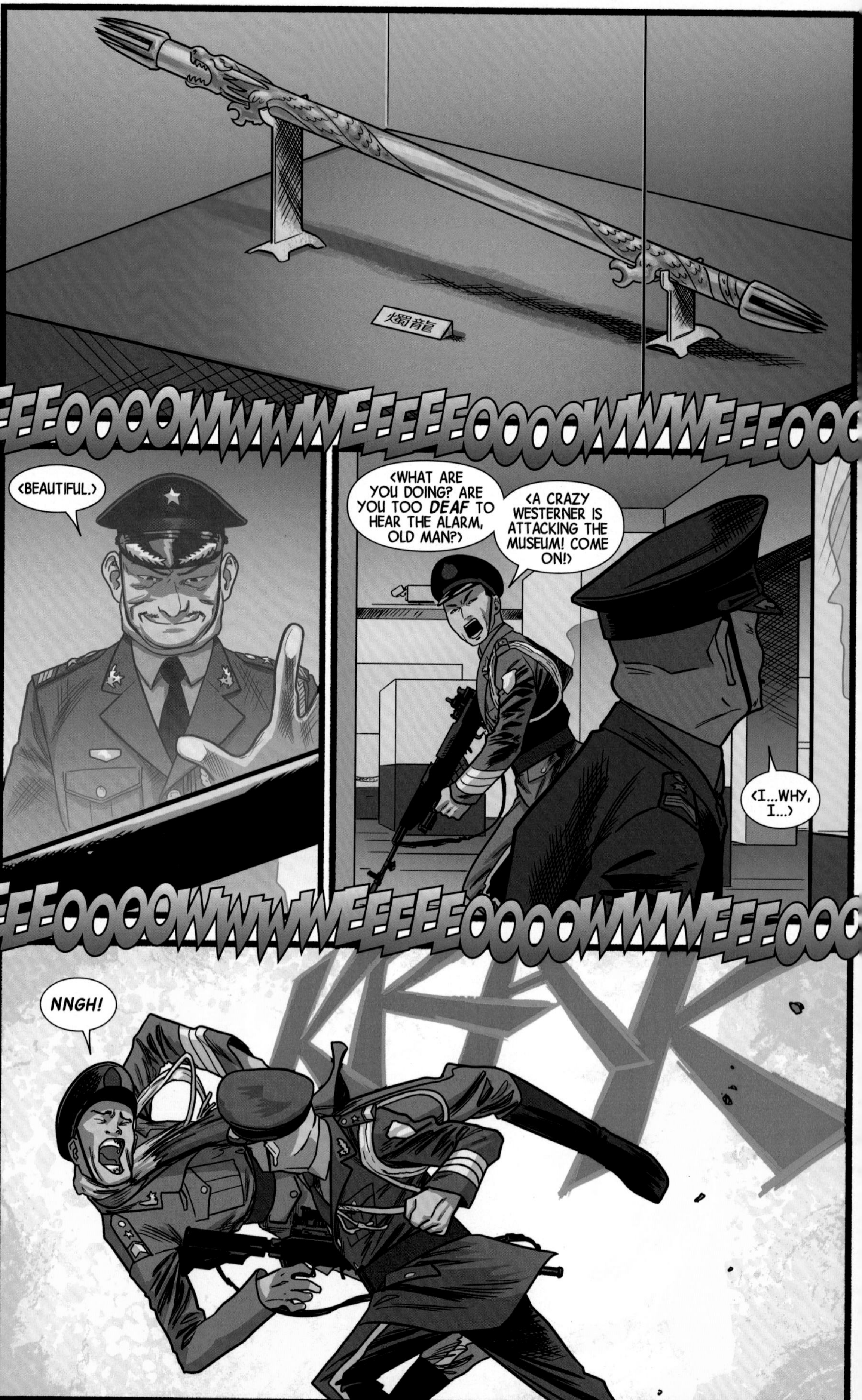
燭龍
EEEOOOOWWWWEEEEEOOOOWWWEEEOOO
<BEAUTIFUL.>
<WHAT ARE YOU DOING? ARE YOU TOO *DEAF* TO HEAR THE ALARM, OLD MAN?>
<A CRAZY WESTERNER IS ATTACKING THE MUSEUM! COME ON!>
<I...WHY, I...>
EEEOOOOWWWWEEEEEOOOOWWWEEEOOO
NNGH!

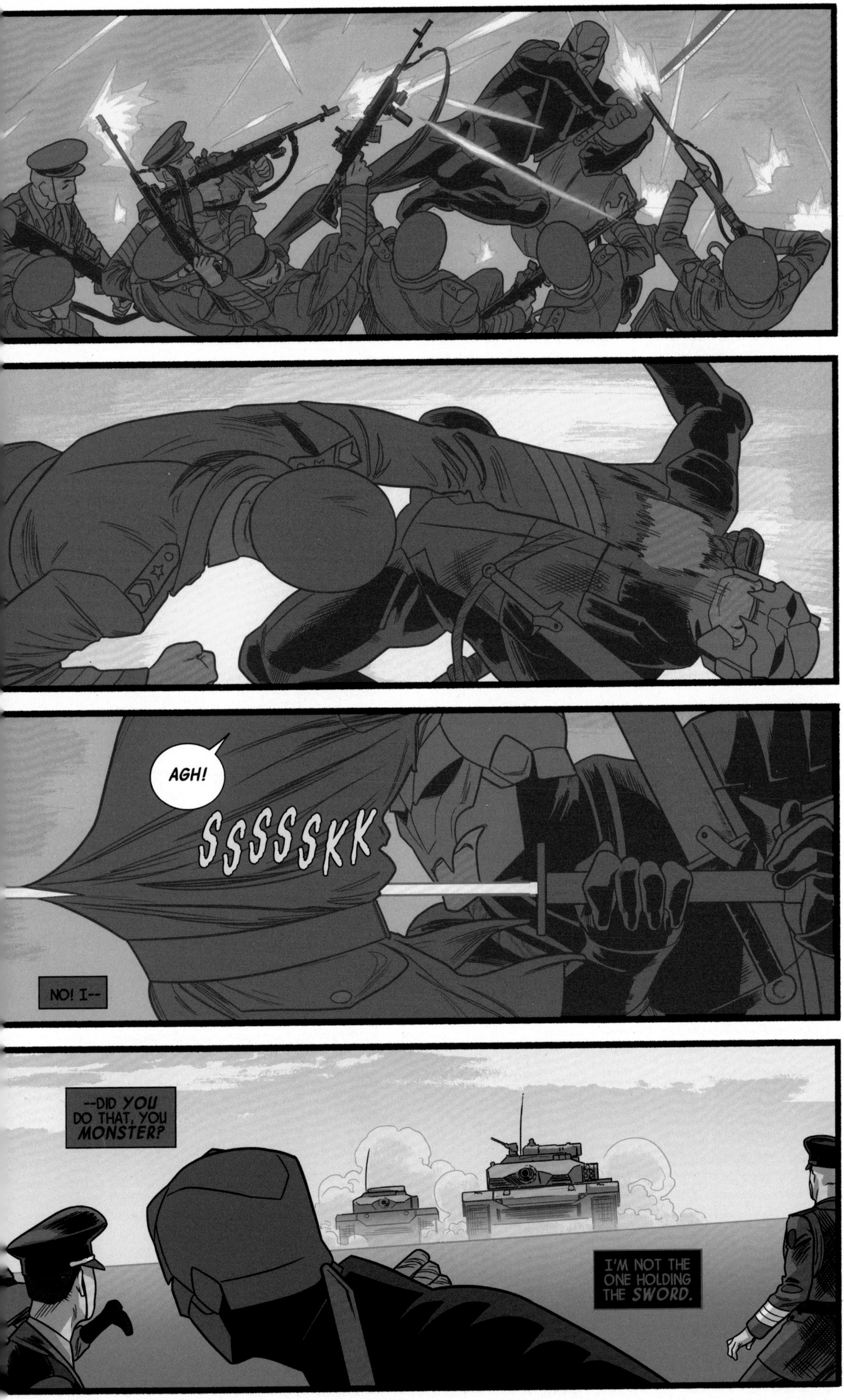
AGH!
SSSSSKK
NO! I--
--DID YOU DO THAT, YOU MONSTER?
I'M NOT THE ONE HOLDING THE SWORD.

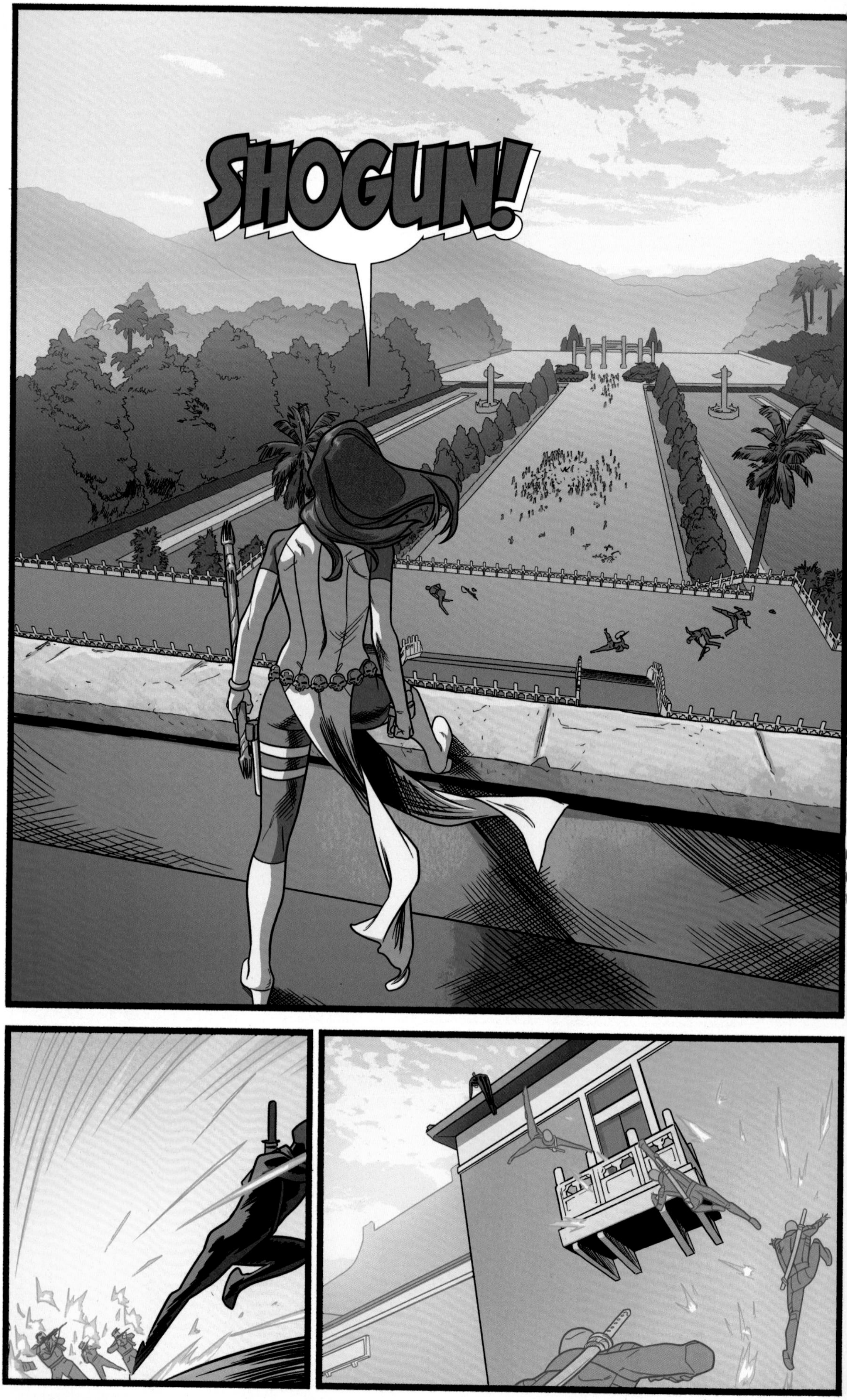
SHOGUN!

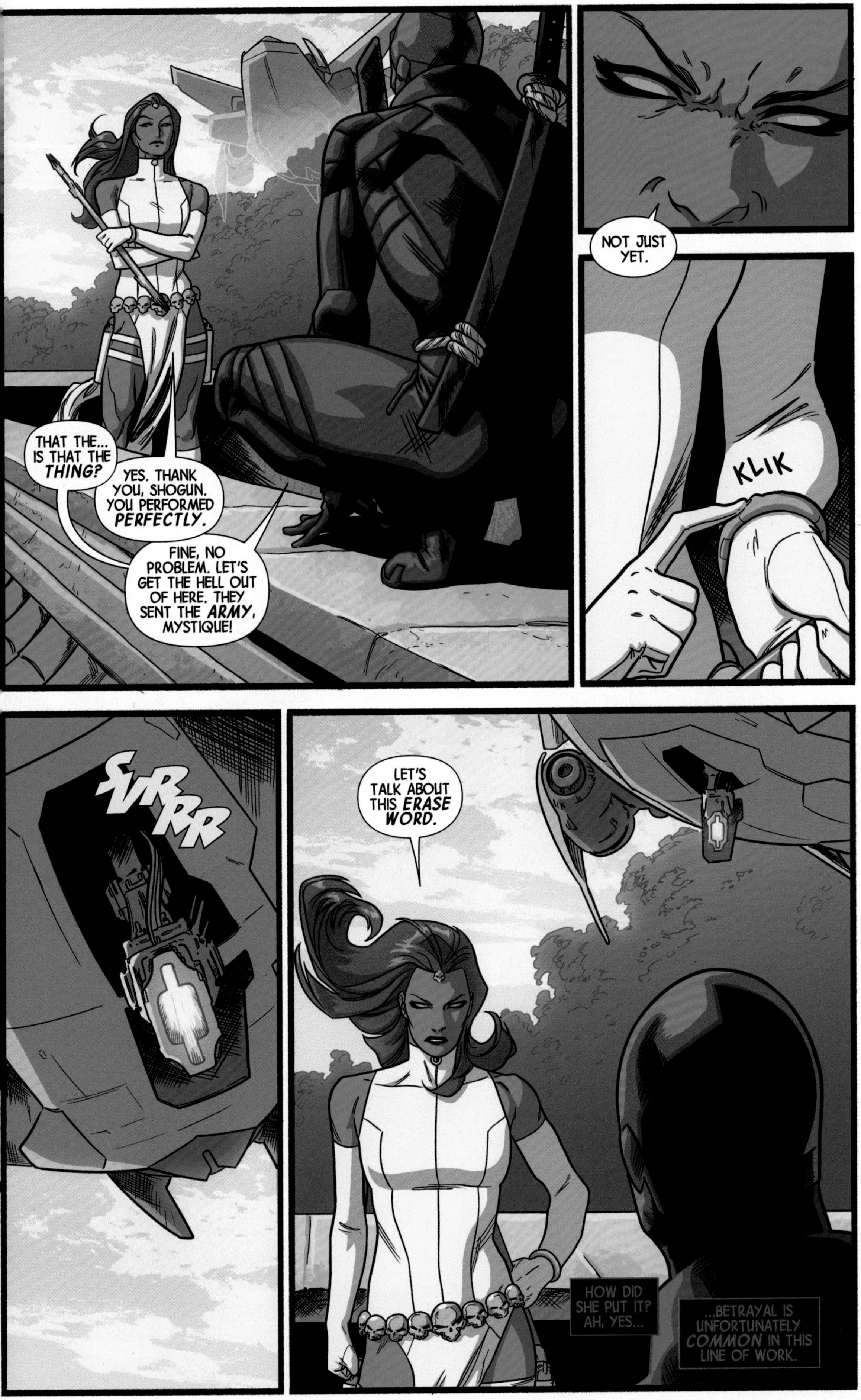
THAT THE... IS THAT THE *THING?*
YES. THANK YOU, SHOGUN. YOU PERFORMED *PERFECTLY.*
FINE, NO PROBLEM. LET'S GET THE HELL OUT OF HERE. THEY SENT THE *ARMY*, MYSTIQUE!
NOT JUST YET.
KLIK
SVRRR
LET'S TALK ABOUT THIS *ERASE WORD.*
HOW DID SHE PUT IT? AH, YES...
...BETRAYAL IS UNFORTUNATELY *COMMON* IN THIS LINE OF WORK.

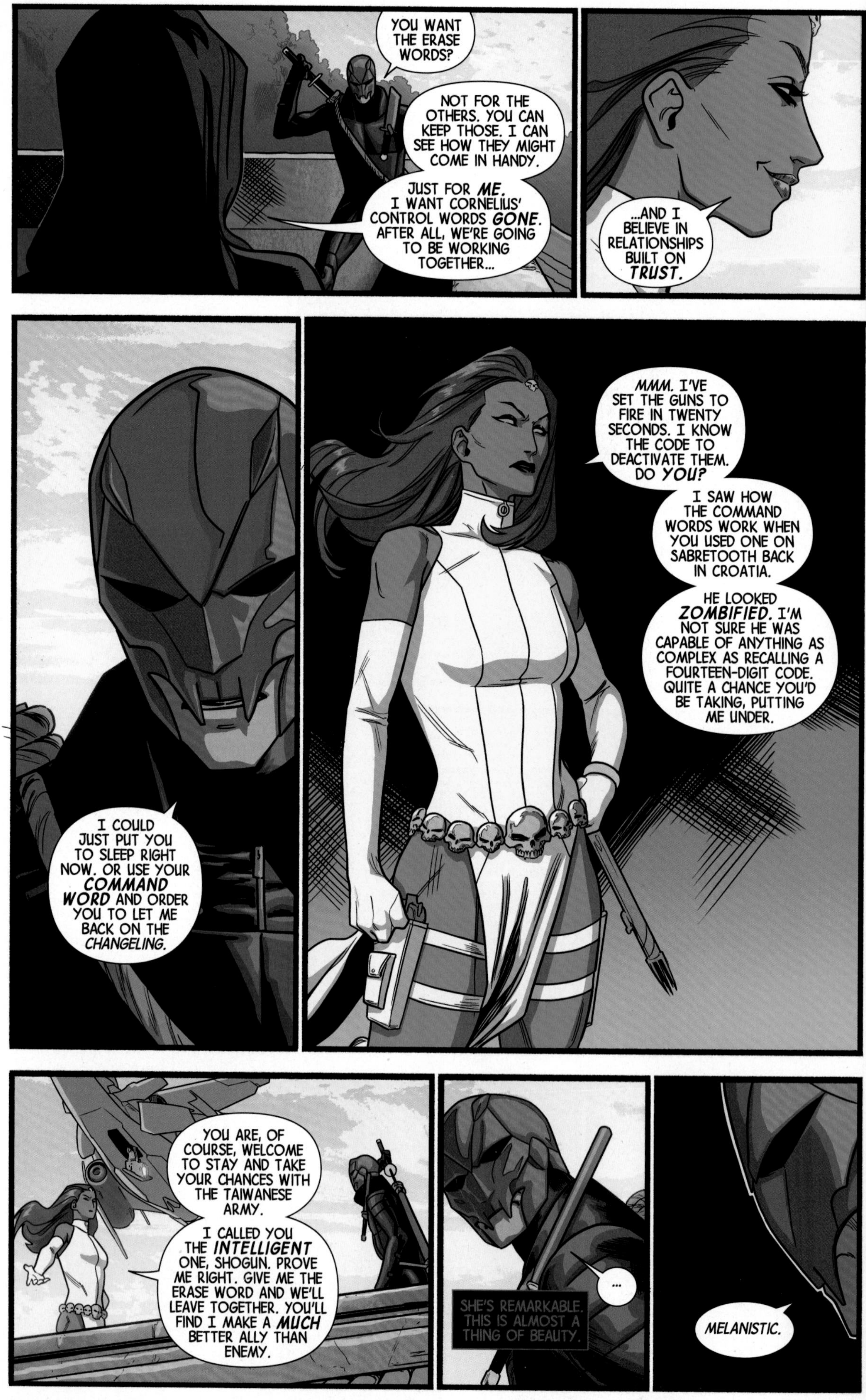
YOU WANT THE ERASE WORDS?
NOT FOR THE OTHERS. YOU CAN KEEP THOSE. I CAN SEE HOW THEY MIGHT COME IN HANDY.
JUST FOR ME. I WANT CORNELIUS' CONTROL WORDS GONE. AFTER ALL, WE'RE GOING TO BE WORKING TOGETHER...
...AND I BELIEVE IN RELATIONSHIPS BUILT ON TRUST.
I COULD JUST PUT YOU TO SLEEP RIGHT NOW. OR USE YOUR COMMAND WORD AND ORDER YOU TO LET ME BACK ON THE CHANGELING.
MMM. I'VE SET THE GUNS TO FIRE IN TWENTY SECONDS. I KNOW THE CODE TO DEACTIVATE THEM. DO YOU?
I SAW HOW THE COMMAND WORDS WORK WHEN YOU USED ONE ON SABRETOOTH BACK IN CROATIA.
HE LOOKED ZOMBIFIED. I'M NOT SURE HE WAS CAPABLE OF ANYTHING AS COMPLEX AS RECALLING A FOURTEEN-DIGIT CODE. QUITE A CHANCE YOU'D BE TAKING, PUTTING ME UNDER.
YOU ARE, OF COURSE, WELCOME TO STAY AND TAKE YOUR CHANCES WITH THE TAIWANESE ARMY.
I CALLED YOU THE INTELLIGENT ONE, SHOGUN. PROVE ME RIGHT. GIVE ME THE ERASE WORD AND WE'LL LEAVE TOGETHER. YOU'LL FIND I MAKE A MUCH BETTER ALLY THAN ENEMY.
...
SHE'S REMARKABLE. THIS IS ALMOST A THING OF BEAUTY.
MELANISTIC.

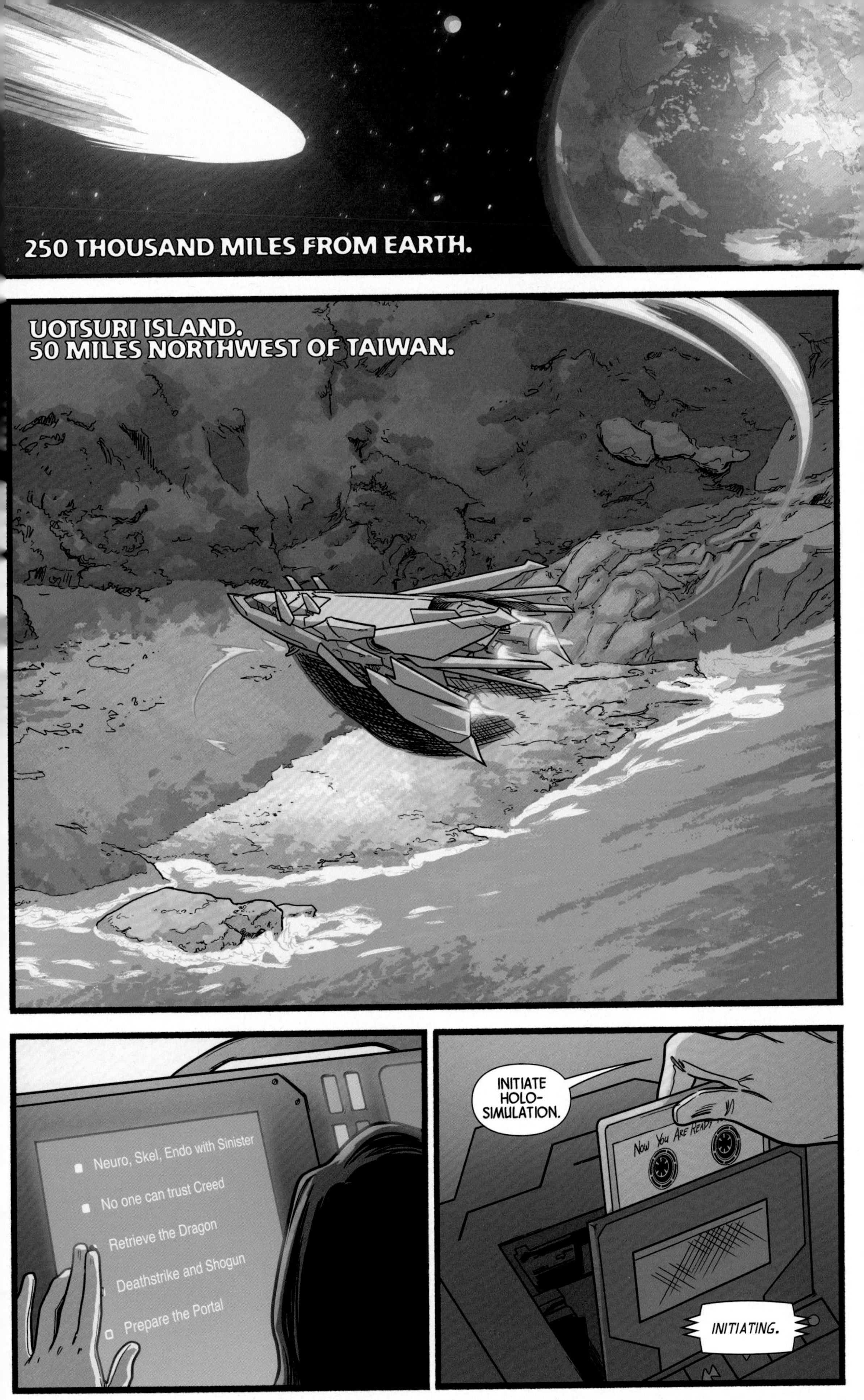
250 THOUSAND MILES FROM EARTH.
UOTSURI ISLAND.
50 MILES NORTHWEST OF TAIWAN.
Neuro, Skel, Endo with Sinister
No one can trust Creed
Retrieve the Dragon
Deathstrike and Shogun
Prepare the Portal
INITIATE HOLO-SIMULATION.
Now You Are Ready
INITIATING.

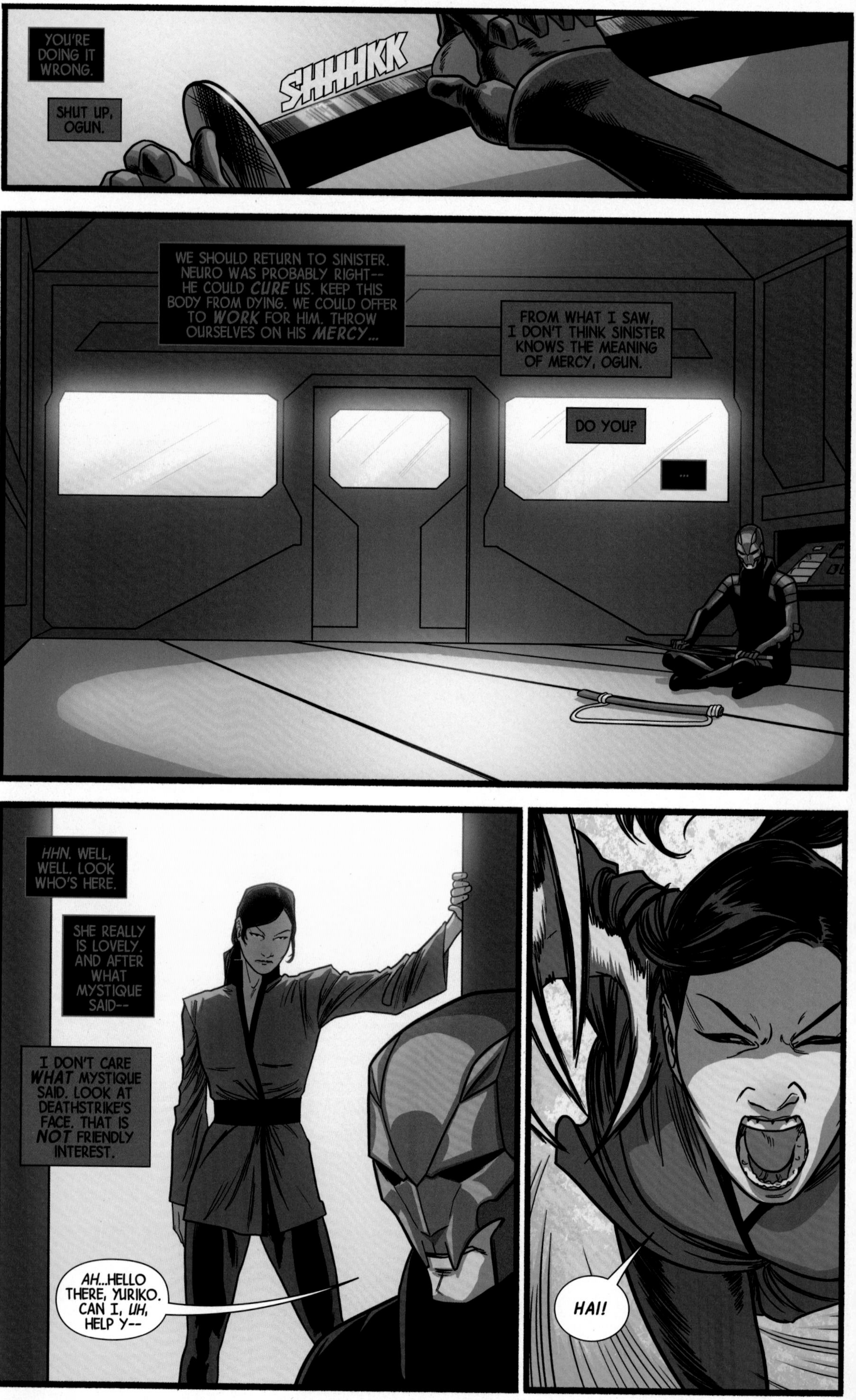
YOU'RE DOING IT WRONG.
SHUT UP, OGUN.
SHHHKK
WE SHOULD RETURN TO SINISTER. NEURO WAS PROBABLY RIGHT-- HE COULD CURE US. KEEP THIS BODY FROM DYING. WE COULD OFFER TO WORK FOR HIM. THROW OURSELVES ON HIS MERCY...
FROM WHAT I SAW, I DON'T THINK SINISTER KNOWS THE MEANING OF MERCY, OGUN.
DO YOU?
...
HHN. WELL, WELL. LOOK WHO'S HERE.
SHE REALLY IS LOVELY. AND AFTER WHAT MYSTIQUE SAID--
I DON'T CARE WHAT MYSTIQUE SAID. LOOK AT DEATHSTRIKE'S FACE. THAT IS NOT FRIENDLY INTEREST.
AH...HELLO THERE, YURIKO. CAN I, UH, HELP Y--
HAI!

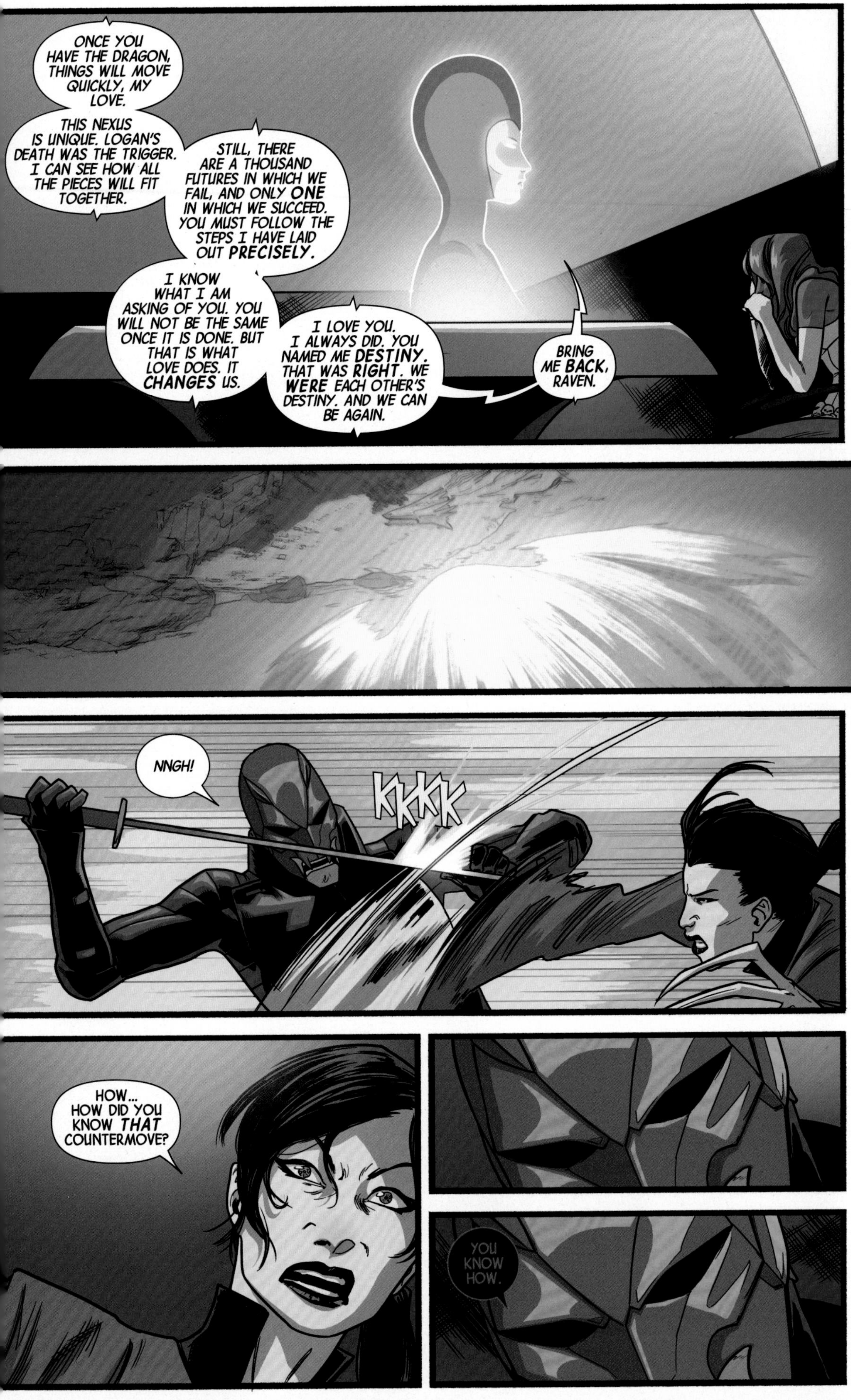
ONCE YOU HAVE THE DRAGON, THINGS WILL MOVE QUICKLY, MY LOVE.
THIS NEXUS IS UNIQUE. LOGAN'S DEATH WAS THE TRIGGER. I CAN SEE HOW ALL THE PIECES WILL FIT TOGETHER.
STILL, THERE ARE A THOUSAND FUTURES IN WHICH WE FAIL, AND ONLY ONE IN WHICH WE SUCCEED. YOU MUST FOLLOW THE STEPS I HAVE LAID OUT PRECISELY.
I KNOW WHAT I AM ASKING OF YOU. YOU WILL NOT BE THE SAME ONCE IT IS DONE. BUT THAT IS WHAT LOVE DOES. IT CHANGES US.
I LOVE YOU. I ALWAYS DID. YOU NAMED ME DESTINY. THAT WAS RIGHT. WE WERE EACH OTHER'S DESTINY. AND WE CAN BE AGAIN.
BRING ME BACK, RAVEN.
NNGH!
KKKK
HOW... HOW DID YOU KNOW THAT COUNTERMOVE?
YOU KNOW HOW.

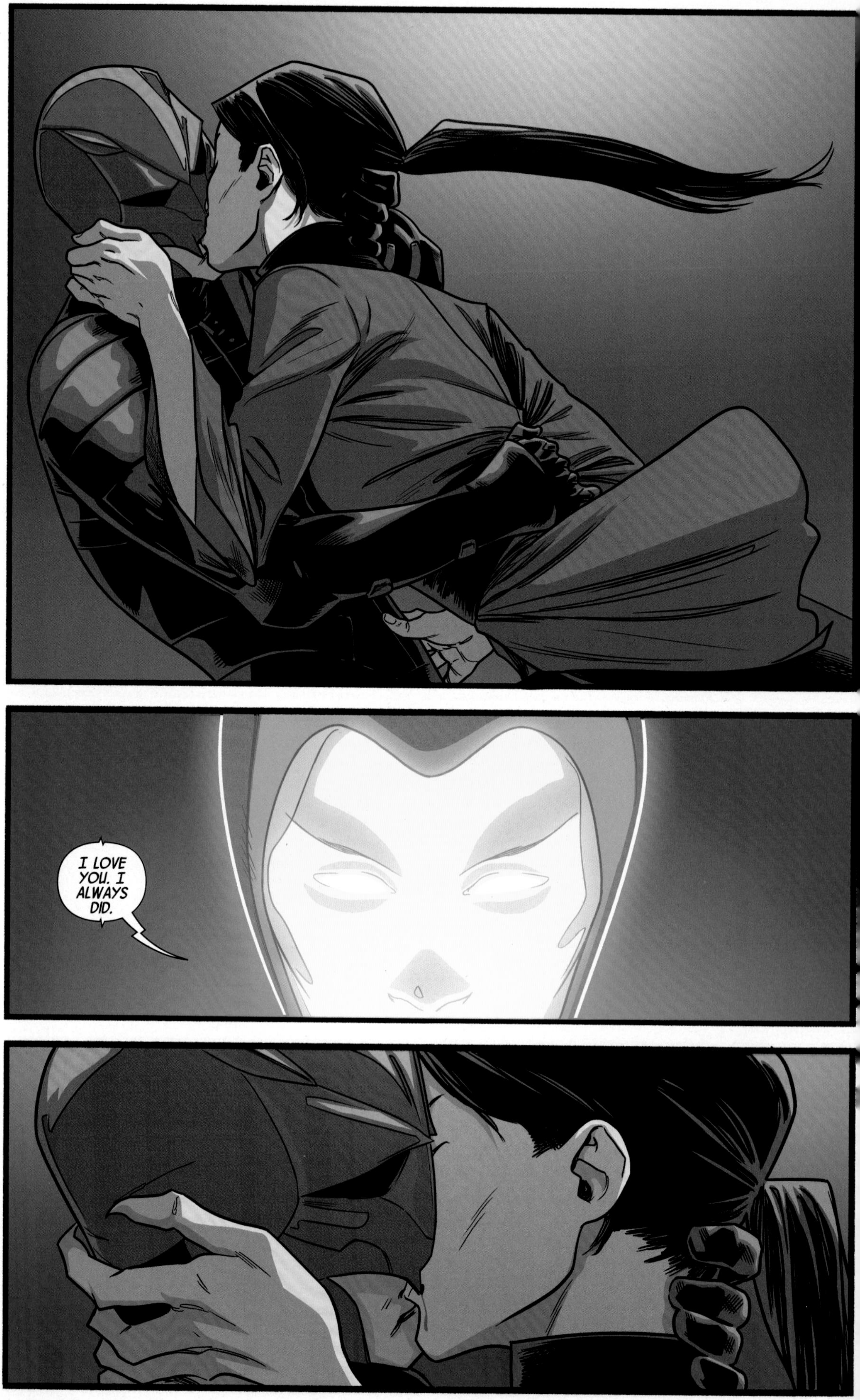
I LOVE YOU. I ALWAYS DID.

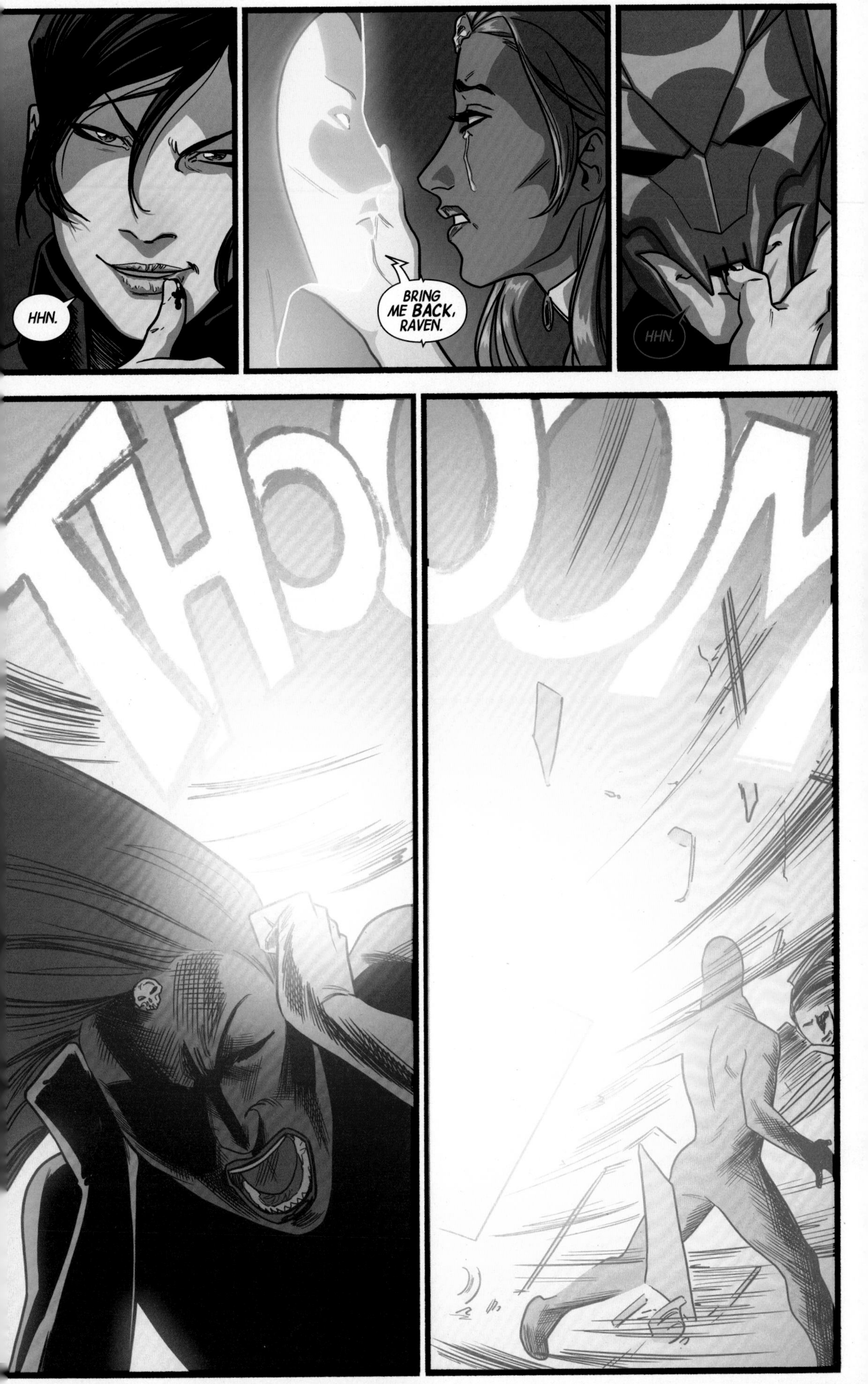
HHN.
BRING ME BACK, RAVEN.
HHN.
THOOM

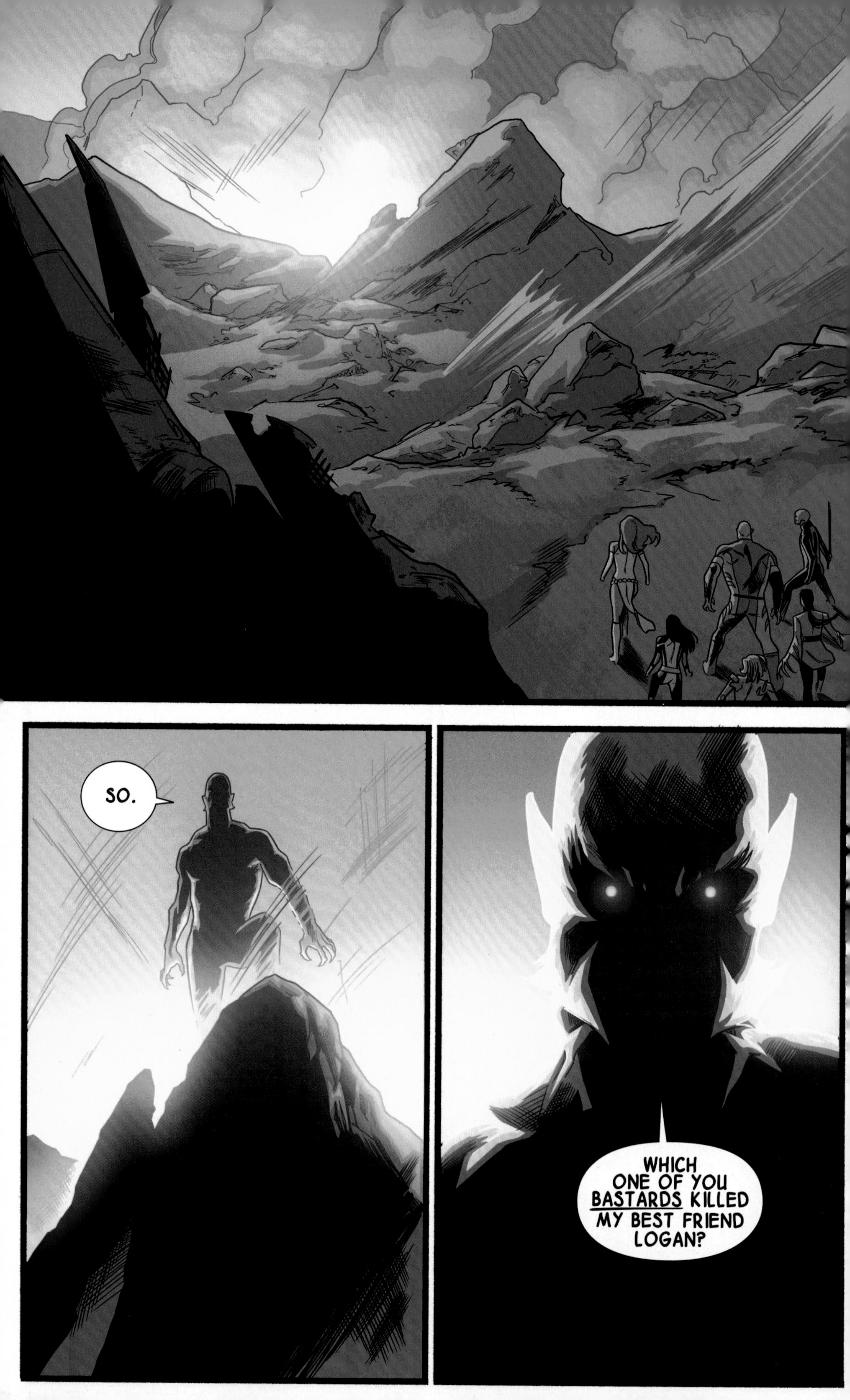
SO.
WHICH ONE OF YOU BASTARDS KILLED MY BEST FRIEND LOGAN?

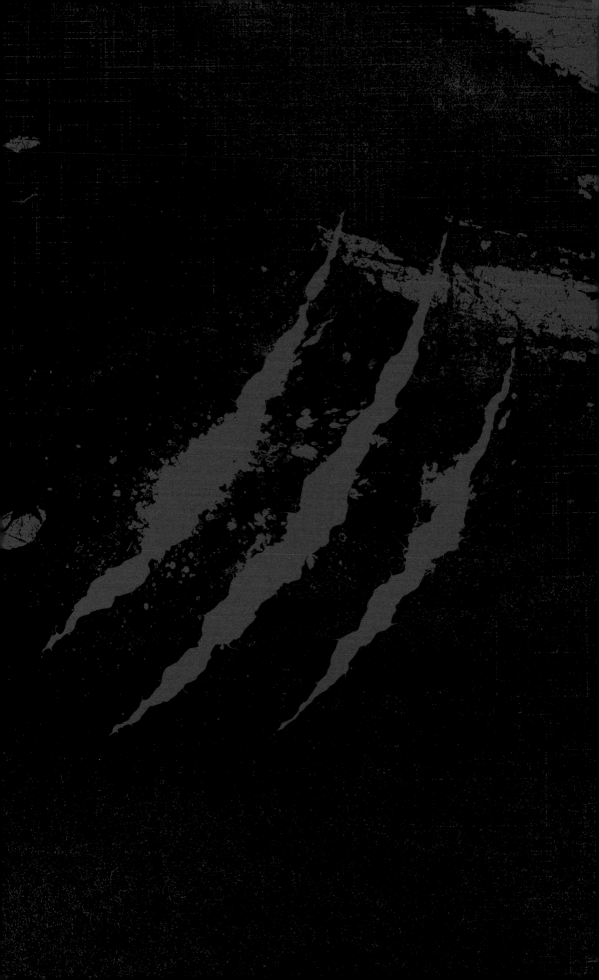

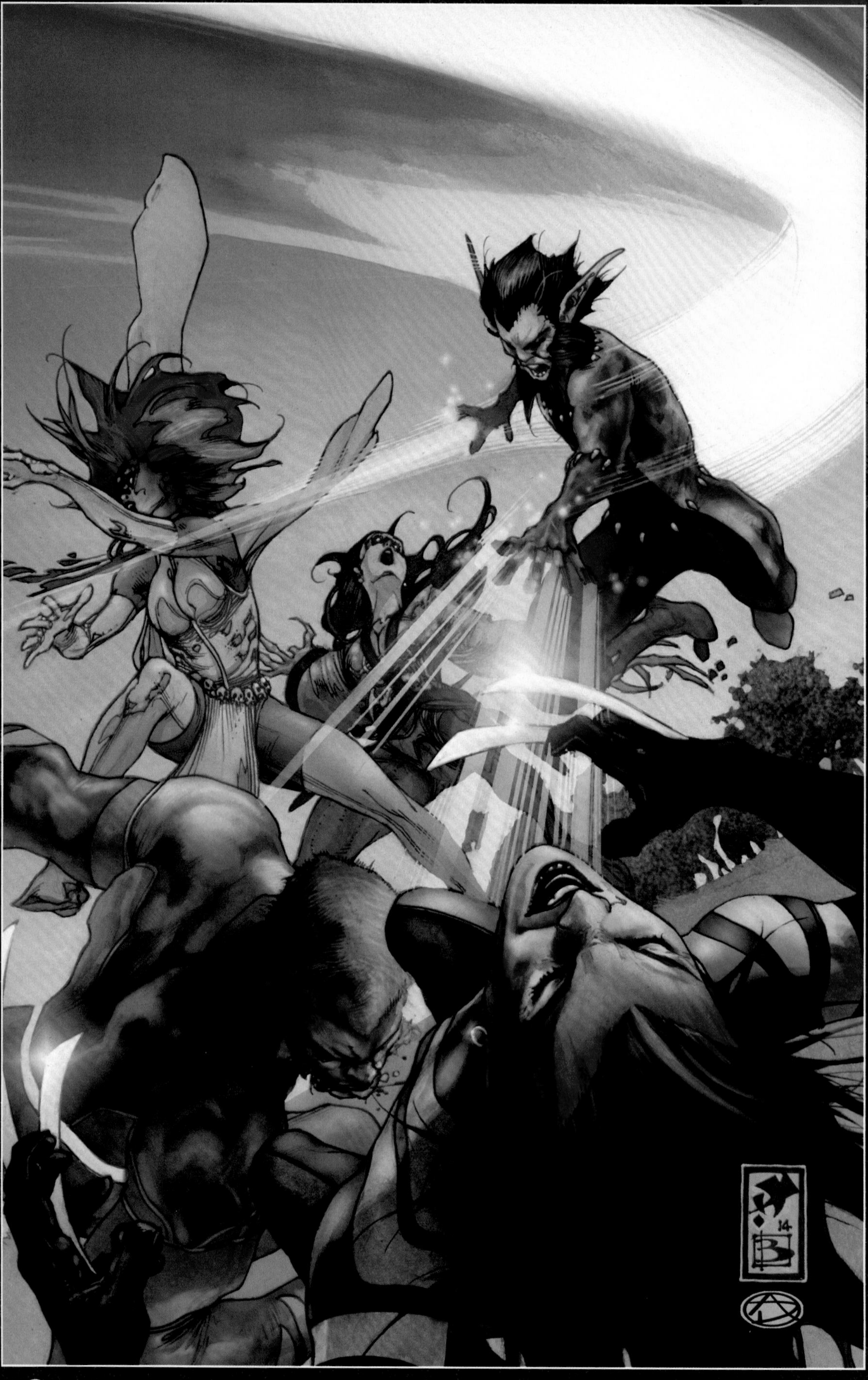

#8

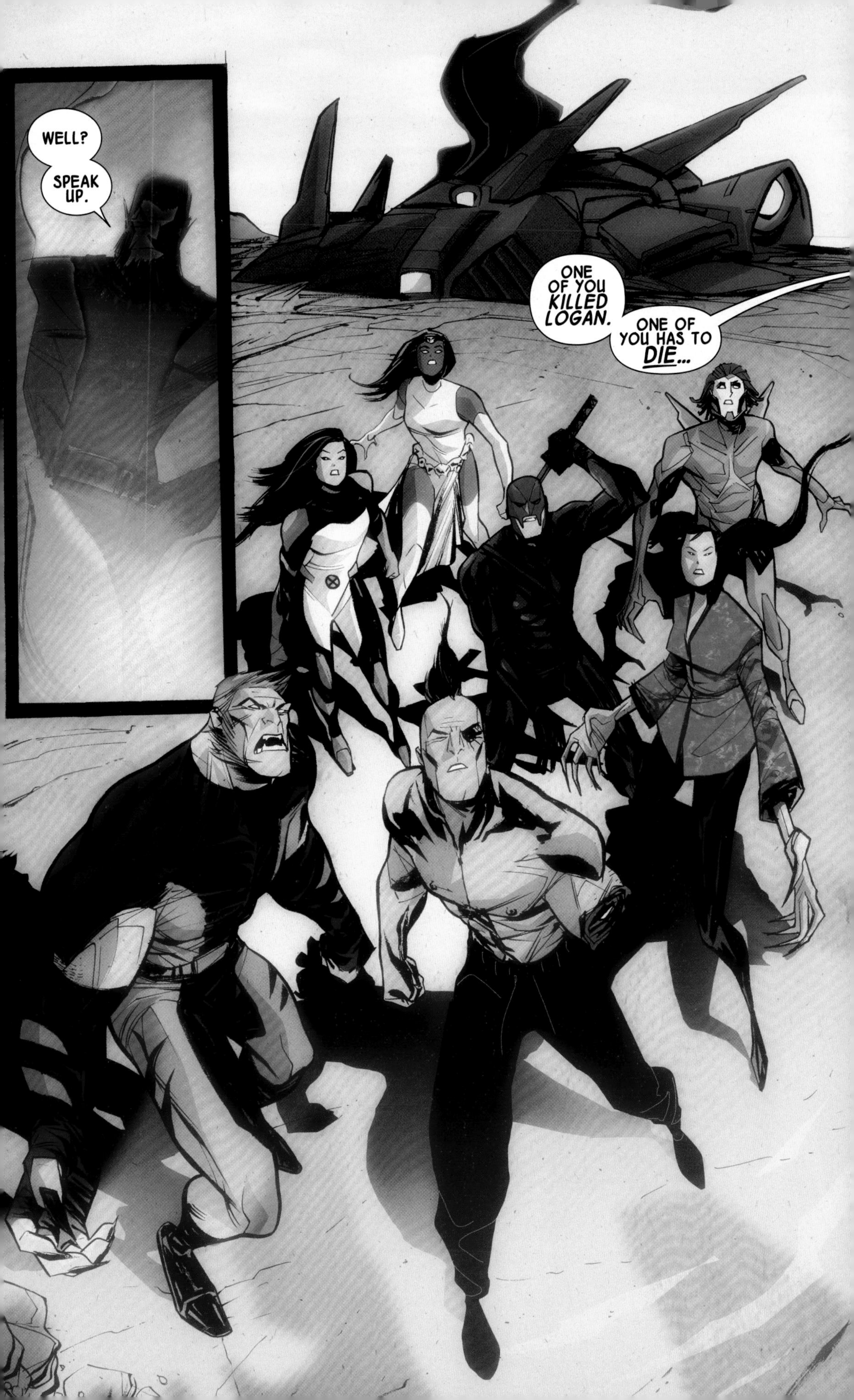
WELL?
SPEAK UP.
ONE OF YOU KILLED LOGAN.
ONE OF YOU HAS TO DIE...

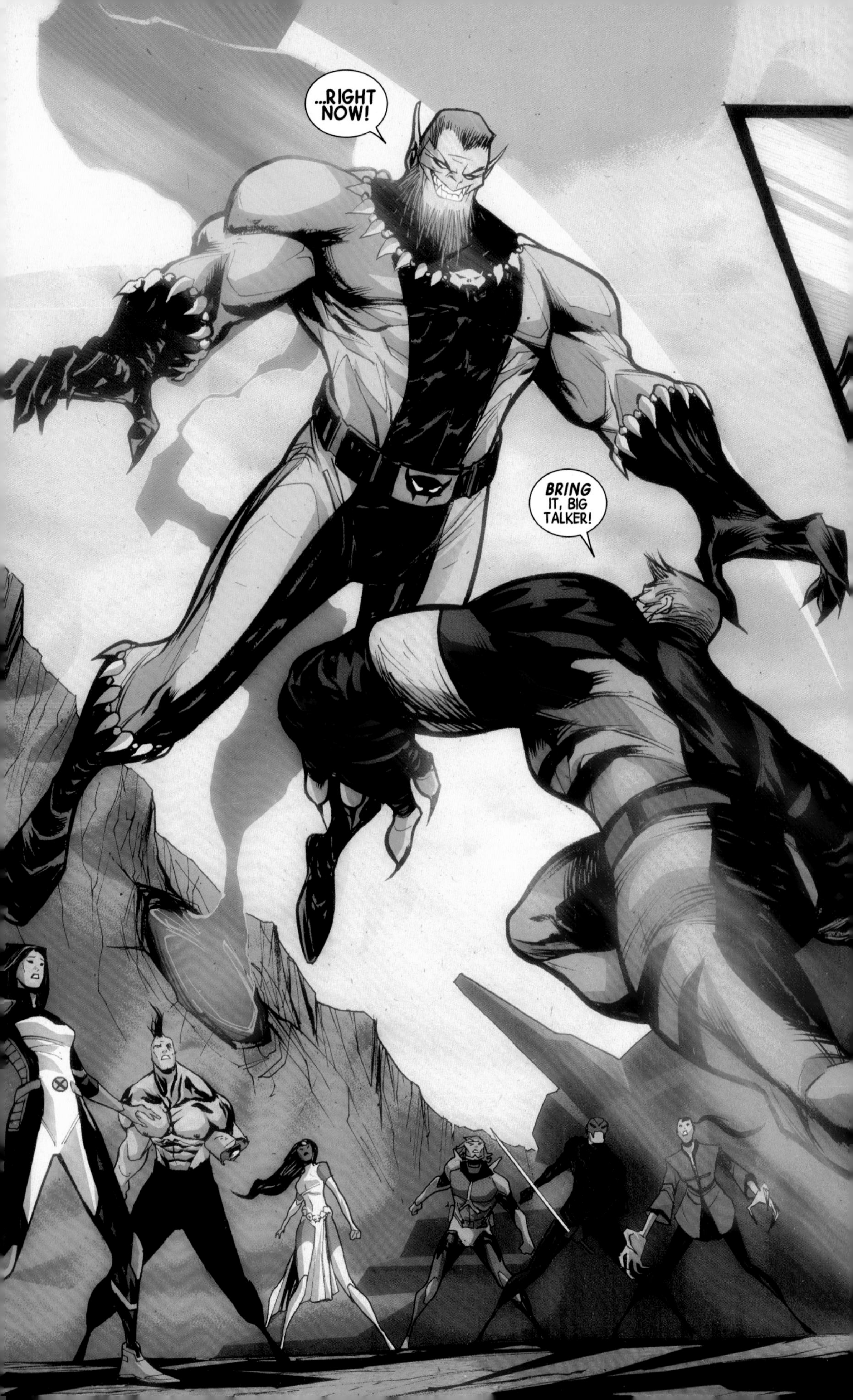
...RIGHT NOW!
*BRING* IT, BIG TALKER!

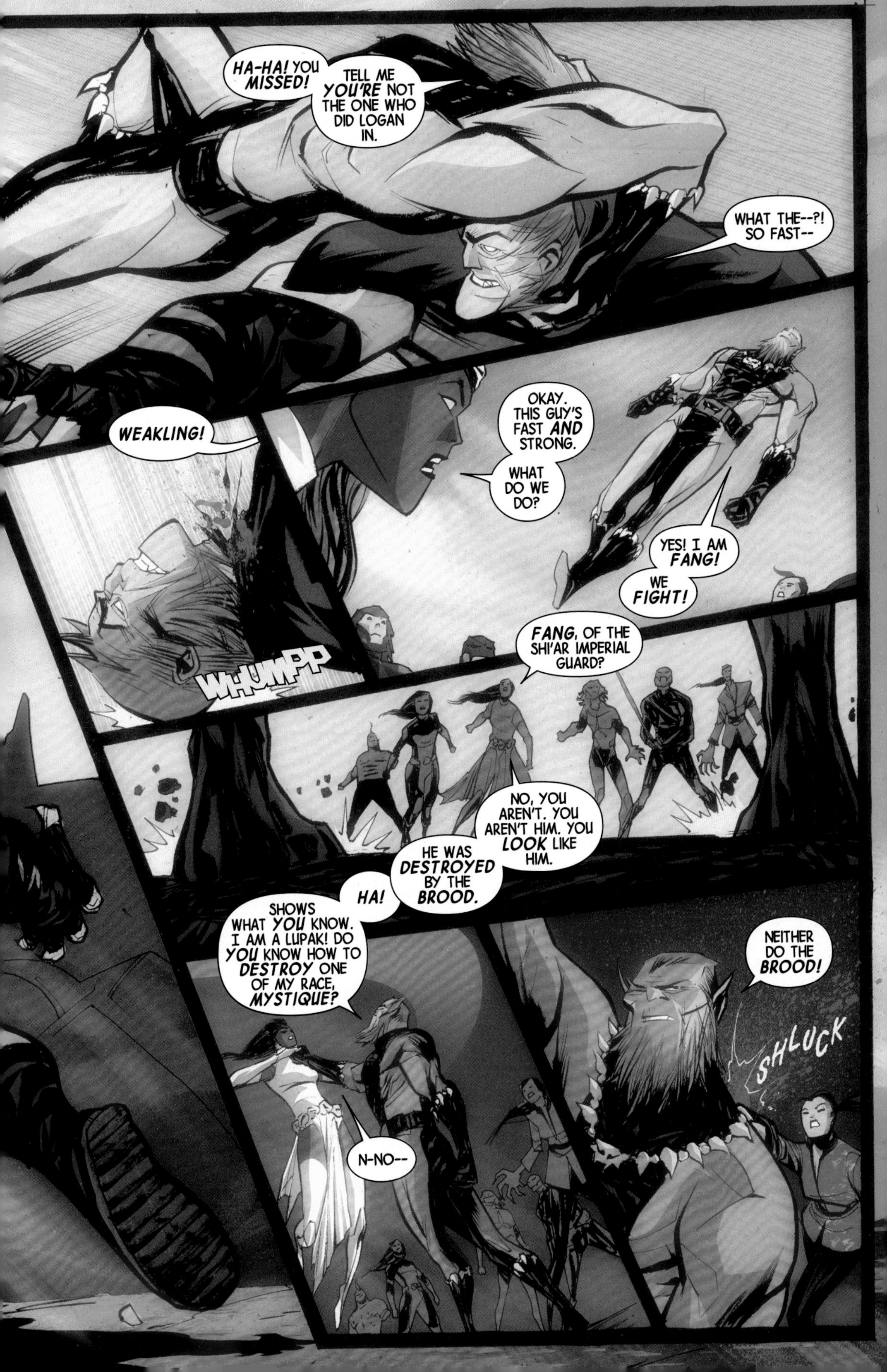

HA-HA! YOU MISSED!
TELL ME YOU'RE NOT THE ONE WHO DID LOGAN IN.
WHAT THE--?! SO FAST--
WEAKLING!
OKAY. THIS GUY'S FAST AND STRONG.
WHAT DO WE DO?
YES! I AM FANG!
WE FIGHT!
WHUMPP
FANG, OF THE SHI'AR IMPERIAL GUARD?
NO, YOU AREN'T. YOU AREN'T HIM. YOU LOOK LIKE HIM.
HE WAS DESTROYED BY THE BROOD.
HA!
SHOWS WHAT YOU KNOW. I AM A LUPAK! DO YOU KNOW HOW TO DESTROY ONE OF MY RACE, MYSTIQUE?
N-NO--
NEITHER DO THE BROOD!
SHLUCK

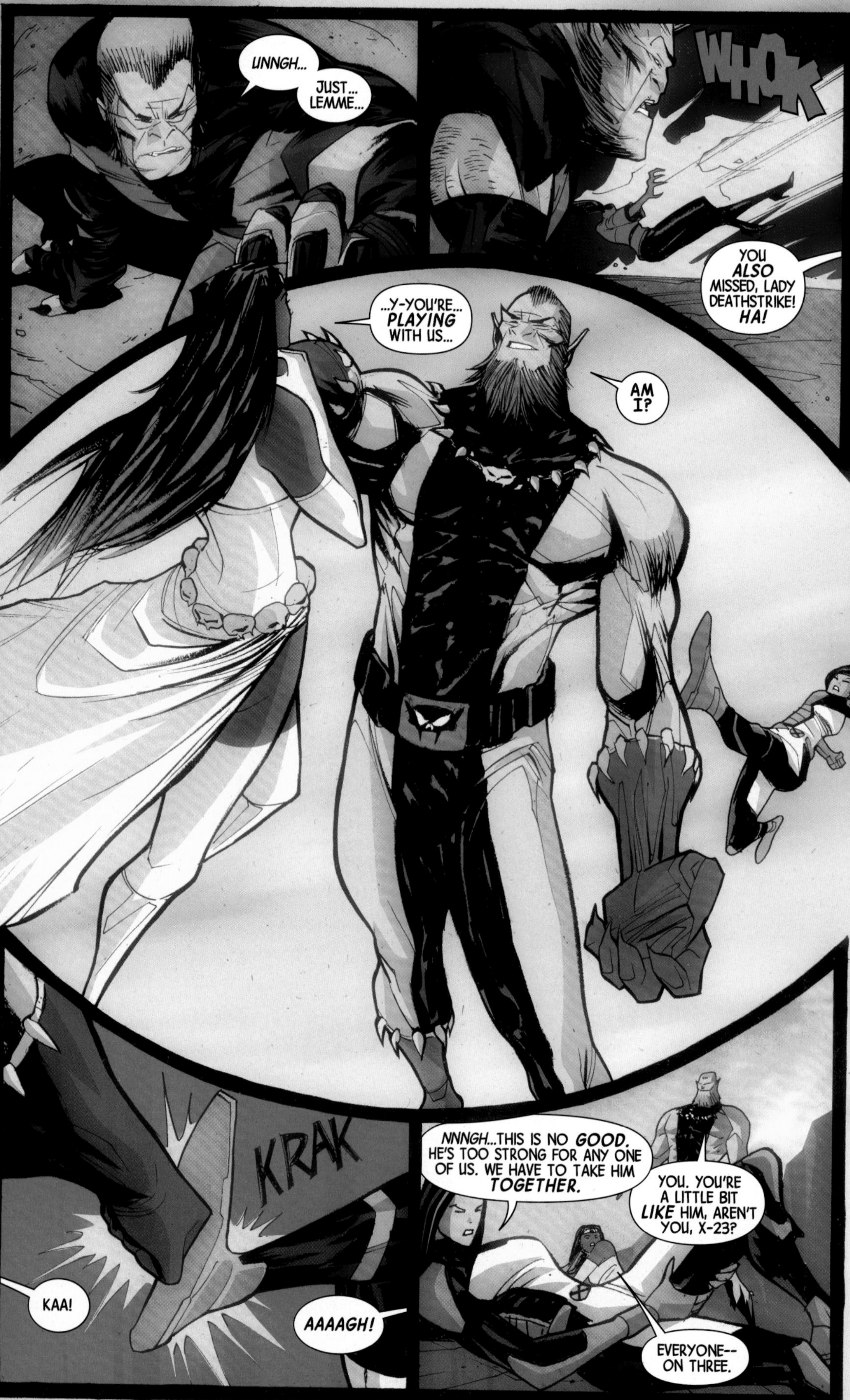
UNNGH...
JUST... LEMME...
WHOK
YOU ALSO MISSED, LADY DEATHSTRIKE! HA!
...Y-YOU'RE... PLAYING WITH US...
AM I?
KRAK
KAA!
AAAAGH!
NNNGH...THIS IS NO GOOD. HE'S TOO STRONG FOR ANY ONE OF US. WE HAVE TO TAKE HIM TOGETHER.
YOU. YOU'RE A LITTLE BIT LIKE HIM, AREN'T YOU, X-23?
EVERYONE-- ON THREE.

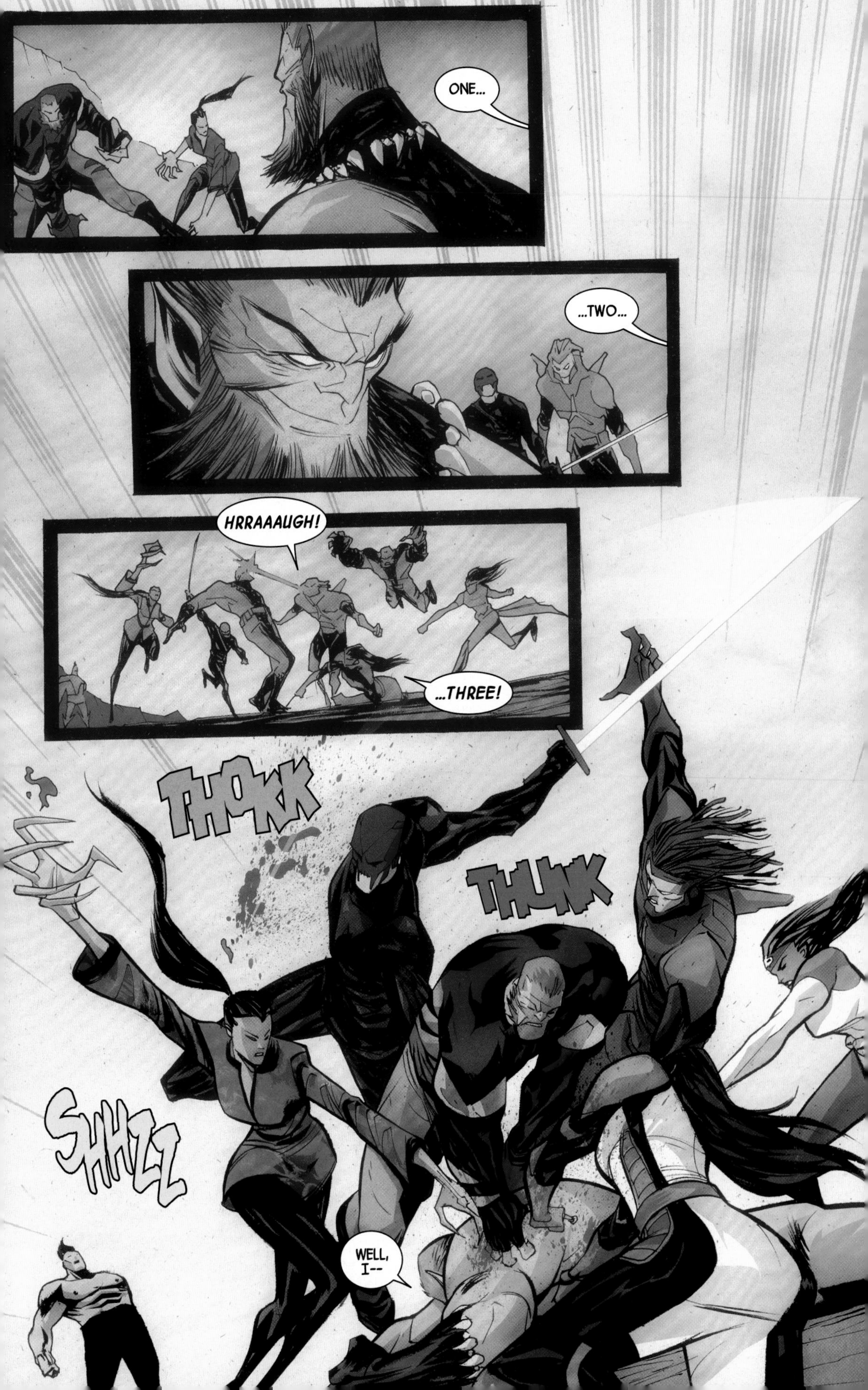
ONE...
...TWO...
HRRAAAUGH!
...THREE!
THOKK
THUNK
SHHZZ
WELL, I--

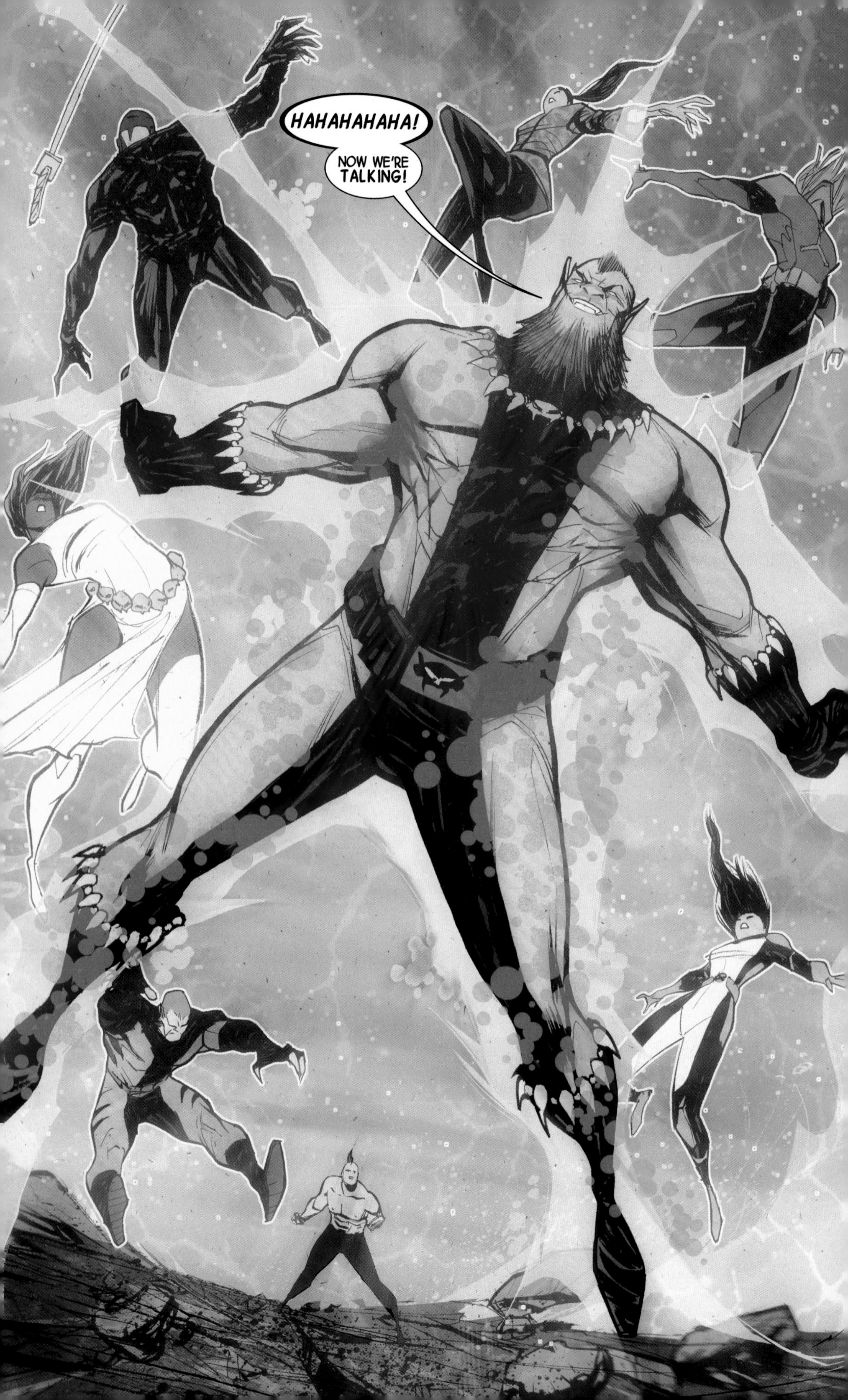
HAHAHAHAHA!
NOW WE'RE TALKING!

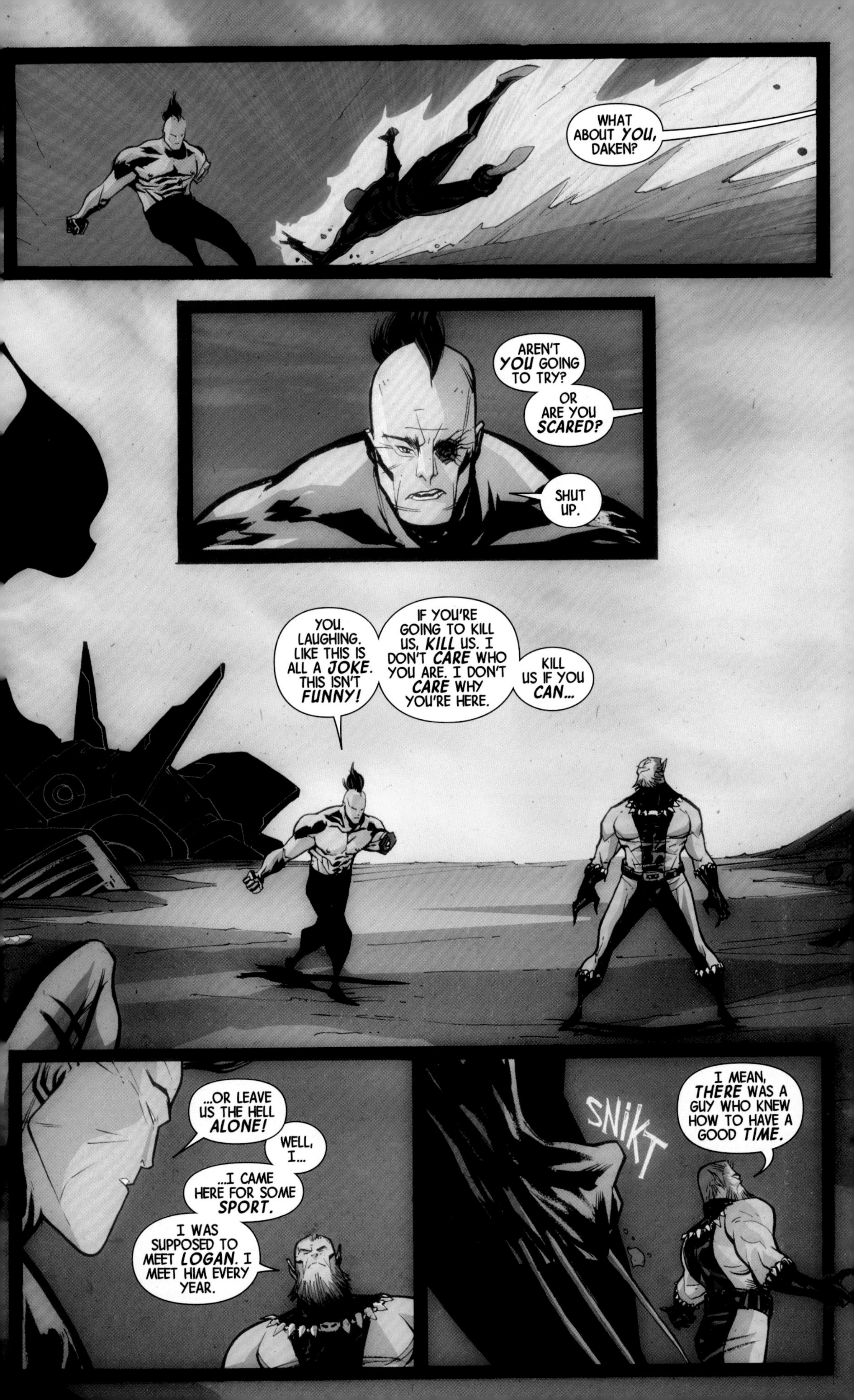
WHAT ABOUT YOU, DAKEN?
AREN'T YOU GOING TO TRY?
OR ARE YOU SCARED?
SHUT UP.
YOU. LAUGHING. LIKE THIS IS ALL A JOKE. THIS ISN'T FUNNY!
IF YOU'RE GOING TO KILL US, KILL US. I DON'T CARE WHO YOU ARE. I DON'T CARE WHY YOU'RE HERE.
KILL US IF YOU CAN...
...OR LEAVE US THE HELL ALONE!
WELL, I...
...I CAME HERE FOR SOME SPORT.
I WAS SUPPOSED TO MEET LOGAN. I MEET HIM EVERY YEAR.
SNIKT
I MEAN, THERE WAS A GUY WHO KNEW HOW TO HAVE A GOOD TIME.

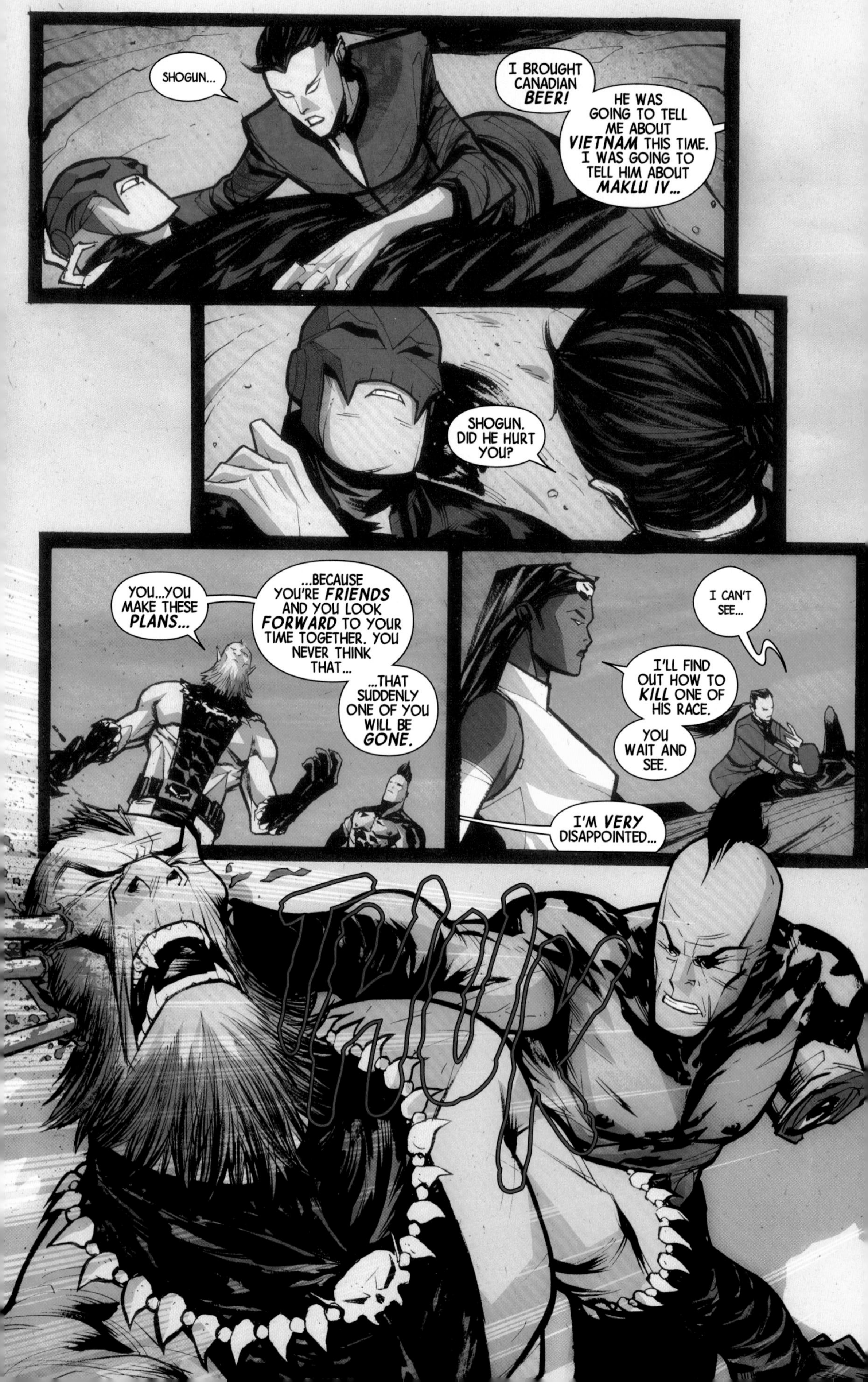
SHOGUN...
I BROUGHT CANADIAN BEER!
HE WAS GOING TO TELL ME ABOUT VIETNAM THIS TIME. I WAS GOING TO TELL HIM ABOUT MAKLU IV...
SHOGUN. DID HE HURT YOU?
YOU...YOU MAKE THESE PLANS...
...BECAUSE YOU'RE FRIENDS AND YOU LOOK FORWARD TO YOUR TIME TOGETHER. YOU NEVER THINK THAT...
...THAT SUDDENLY ONE OF YOU WILL BE GONE.
I CAN'T SEE...
I'LL FIND OUT HOW TO KILL ONE OF HIS RACE.
YOU WAIT AND SEE.
I'M VERY DISAPPOINTED...

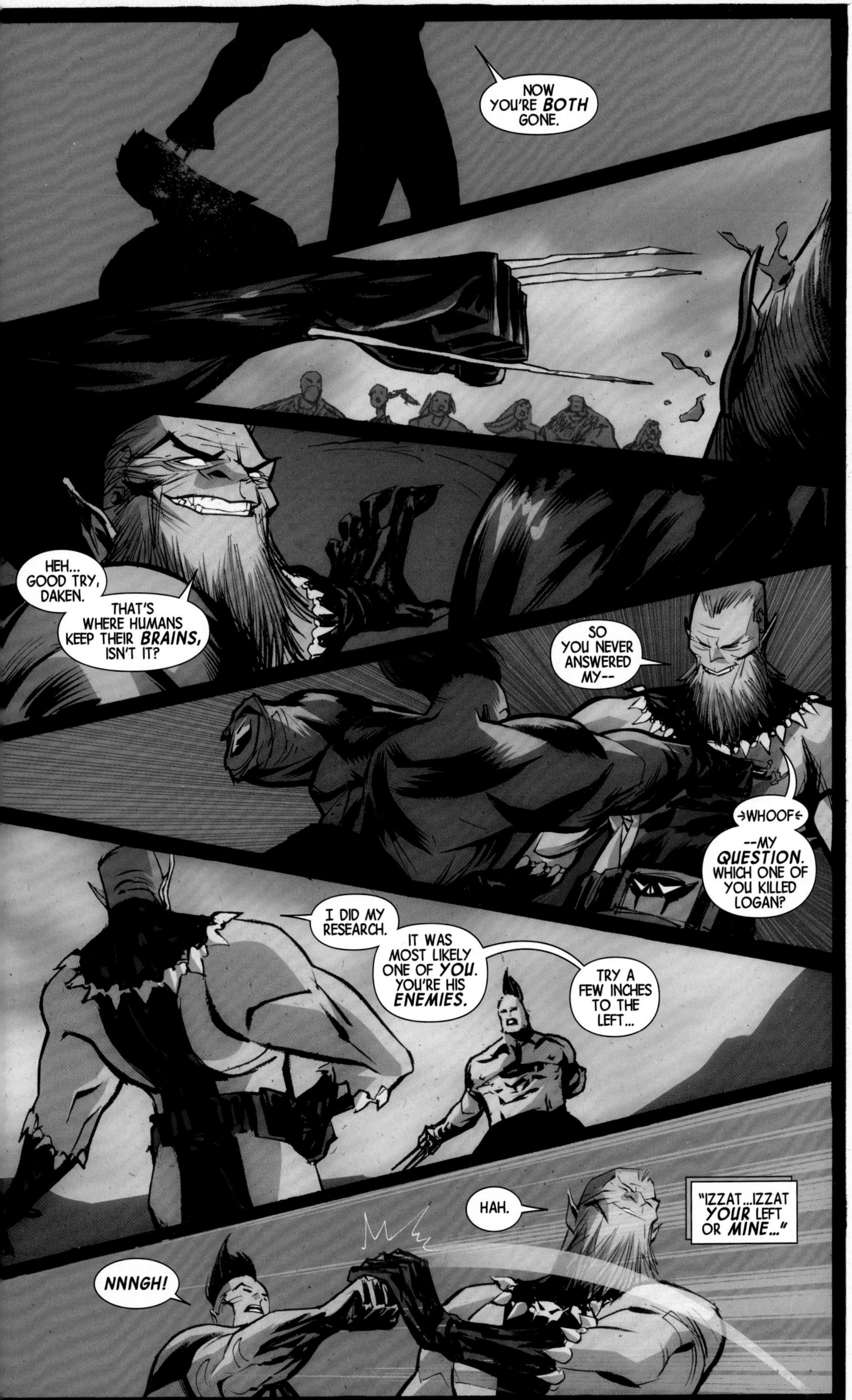

NOW YOU'RE *BOTH* GONE.
HEH... GOOD TRY, DAKEN.
THAT'S WHERE HUMANS KEEP THEIR *BRAINS,* ISN'T IT?
SO YOU NEVER ANSWERED MY--
→WHOOF←
--MY *QUESTION.* WHICH ONE OF YOU KILLED LOGAN?
I DID MY RESEARCH.
IT WAS MOST LIKELY ONE OF *YOU.* YOU'RE HIS *ENEMIES.*
TRY A FEW INCHES TO THE LEFT...
HAH.
"IZZAT...IZZAT *YOUR* LEFT OR *MINE*..."
*NNNGH!*

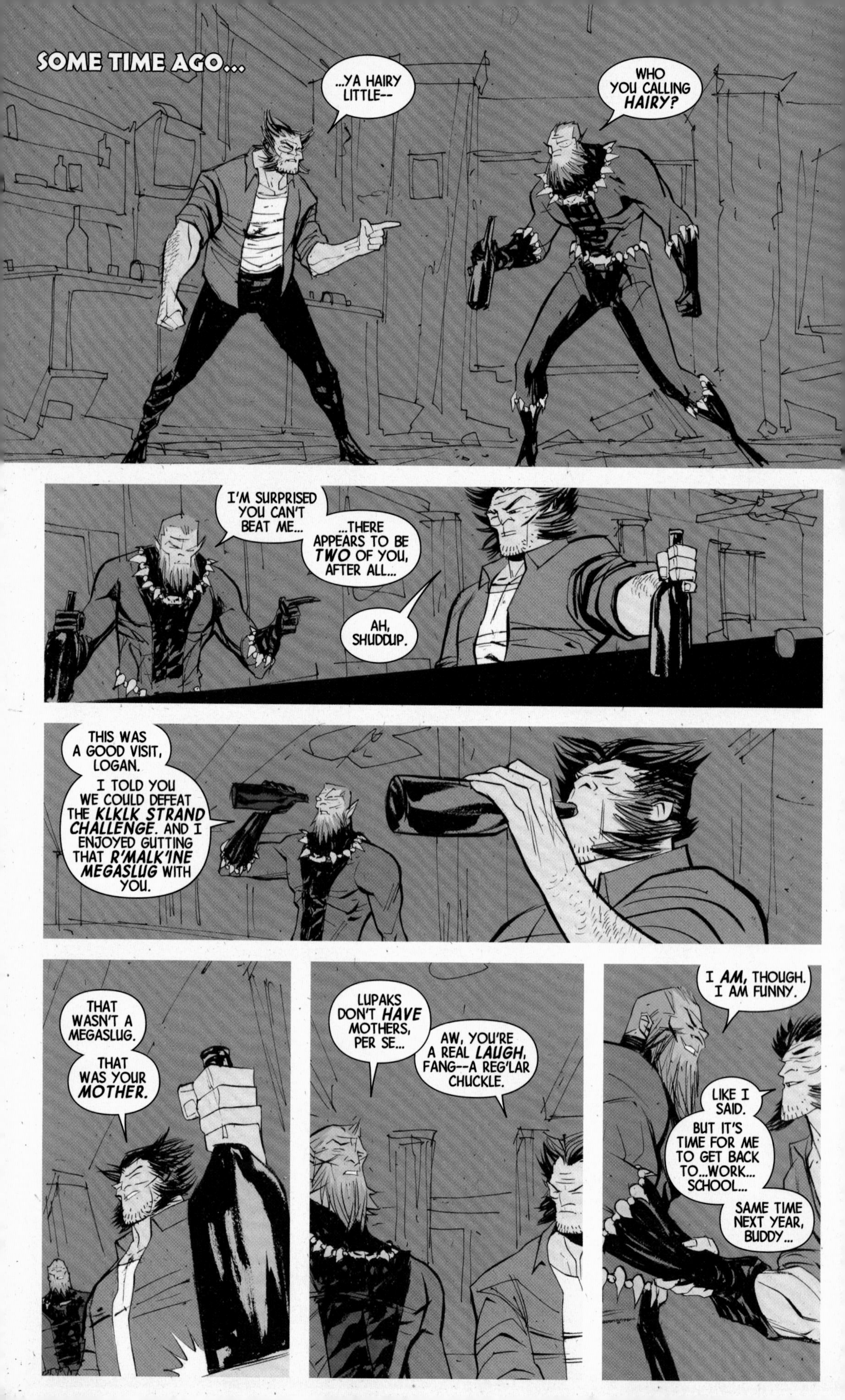
SOME TIME AGO...
...YA HAIRY LITTLE--
WHO YOU CALLING HAIRY?
I'M SURPRISED YOU CAN'T BEAT ME...
...THERE APPEARS TO BE TWO OF YOU, AFTER ALL...
AH, SHUDDUP.
THIS WAS A GOOD VISIT, LOGAN.
I TOLD YOU WE COULD DEFEAT THE KLKLK STRAND CHALLENGE. AND I ENJOYED GUTTING THAT R'MALK'INE MEGASLUG WITH YOU.
THAT WASN'T A MEGASLUG.
THAT WAS YOUR MOTHER.
LUPAKS DON'T HAVE MOTHERS, PER SE...
AW, YOU'RE A REAL LAUGH, FANG--A REG'LAR CHUCKLE.
I AM, THOUGH. I AM FUNNY.
LIKE I SAID.
BUT IT'S TIME FOR ME TO GET BACK TO...WORK... SCHOOL...
SAME TIME NEXT YEAR, BUDDY...

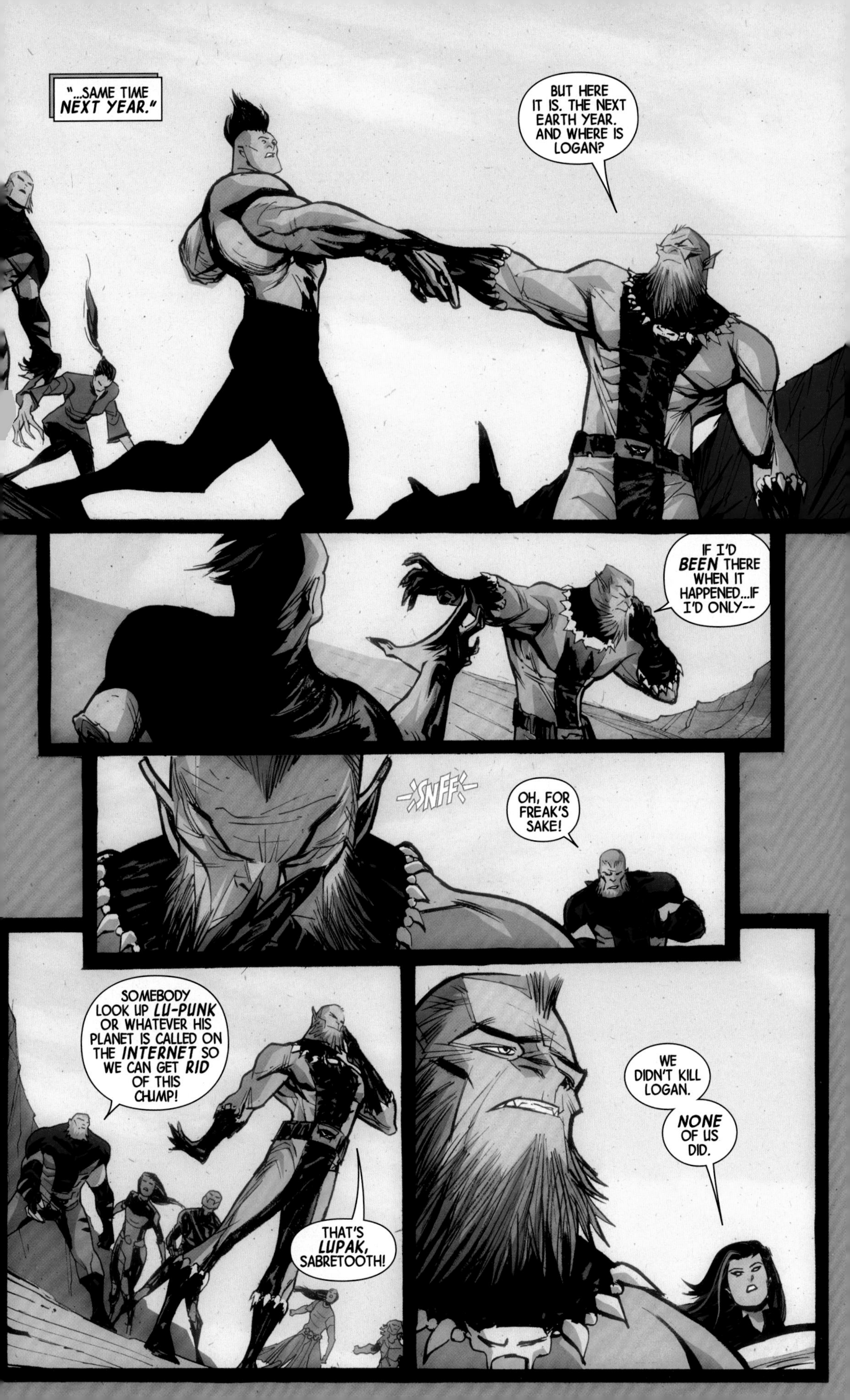
"...SAME TIME NEXT YEAR."
BUT HERE IT IS. THE NEXT EARTH YEAR. AND WHERE IS LOGAN?
IF I'D BEEN THERE WHEN IT HAPPENED...IF I'D ONLY--
SNFF
OH, FOR FREAK'S SAKE!
SOMEBODY LOOK UP LU-PUNK OR WHATEVER HIS PLANET IS CALLED ON THE INTERNET SO WE CAN GET RID OF THIS CHUMP!
THAT'S LUPAK, SABRETOOTH!
WE DIDN'T KILL LOGAN.
NONE OF US DID.

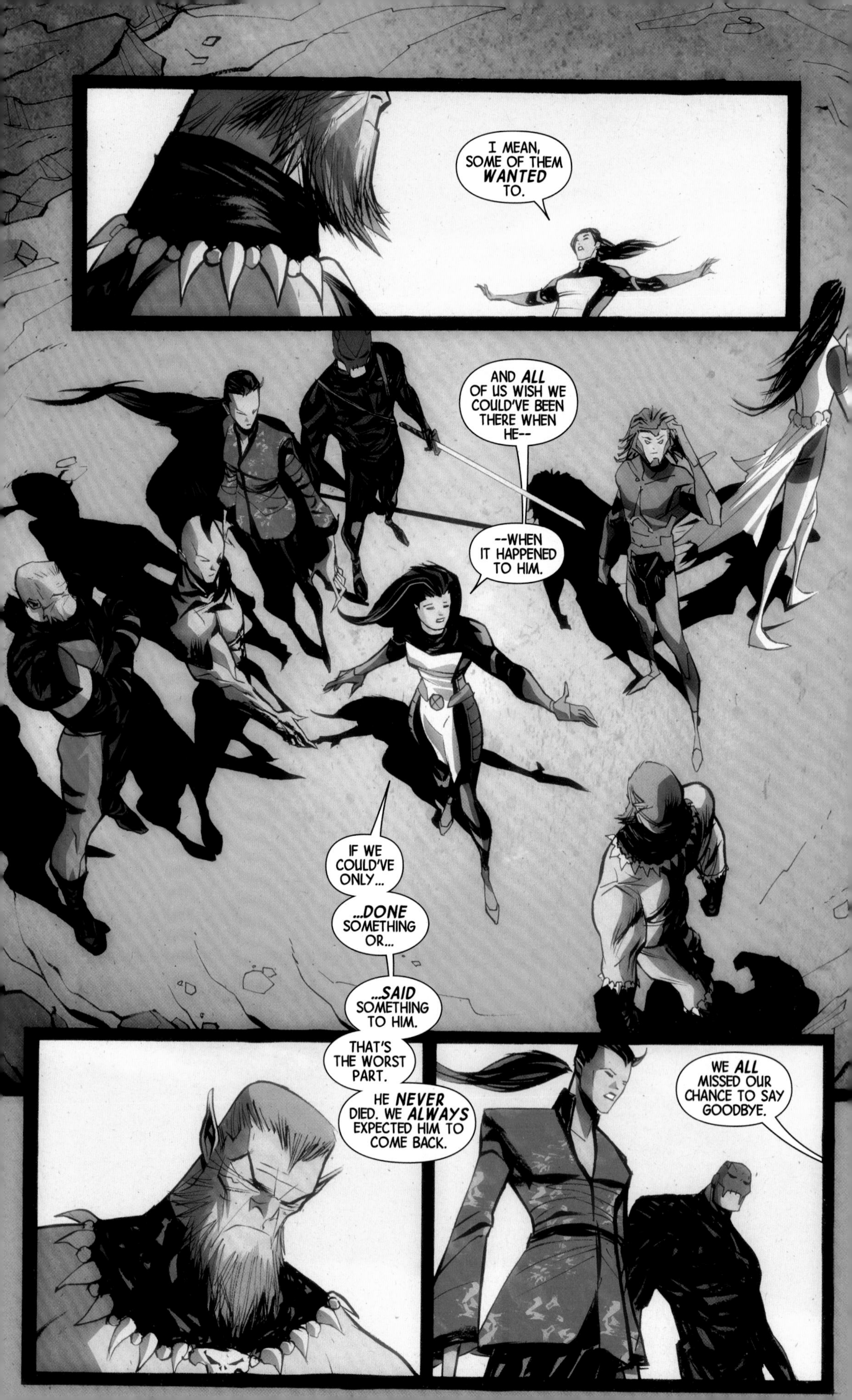
I MEAN, SOME OF THEM WANTED TO.
AND ALL OF US WISH WE COULD'VE BEEN THERE WHEN HE--
--WHEN IT HAPPENED TO HIM.
IF WE COULD'VE ONLY...
...DONE SOMETHING OR...
...SAID SOMETHING TO HIM.
THAT'S THE WORST PART.
HE NEVER DIED. WE ALWAYS EXPECTED HIM TO COME BACK.
WE ALL MISSED OUR CHANCE TO SAY GOODBYE.

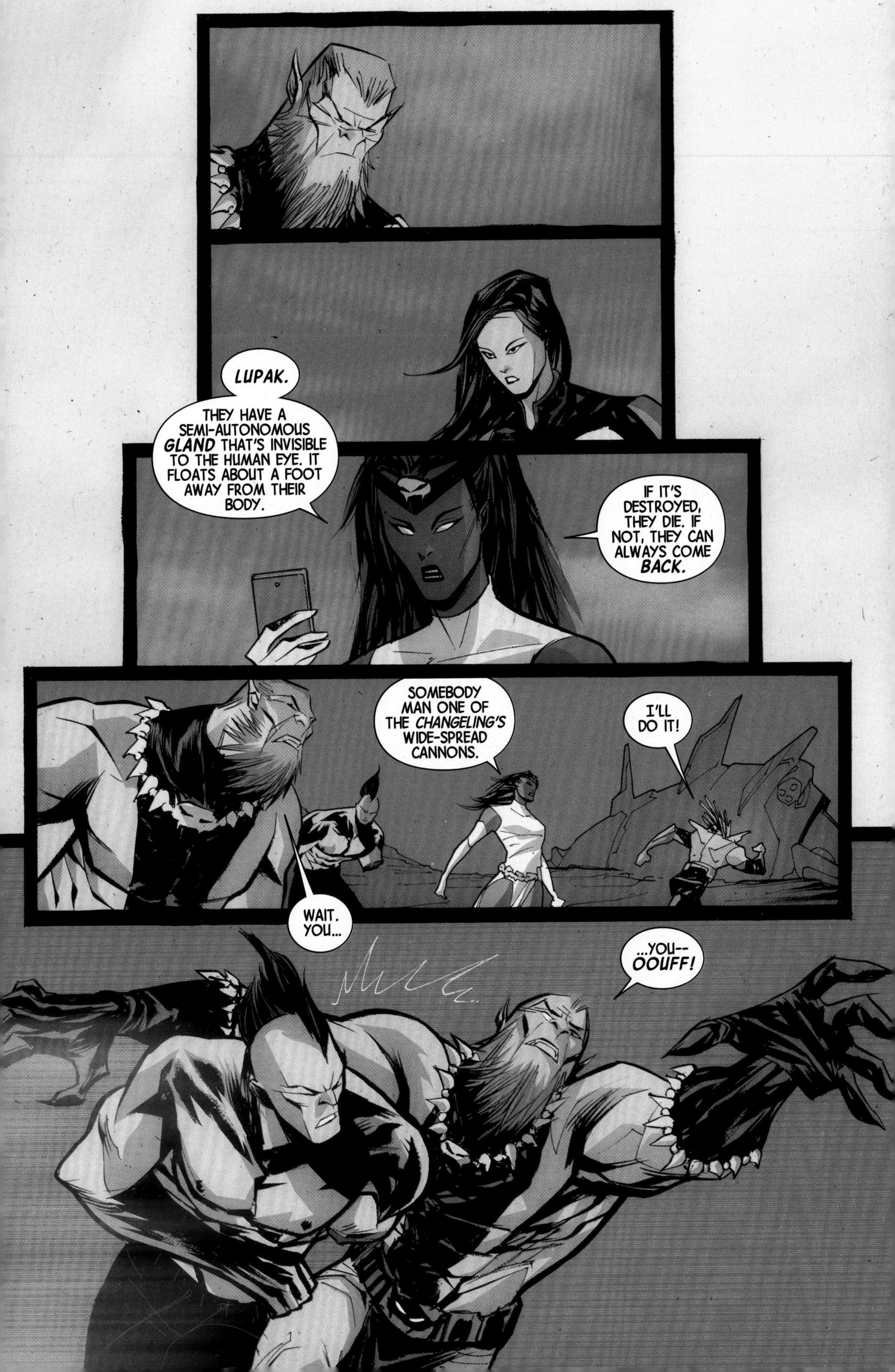

LUPAK.
THEY HAVE A SEMI-AUTONOMOUS GLAND THAT'S INVISIBLE TO THE HUMAN EYE. IT FLOATS ABOUT A FOOT AWAY FROM THEIR BODY.
IF IT'S DESTROYED, THEY DIE. IF NOT, THEY CAN ALWAYS COME BACK.
SOMEBODY MAN ONE OF THE CHANGELING'S WIDE-SPREAD CANNONS.
I'LL DO IT!
WAIT. YOU...
...YOU--OOUFF!

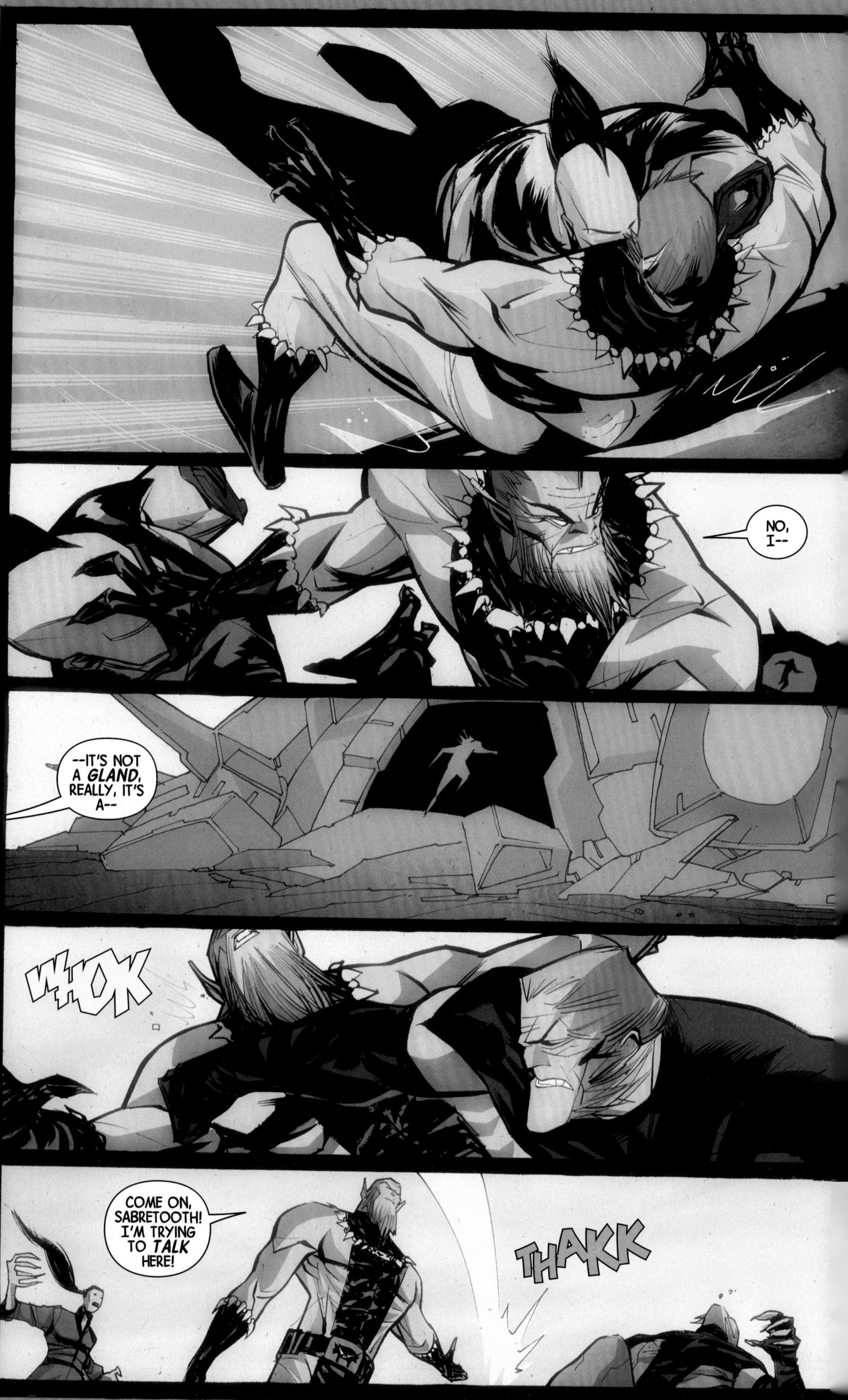
NO, I--
--IT'S NOT A GLAND, REALLY, IT'S A--
WHOK
COME ON, SABRETOOTH! I'M TRYING TO TALK HERE!
THAKK

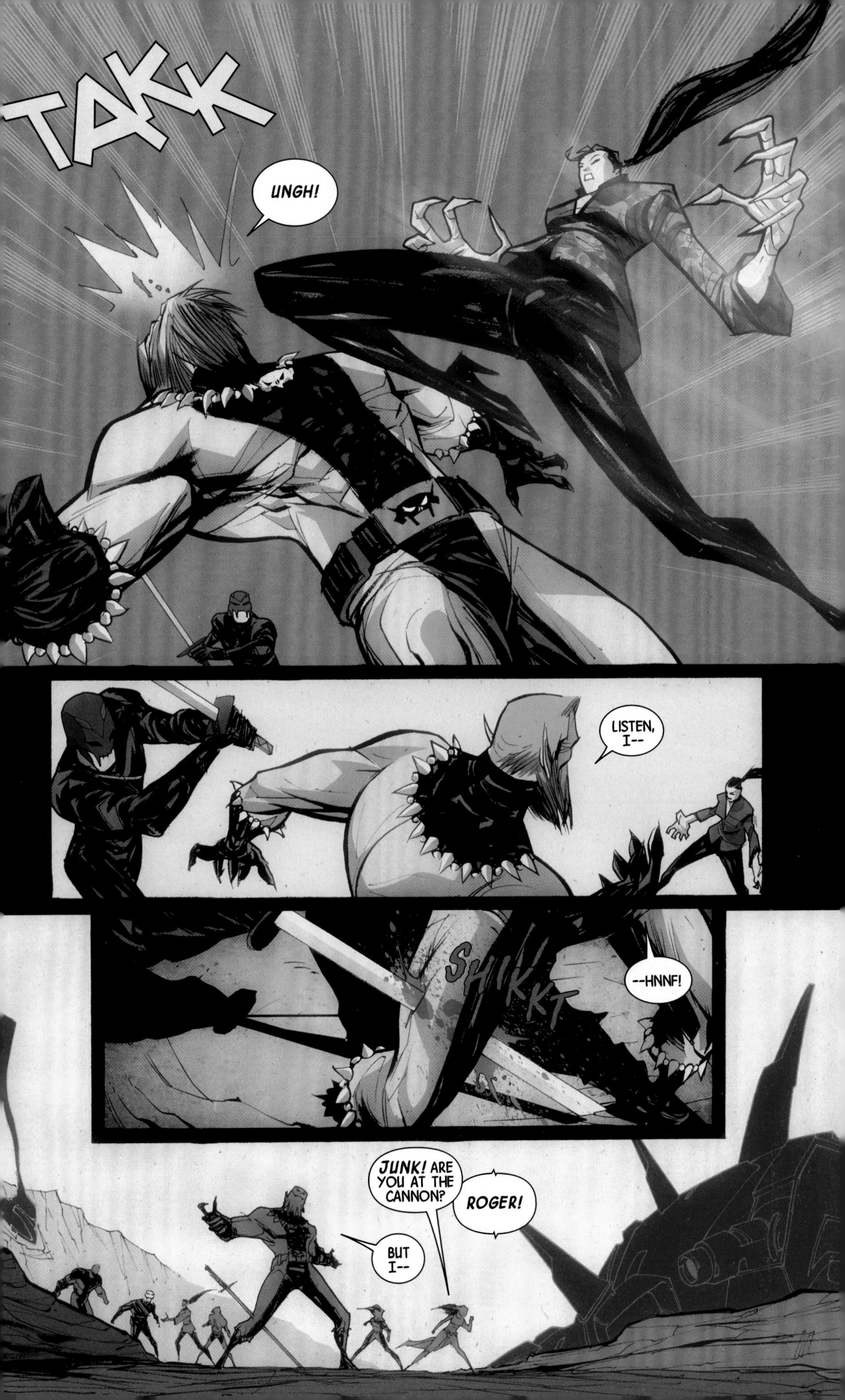
TAKK
UNGH!
LISTEN, I--
SHIKKT
--HNNF!
JUNK! ARE YOU AT THE CANNON?
ROGER!
BUT I--

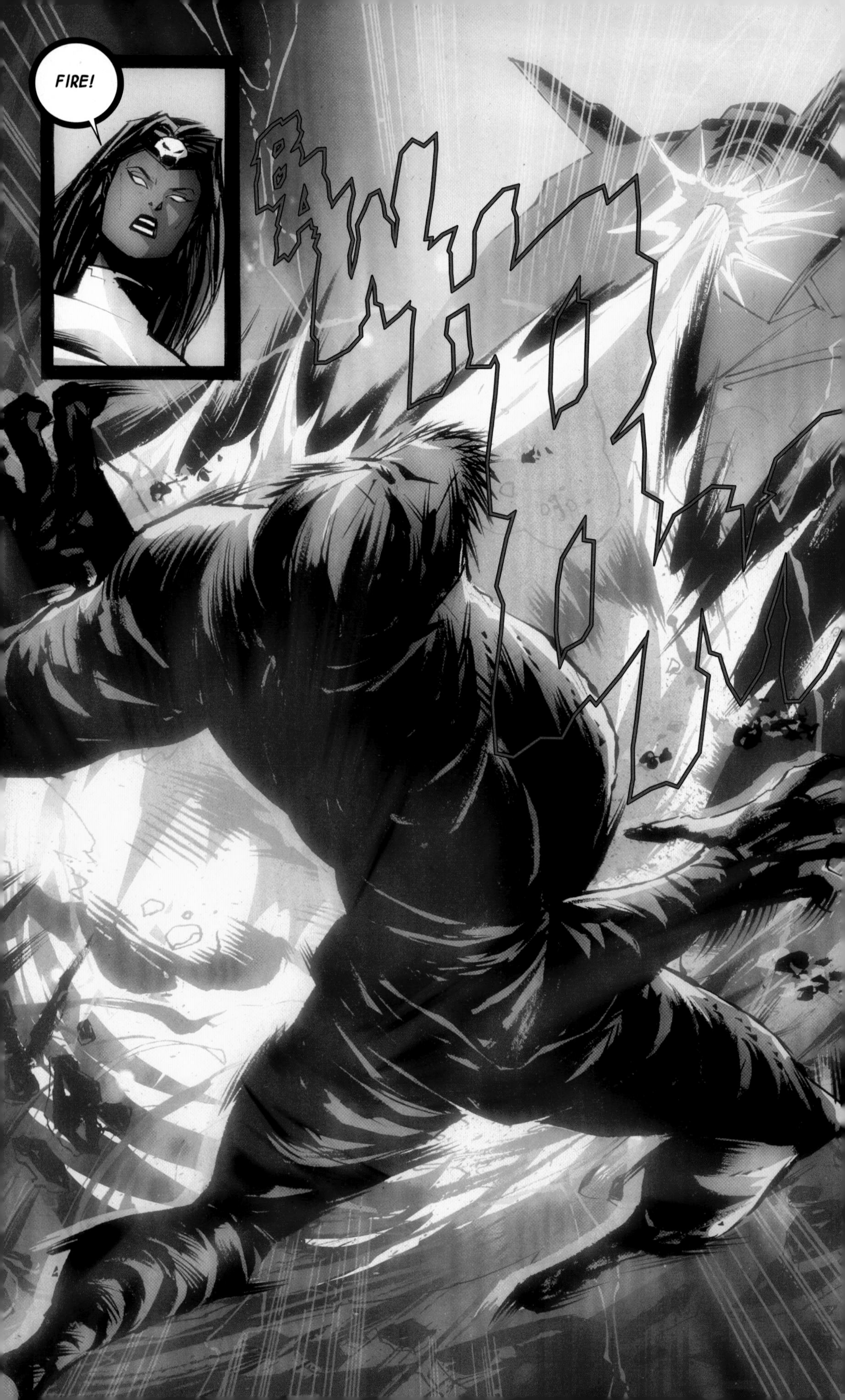
FIRE!

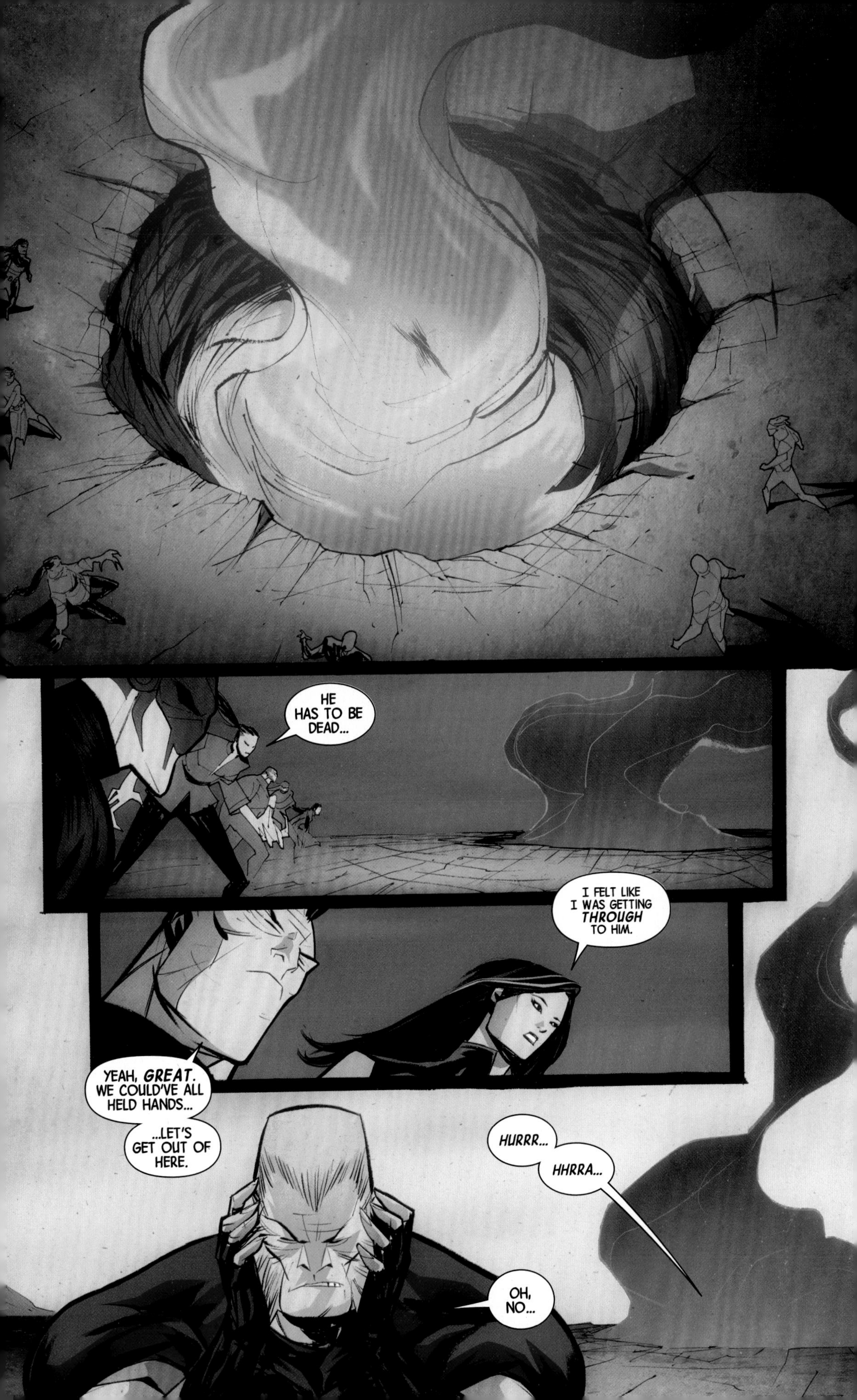
HE HAS TO BE DEAD...
I FELT LIKE I WAS GETTING THROUGH TO HIM.
YEAH, GREAT. WE COULD'VE ALL HELD HANDS...
...LET'S GET OUT OF HERE.
HURRR...
HHRRA...
OH, NO...

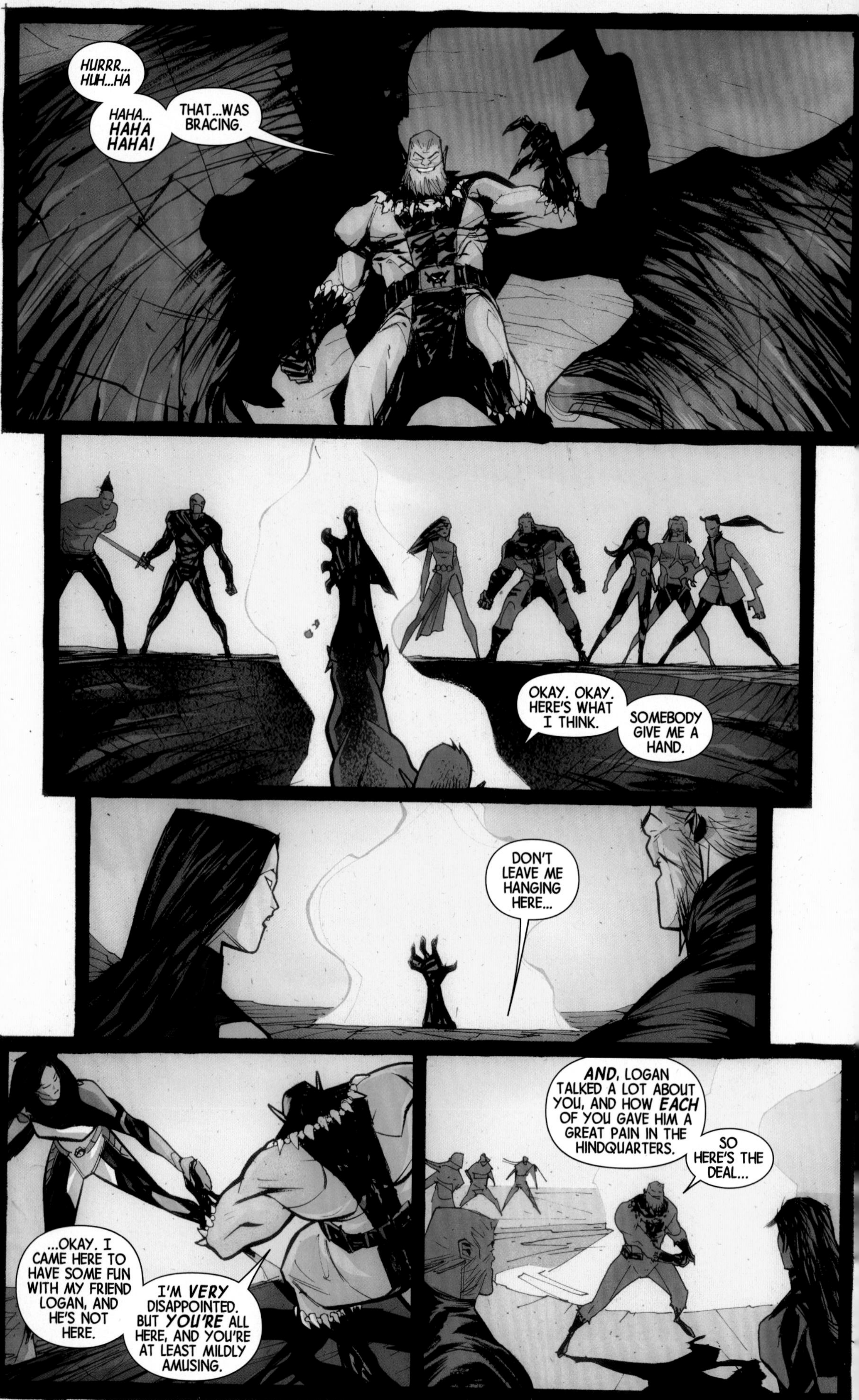
HURRR... HUH...HA
HAHA... HAHA HAHA!
THAT...WAS BRACING.
OKAY. OKAY. HERE'S WHAT I THINK.
SOMEBODY GIVE ME A HAND.
DON'T LEAVE ME HANGING HERE...
...OKAY. I CAME HERE TO HAVE SOME FUN WITH MY FRIEND LOGAN, AND HE'S NOT HERE.
I'M VERY DISAPPOINTED. BUT YOU'RE ALL HERE, AND YOU'RE AT LEAST MILDLY AMUSING.
AND, LOGAN TALKED A LOT ABOUT YOU, AND HOW EACH OF YOU GAVE HIM A GREAT PAIN IN THE HINDQUARTERS.
SO HERE'S THE DEAL...

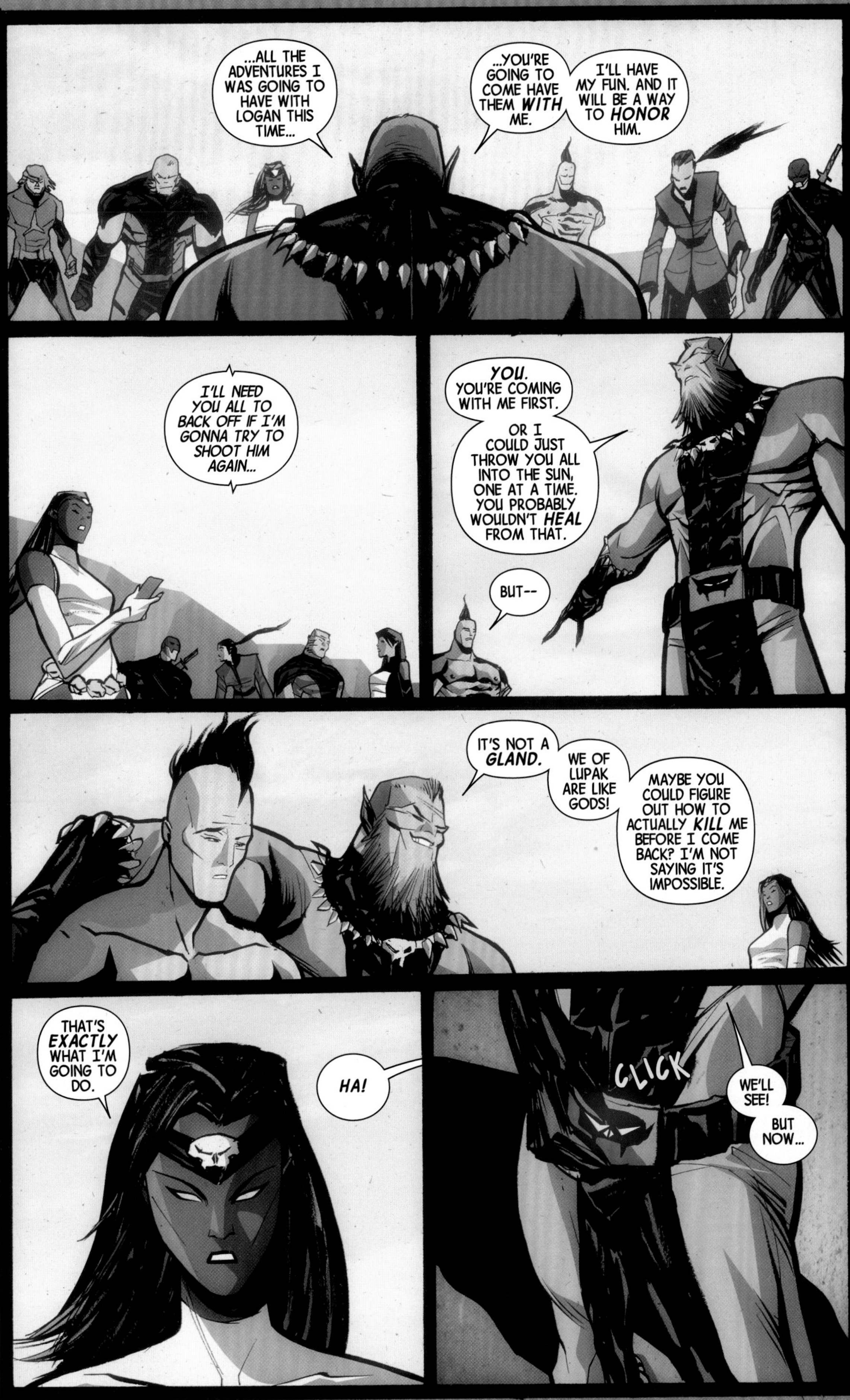
...ALL THE ADVENTURES I WAS GOING TO HAVE WITH LOGAN THIS TIME...
...YOU'RE GOING TO COME HAVE THEM WITH ME.
I'LL HAVE MY FUN. AND IT WILL BE A WAY TO HONOR HIM.
I'LL NEED YOU ALL TO BACK OFF IF I'M GONNA TRY TO SHOOT HIM AGAIN...
YOU. YOU'RE COMING WITH ME FIRST.
OR I COULD JUST THROW YOU ALL INTO THE SUN, ONE AT A TIME. YOU PROBABLY WOULDN'T HEAL FROM THAT.
BUT--
IT'S NOT A GLAND.
WE OF LUPAK ARE LIKE GODS!
MAYBE YOU COULD FIGURE OUT HOW TO ACTUALLY KILL ME BEFORE I COME BACK? I'M NOT SAYING IT'S IMPOSSIBLE.
THAT'S EXACTLY WHAT I'M GOING TO DO.
HA!
CLICK
WE'LL SEE!
BUT NOW...

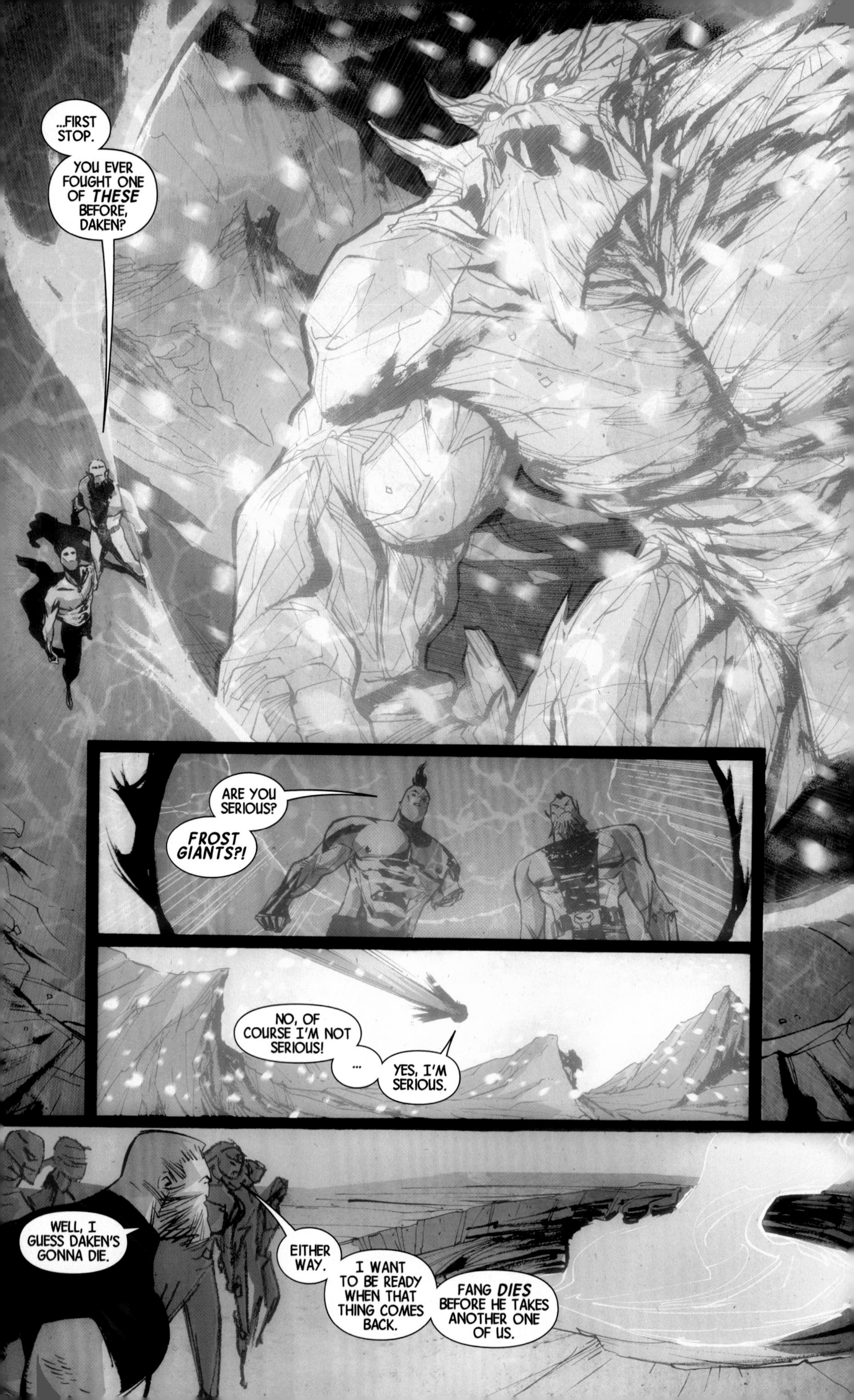
...FIRST STOP.
YOU EVER FOUGHT ONE OF *THESE* BEFORE, DAKEN?
ARE YOU SERIOUS?
*FROST GIANTS?!*
NO, OF COURSE I'M NOT SERIOUS!
...
YES, I'M SERIOUS.
WELL, I GUESS DAKEN'S GONNA DIE.
EITHER WAY.
I WANT TO BE READY WHEN THAT THING COMES BACK.
FANG *DIES* BEFORE HE TAKES ANOTHER ONE OF US.

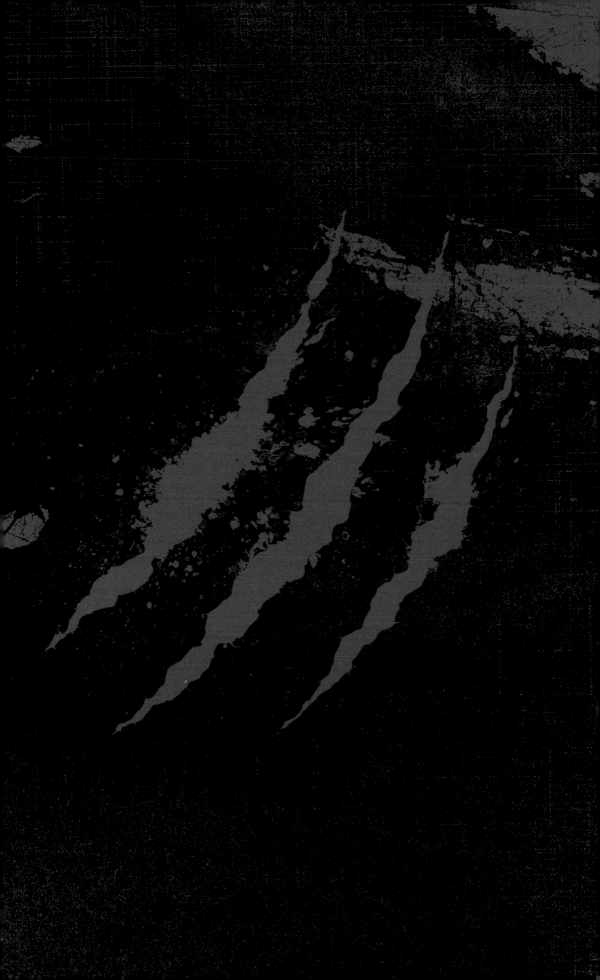

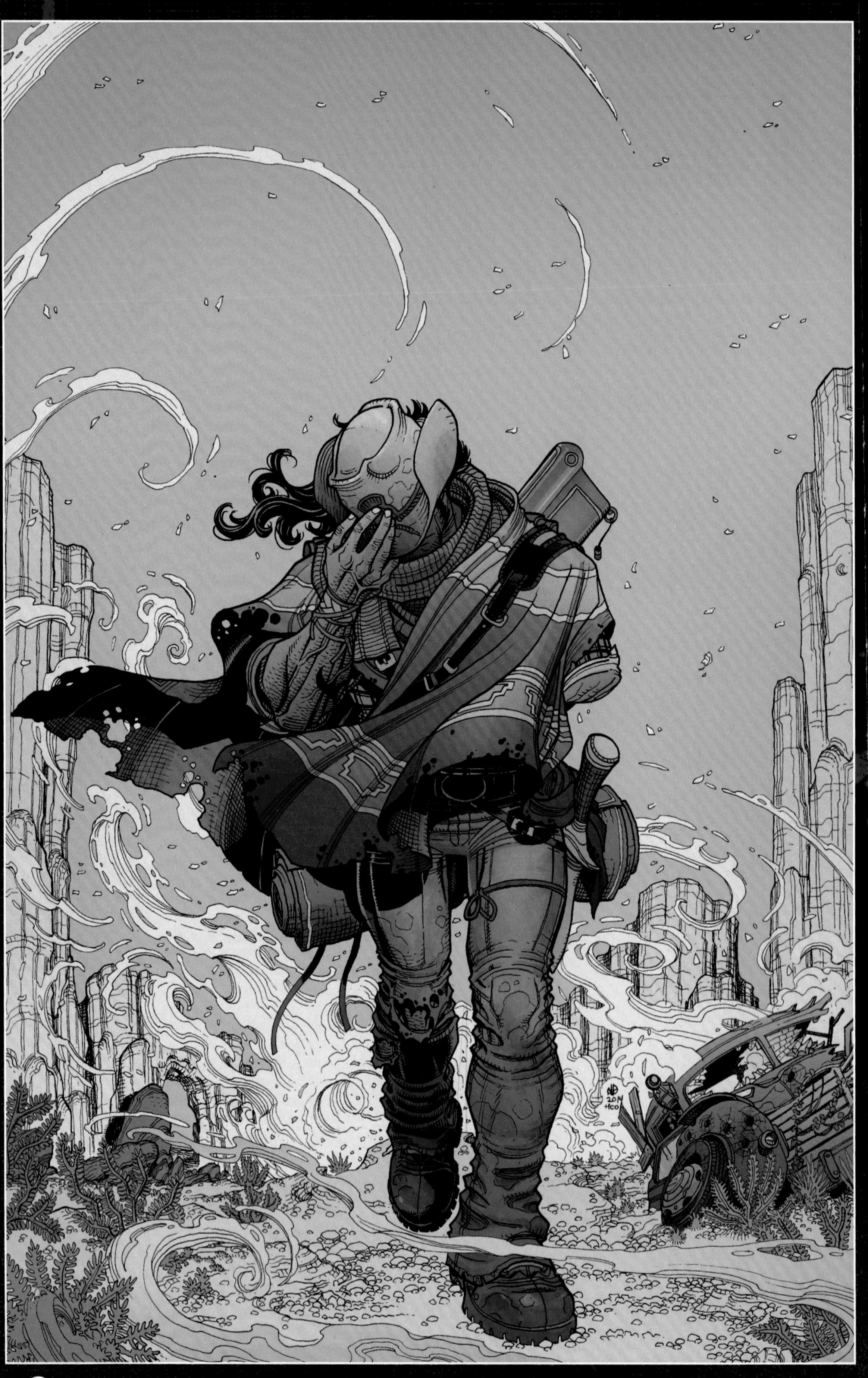

#9

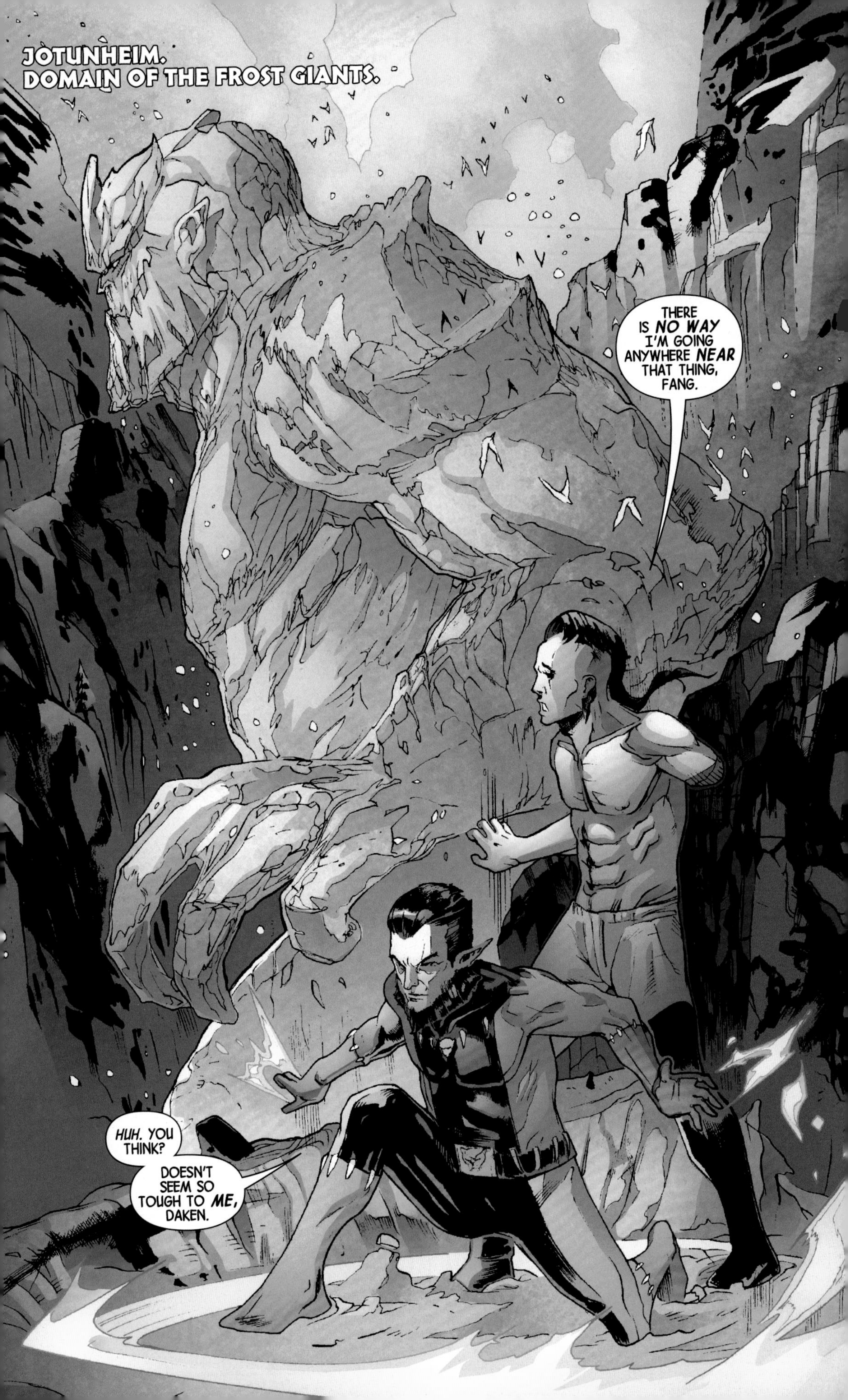
JOTUNHEIM.
DOMAIN OF THE FROST GIANTS.
THERE IS NO WAY I'M GOING ANYWHERE NEAR THAT THING, FANG.
HUH. YOU THINK?
DOESN'T SEEM SO TOUGH TO ME, DAKEN.

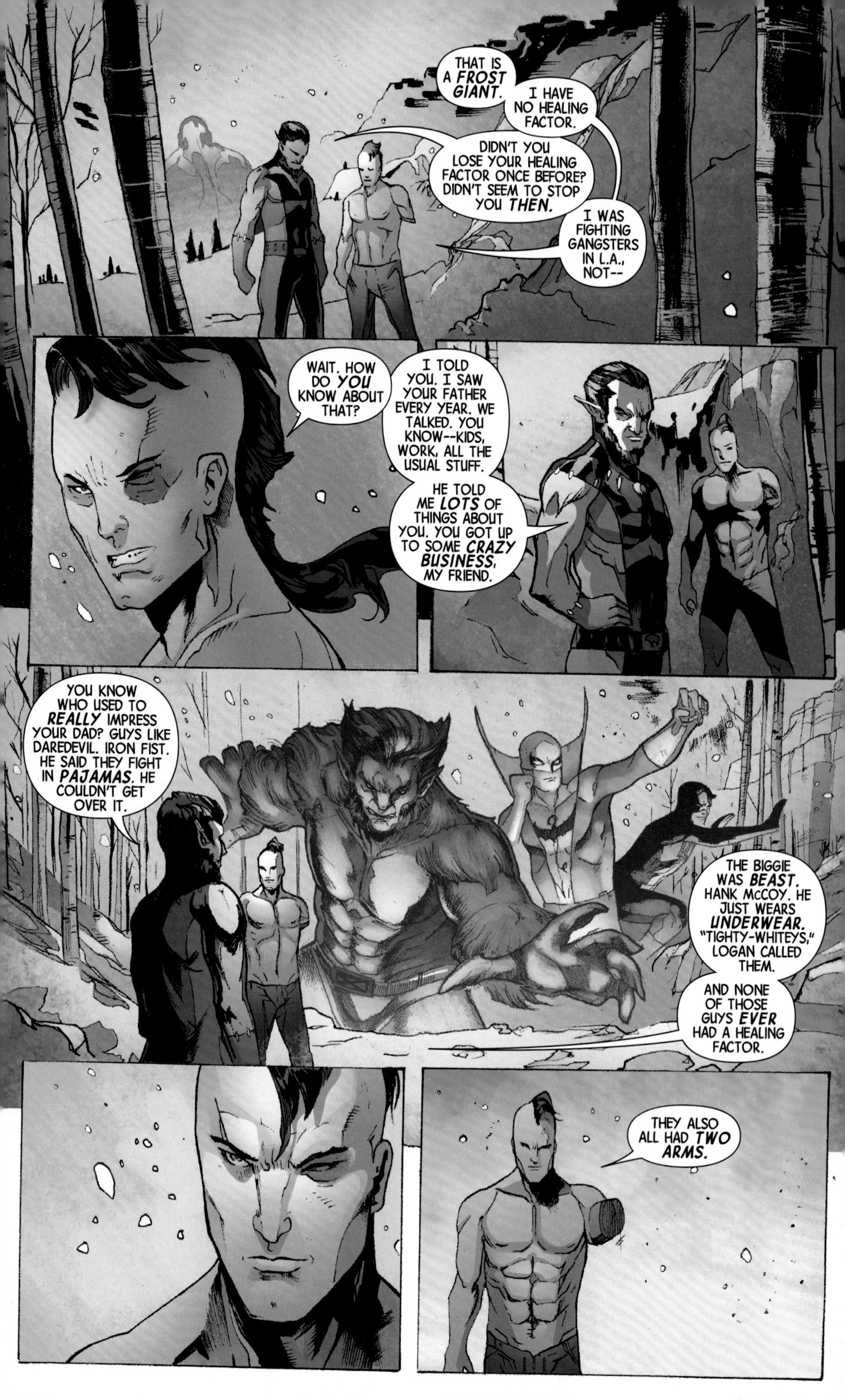
THAT IS A FROST GIANT.
I HAVE NO HEALING FACTOR.
DIDN'T YOU LOSE YOUR HEALING FACTOR ONCE BEFORE? DIDN'T SEEM TO STOP YOU THEN.
I WAS FIGHTING GANGSTERS IN L.A., NOT--
WAIT. HOW DO YOU KNOW ABOUT THAT?
I TOLD YOU. I SAW YOUR FATHER EVERY YEAR. WE TALKED. YOU KNOW--KIDS, WORK, ALL THE USUAL STUFF.
HE TOLD ME LOTS OF THINGS ABOUT YOU. YOU GOT UP TO SOME CRAZY BUSINESS, MY FRIEND.
YOU KNOW WHO USED TO REALLY IMPRESS YOUR DAD? GUYS LIKE DAREDEVIL. IRON FIST. HE SAID THEY FIGHT IN PAJAMAS. HE COULDN'T GET OVER IT.
THE BIGGIE WAS BEAST. HANK McCOY. HE JUST WEARS UNDERWEAR. "TIGHTY-WHITEYS," LOGAN CALLED THEM.
AND NONE OF THOSE GUYS EVER HAD A HEALING FACTOR.
THEY ALSO ALL HAD TWO ARMS.

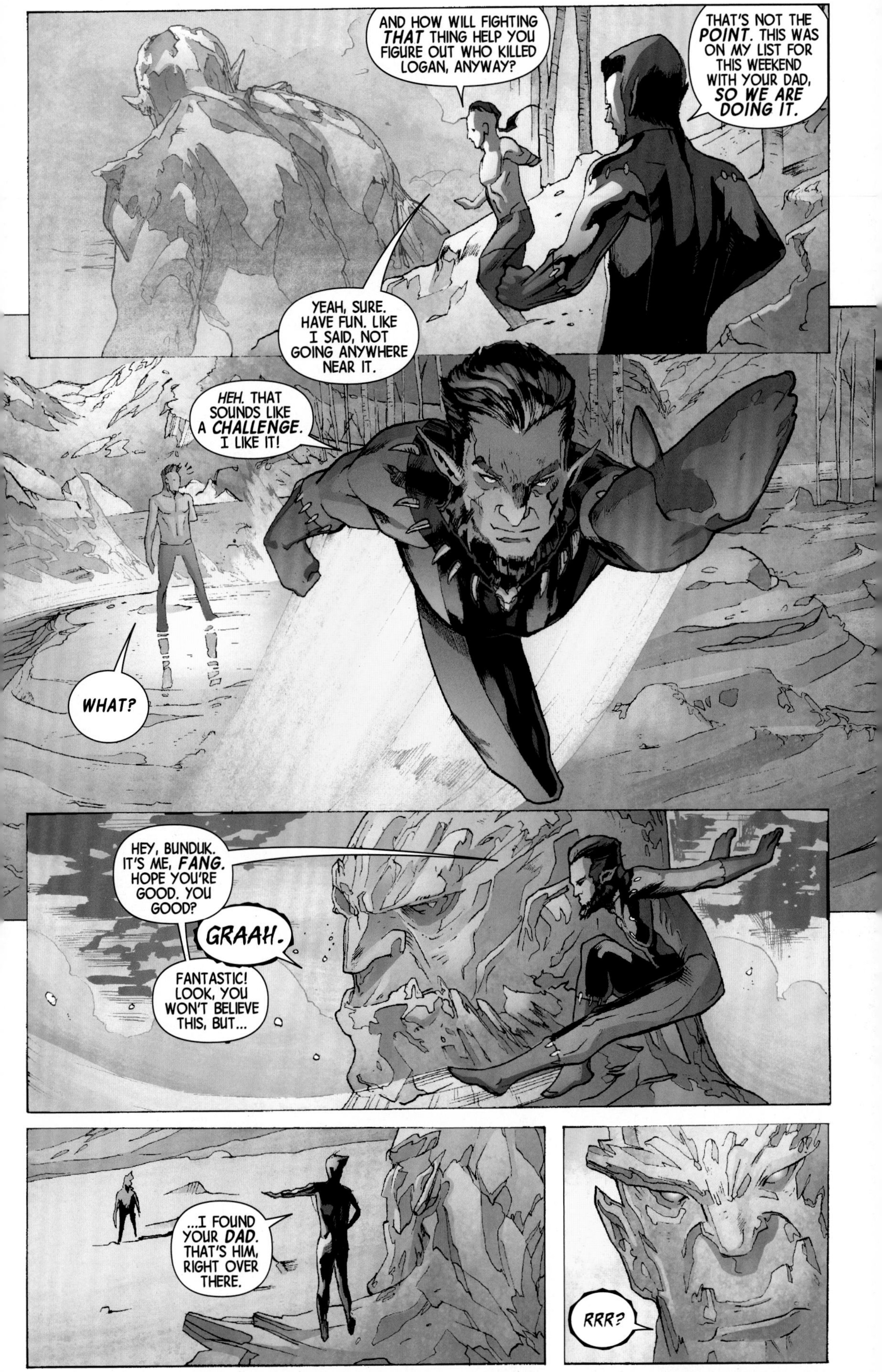
AND HOW WILL FIGHTING THAT THING HELP YOU FIGURE OUT WHO KILLED LOGAN, ANYWAY?
THAT'S NOT THE POINT. THIS WAS ON MY LIST FOR THIS WEEKEND WITH YOUR DAD, SO WE ARE DOING IT.
YEAH, SURE. HAVE FUN. LIKE I SAID, NOT GOING ANYWHERE NEAR IT.
HEH. THAT SOUNDS LIKE A CHALLENGE. I LIKE IT!
WHAT?
HEY, BUNDUK. IT'S ME, FANG. HOPE YOU'RE GOOD. YOU GOOD?
GRAAH.
FANTASTIC! LOOK, YOU WON'T BELIEVE THIS, BUT...
...I FOUND YOUR DAD. THAT'S HIM, RIGHT OVER THERE.
RRR?

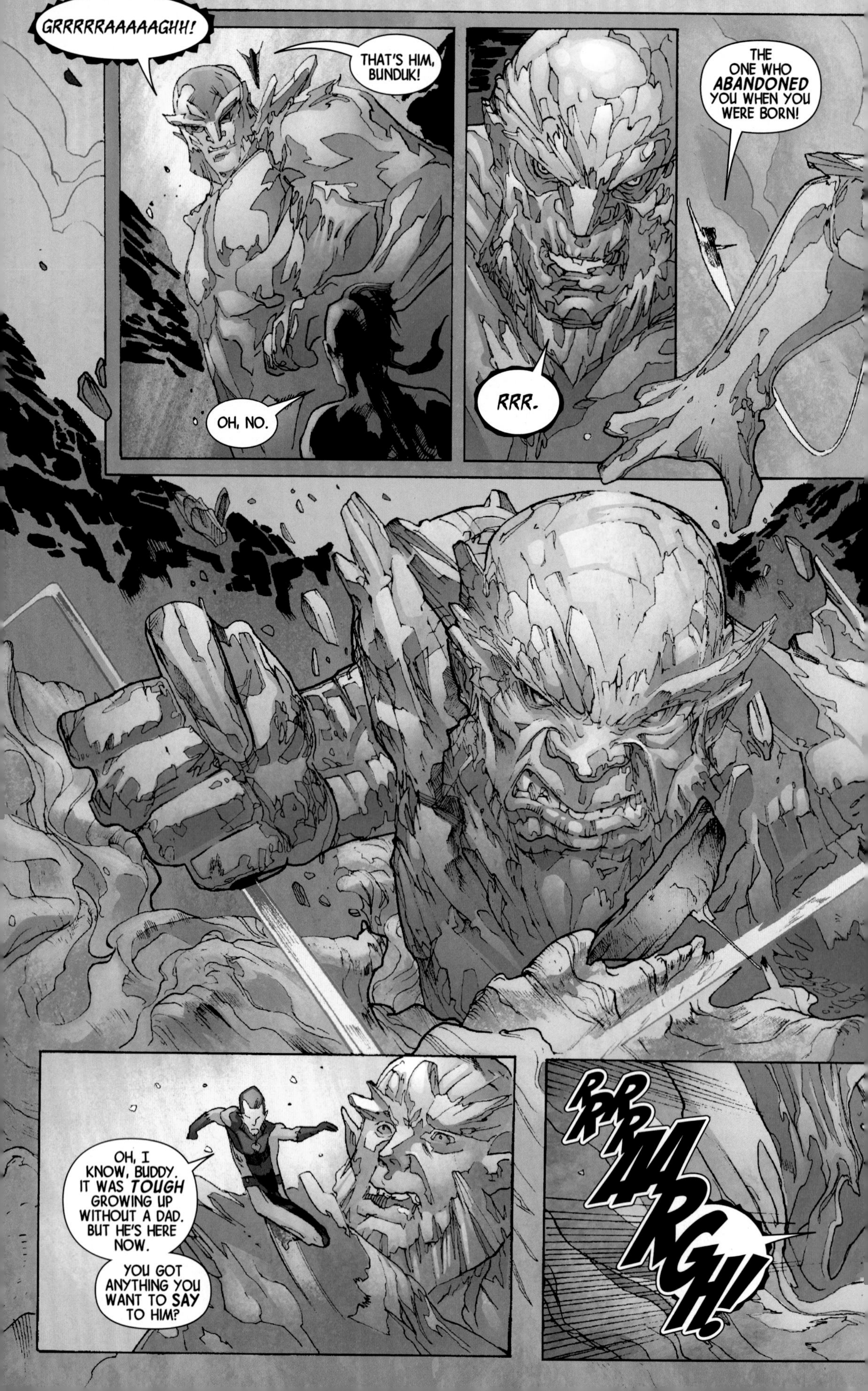
GRRRRRAAAAAGHH!
THAT'S HIM, BUNDUK!
OH, NO.
THE ONE WHO ABANDONED YOU WHEN YOU WERE BORN!
RRR.
OH, I KNOW, BUDDY. IT WAS TOUGH GROWING UP WITHOUT A DAD. BUT HE'S HERE NOW.
YOU GOT ANYTHING YOU WANT TO SAY TO HIM?
RRRRAARGH!

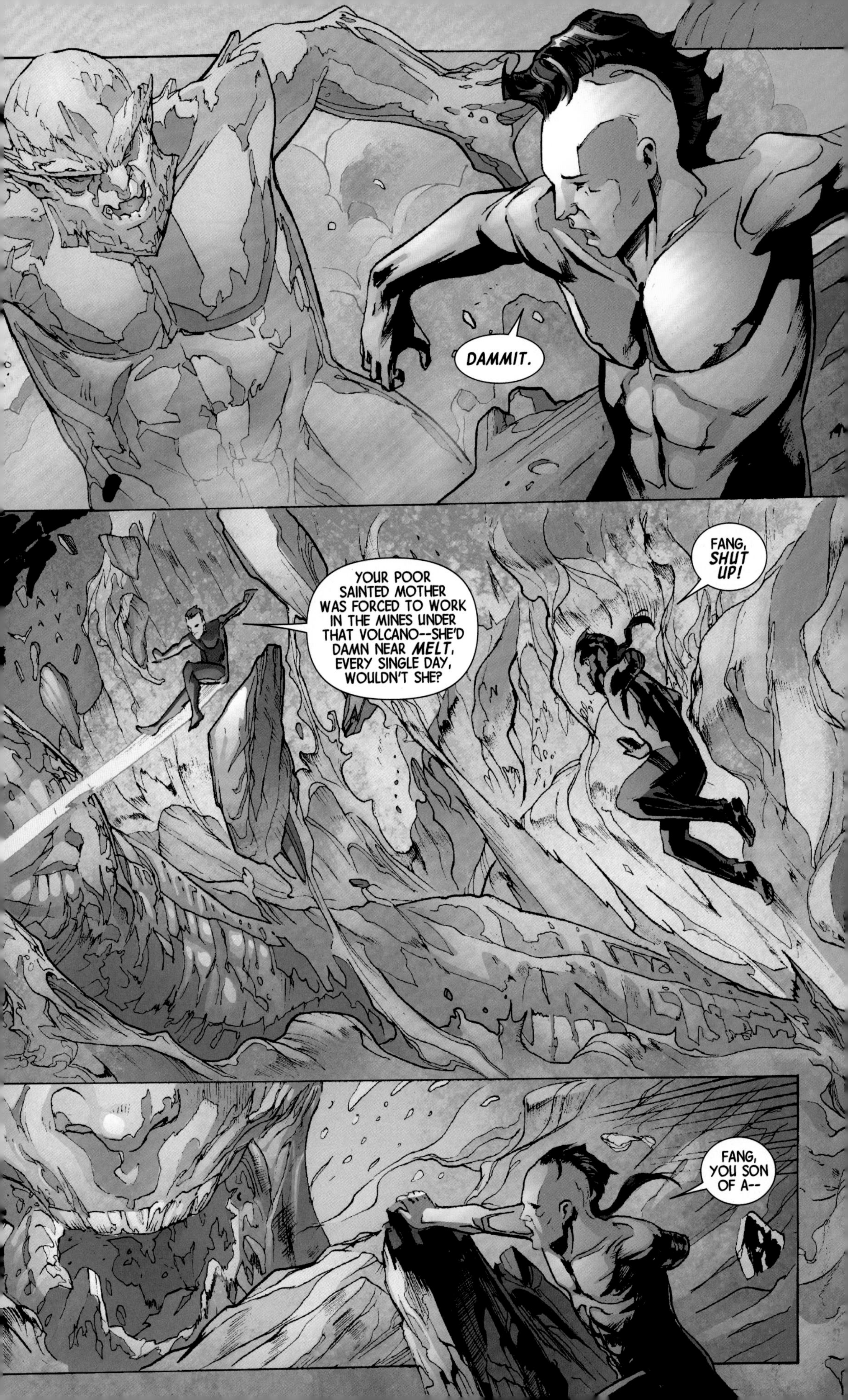
DAMMIT.
YOUR POOR SAINTED MOTHER WAS FORCED TO WORK IN THE MINES UNDER THAT VOLCANO--SHE'D DAMN NEAR MELT, EVERY SINGLE DAY, WOULDN'T SHE?
FANG, SHUT UP!
FANG, YOU SON OF A--

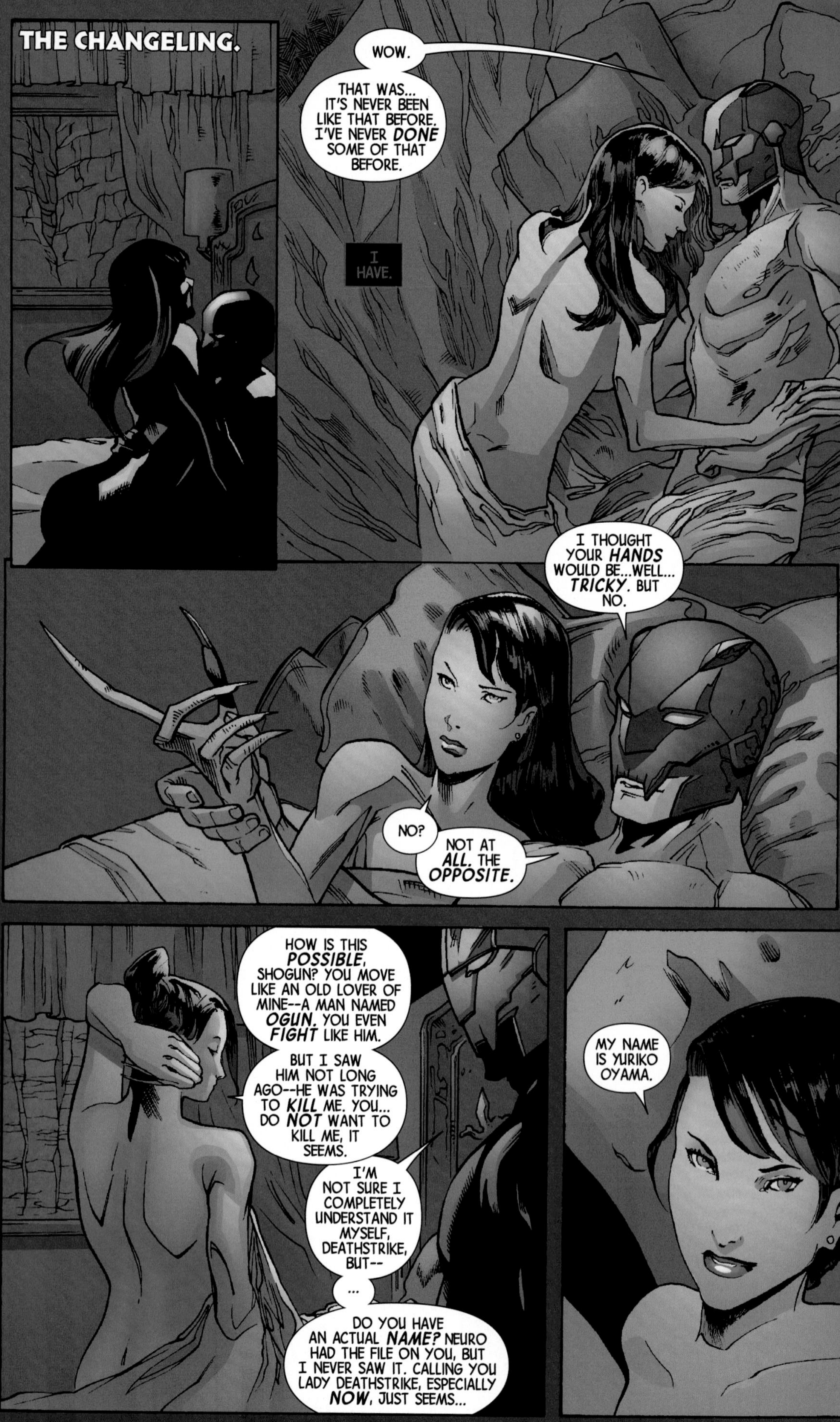
THE CHANGELING.
WOW.
THAT WAS... IT'S NEVER BEEN LIKE THAT BEFORE. I'VE NEVER DONE SOME OF THAT BEFORE.
I HAVE.
I THOUGHT YOUR HANDS WOULD BE...WELL... TRICKY. BUT NO.
NO?
NOT AT ALL. THE OPPOSITE.
HOW IS THIS POSSIBLE, SHOGUN? YOU MOVE LIKE AN OLD LOVER OF MINE--A MAN NAMED OGUN. YOU EVEN FIGHT LIKE HIM.
BUT I SAW HIM NOT LONG AGO--HE WAS TRYING TO KILL ME. YOU... DO NOT WANT TO KILL ME, IT SEEMS.
I'M NOT SURE I COMPLETELY UNDERSTAND IT MYSELF, DEATHSTRIKE, BUT--
...
DO YOU HAVE AN ACTUAL NAME? NEURO HAD THE FILE ON YOU, BUT I NEVER SAW IT. CALLING YOU LADY DEATHSTRIKE, ESPECIALLY NOW, JUST SEEMS...
MY NAME IS YURIKO OYAMA.

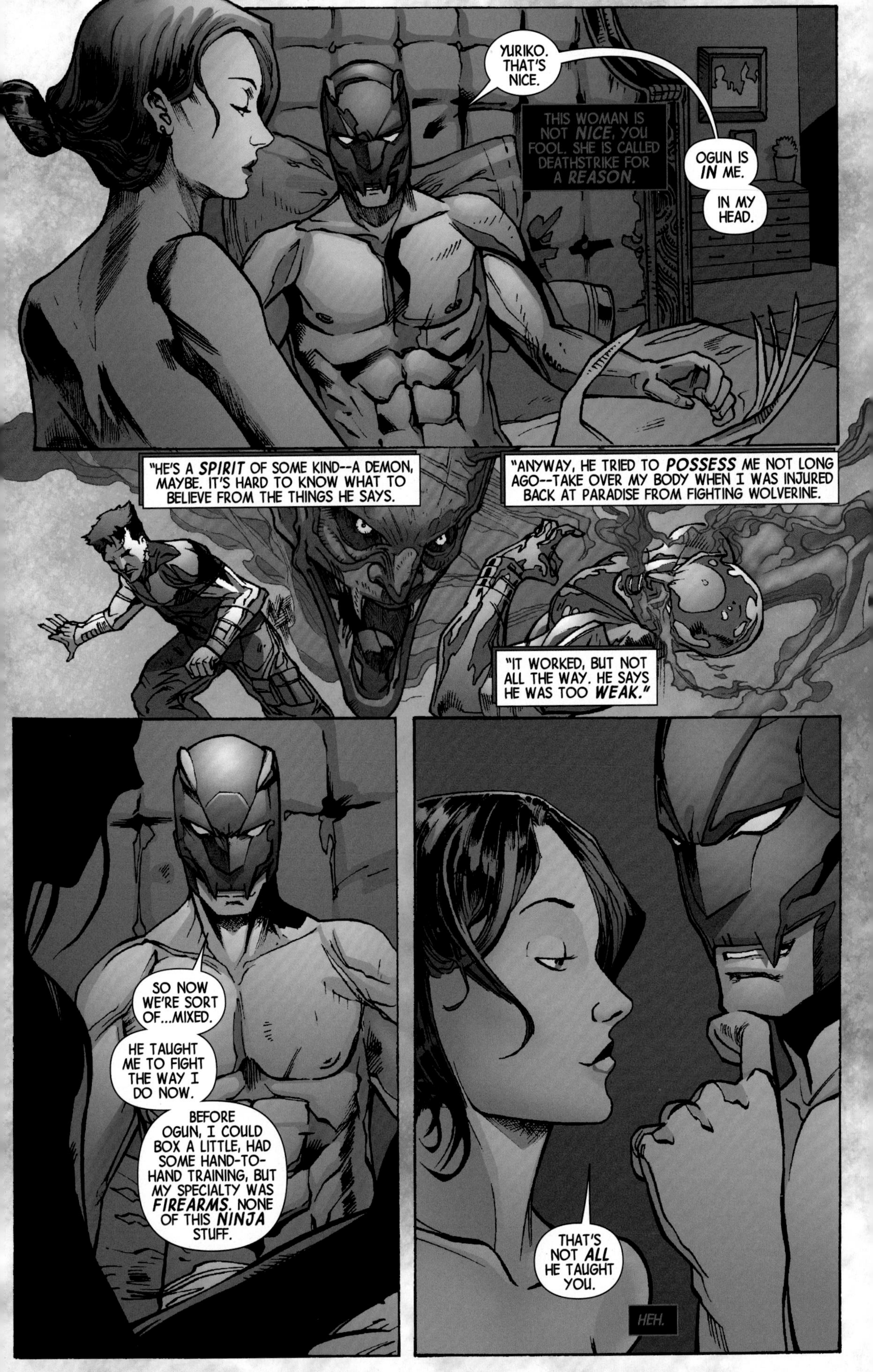

YURIKO. THAT'S NICE.
THIS WOMAN IS NOT NICE, YOU FOOL. SHE IS CALLED DEATHSTRIKE FOR A REASON.
OGUN IS IN ME.
IN MY HEAD.
"HE'S A SPIRIT OF SOME KIND--A DEMON, MAYBE. IT'S HARD TO KNOW WHAT TO BELIEVE FROM THE THINGS HE SAYS.
"ANYWAY, HE TRIED TO POSSESS ME NOT LONG AGO--TAKE OVER MY BODY WHEN I WAS INJURED BACK AT PARADISE FROM FIGHTING WOLVERINE.
"IT WORKED, BUT NOT ALL THE WAY. HE SAYS HE WAS TOO WEAK."
SO NOW WE'RE SORT OF...MIXED.
HE TAUGHT ME TO FIGHT THE WAY I DO NOW.
BEFORE OGUN, I COULD BOX A LITTLE, HAD SOME HAND-TO-HAND TRAINING, BUT MY SPECIALTY WAS FIREARMS. NONE OF THIS NINJA STUFF.
THAT'S NOT ALL HE TAUGHT YOU.
HEH.

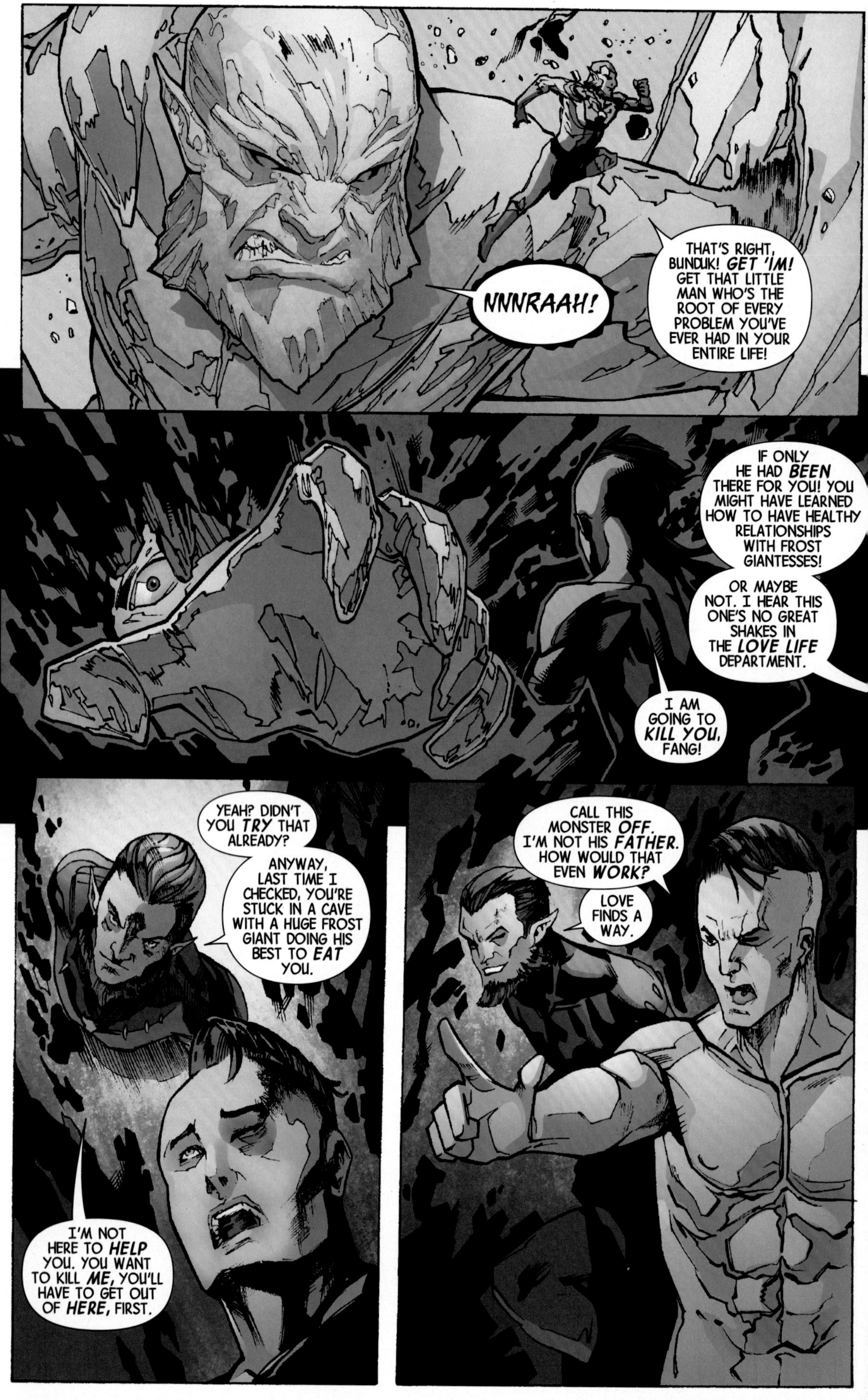
THAT'S RIGHT, BUNDUK! GET 'IM! GET THAT LITTLE MAN WHO'S THE ROOT OF EVERY PROBLEM YOU'VE EVER HAD IN YOUR ENTIRE LIFE!
NNNRAAH!
IF ONLY HE HAD BEEN THERE FOR YOU! YOU MIGHT HAVE LEARNED HOW TO HAVE HEALTHY RELATIONSHIPS WITH FROST GIANTESSES!
OR MAYBE NOT. I HEAR THIS ONE'S NO GREAT SHAKES IN THE LOVE LIFE DEPARTMENT.
I AM GOING TO KILL YOU, FANG!
YEAH? DIDN'T YOU TRY THAT ALREADY?
ANYWAY, LAST TIME I CHECKED, YOU'RE STUCK IN A CAVE WITH A HUGE FROST GIANT DOING HIS BEST TO EAT YOU.
I'M NOT HERE TO HELP YOU. YOU WANT TO KILL ME, YOU'LL HAVE TO GET OUT OF HERE, FIRST.
CALL THIS MONSTER OFF. I'M NOT HIS FATHER. HOW WOULD THAT EVEN WORK?
LOVE FINDS A WAY.

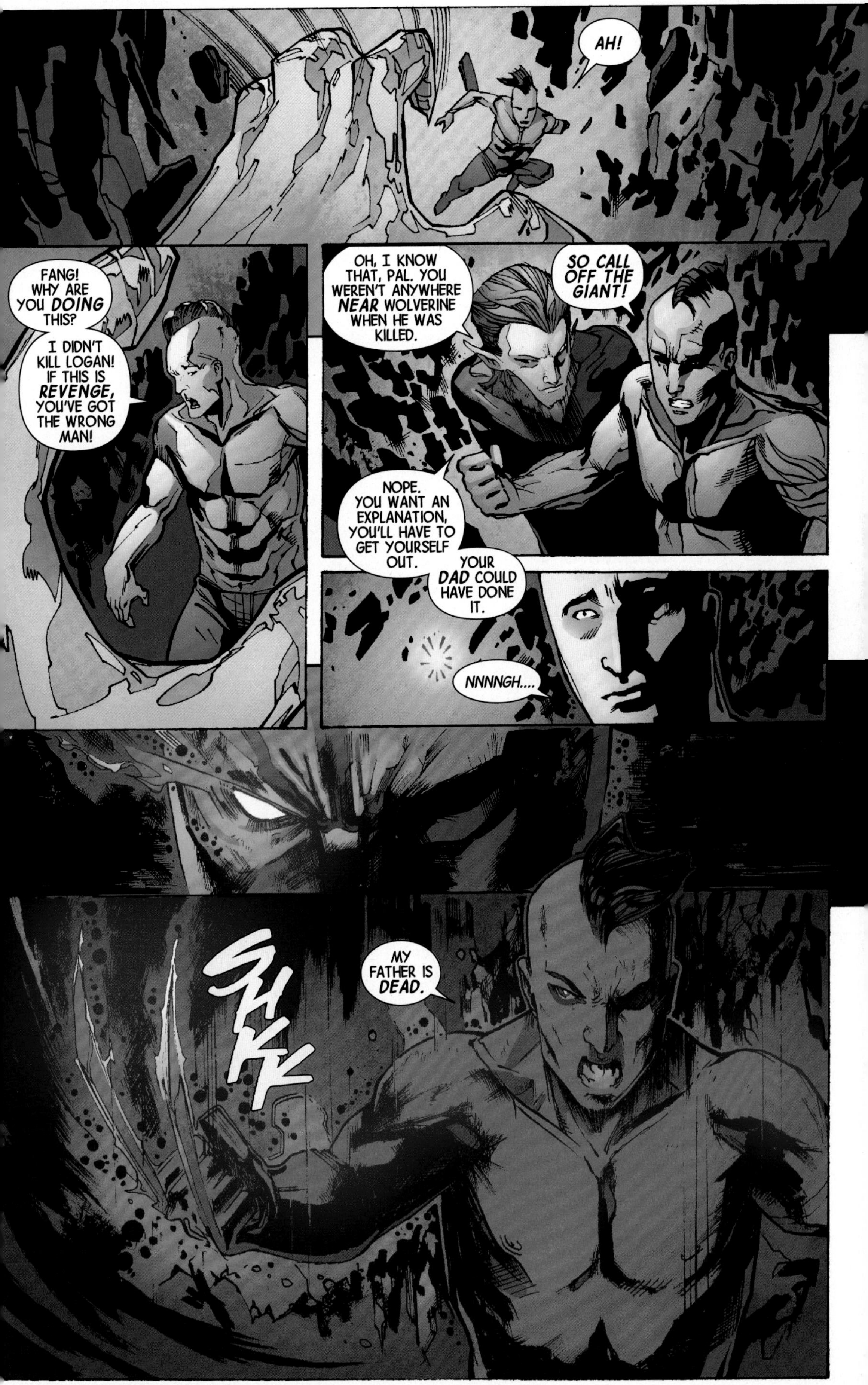
AH!
FANG! WHY ARE YOU DOING THIS?
I DIDN'T KILL LOGAN! IF THIS IS REVENGE, YOU'VE GOT THE WRONG MAN!
OH, I KNOW THAT, PAL. YOU WEREN'T ANYWHERE NEAR WOLVERINE WHEN HE WAS KILLED.
SO CALL OFF THE GIANT!
NOPE. YOU WANT AN EXPLANATION, YOU'LL HAVE TO GET YOURSELF OUT.
YOUR DAD COULD HAVE DONE IT.
NNNNGH....
SHKK
MY FATHER IS DEAD.

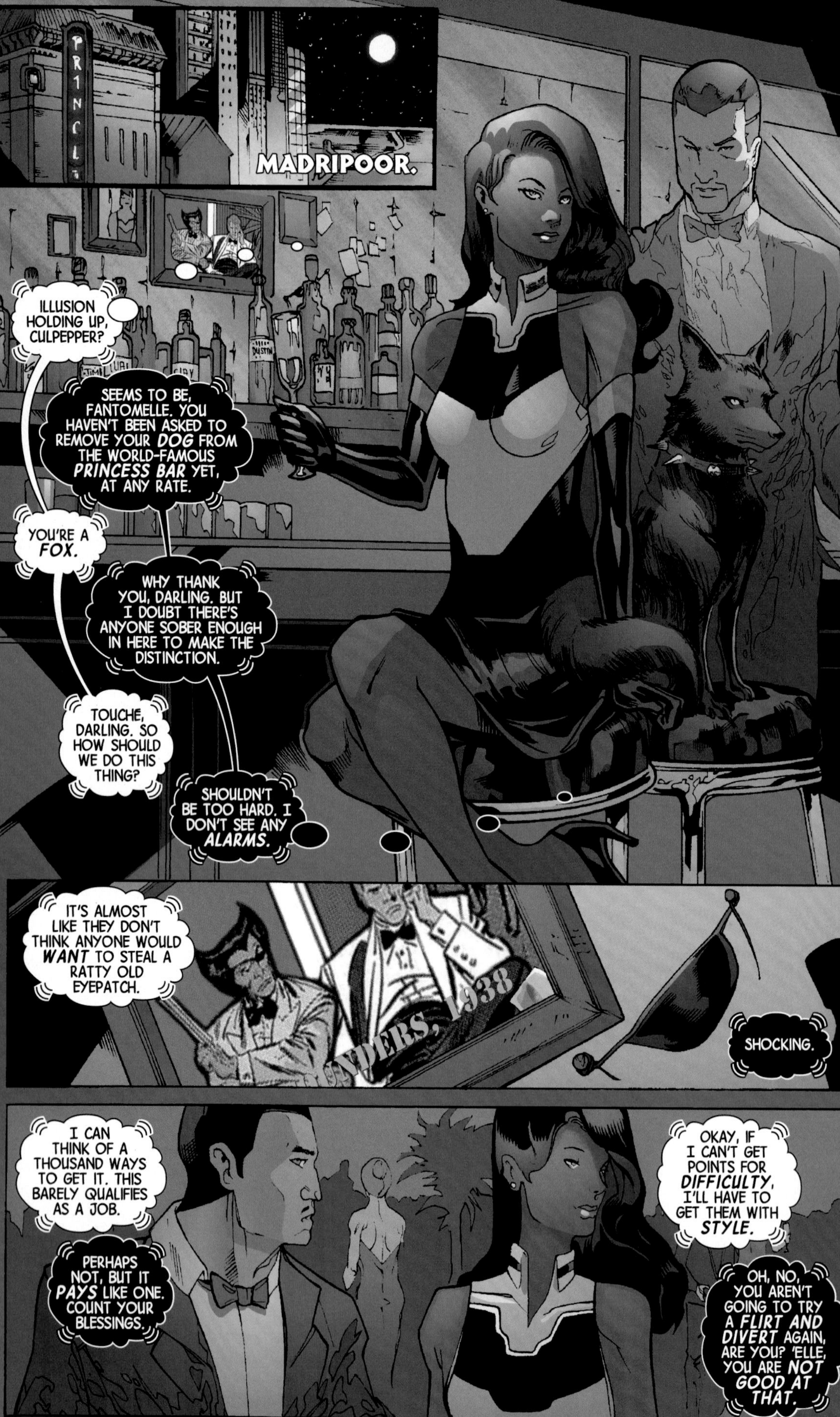
MADRIPOOR.
ILLUSION HOLDING UP, CULPEPPER?
SEEMS TO BE, FANTOMELLE. YOU HAVEN'T BEEN ASKED TO REMOVE YOUR DOG FROM THE WORLD-FAMOUS PRINCESS BAR YET, AT ANY RATE.
YOU'RE A FOX.
WHY THANK YOU, DARLING. BUT I DOUBT THERE'S ANYONE SOBER ENOUGH IN HERE TO MAKE THE DISTINCTION.
TOUCHE, DARLING. SO HOW SHOULD WE DO THIS THING?
SHOULDN'T BE TOO HARD. I DON'T SEE ANY ALARMS.
IT'S ALMOST LIKE THEY DON'T THINK ANYONE WOULD WANT TO STEAL A RATTY OLD EYEPATCH.
SHOCKING.
I CAN THINK OF A THOUSAND WAYS TO GET IT. THIS BARELY QUALIFIES AS A JOB.
PERHAPS NOT, BUT IT PAYS LIKE ONE. COUNT YOUR BLESSINGS.
OKAY, IF I CAN'T GET POINTS FOR DIFFICULTY, I'LL HAVE TO GET THEM WITH STYLE.
OH, NO, YOU AREN'T GOING TO TRY A FLIRT AND DIVERT AGAIN, ARE YOU? 'ELLE, YOU ARE NOT GOOD AT THAT.

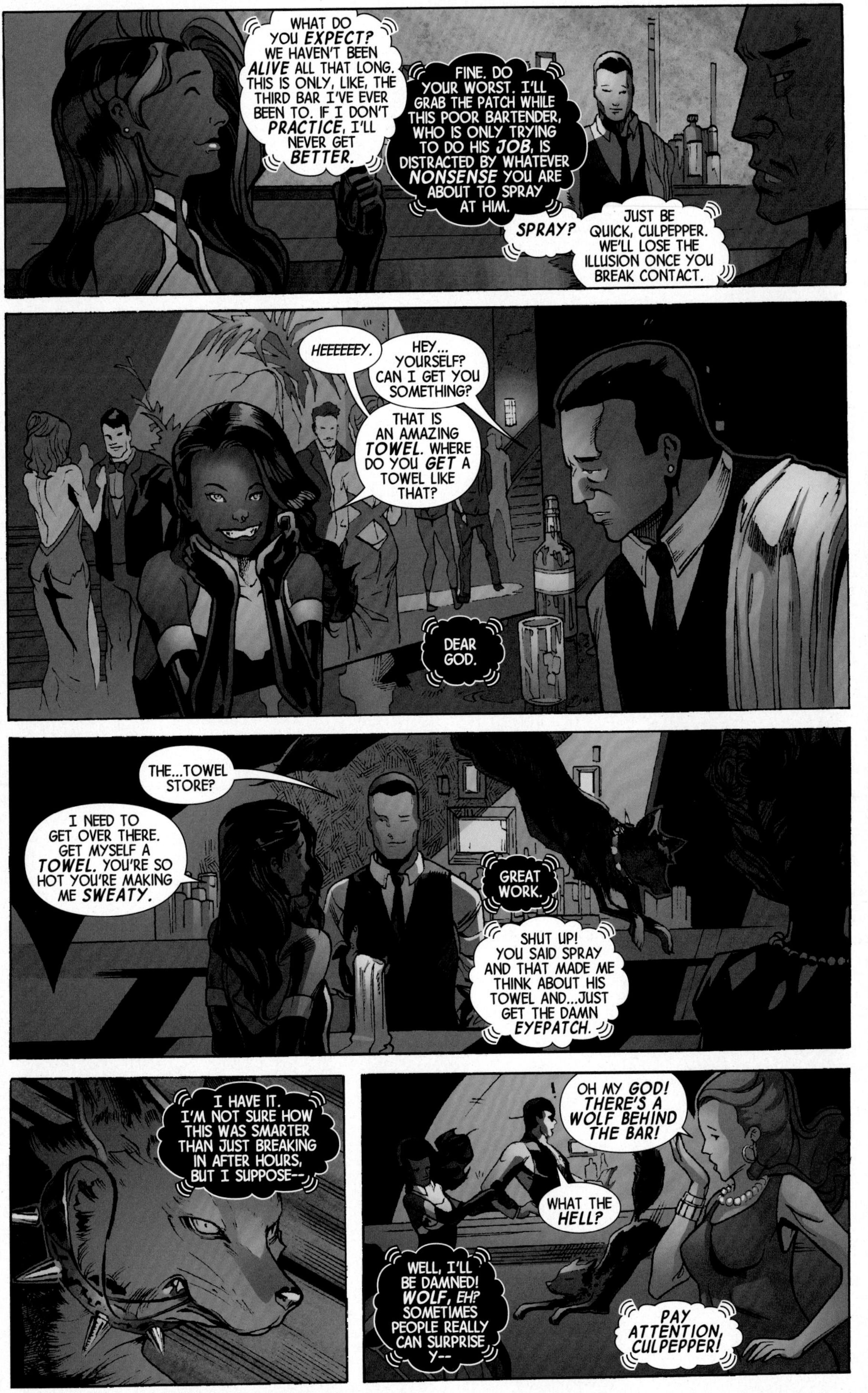

WHAT DO YOU EXPECT? WE HAVEN'T BEEN ALIVE ALL THAT LONG. THIS IS ONLY, LIKE, THE THIRD BAR I'VE EVER BEEN TO. IF I DON'T PRACTICE, I'LL NEVER GET BETTER.
FINE. DO YOUR WORST. I'LL GRAB THE PATCH WHILE THIS POOR BARTENDER, WHO IS ONLY TRYING TO DO HIS JOB, IS DISTRACTED BY WHATEVER NONSENSE YOU ARE ABOUT TO SPRAY AT HIM.
SPRAY?
JUST BE QUICK, CULPEPPER. WE'LL LOSE THE ILLUSION ONCE YOU BREAK CONTACT.
HEEEEEEY.
HEY... YOURSELF? CAN I GET YOU SOMETHING?
THAT IS AN AMAZING TOWEL. WHERE DO YOU GET A TOWEL LIKE THAT?
DEAR GOD.
THE...TOWEL STORE?
I NEED TO GET OVER THERE. GET MYSELF A TOWEL. YOU'RE SO HOT YOU'RE MAKING ME SWEATY.
GREAT WORK.
SHUT UP! YOU SAID SPRAY AND THAT MADE ME THINK ABOUT HIS TOWEL AND...JUST GET THE DAMN EYEPATCH.
I HAVE IT. I'M NOT SURE HOW THIS WAS SMARTER THAN JUST BREAKING IN AFTER HOURS, BUT I SUPPOSE--
!
OH MY GOD! THERE'S A WOLF BEHIND THE BAR!
WHAT THE HELL?
WELL, I'LL BE DAMNED! WOLF, EH? SOMETIMES PEOPLE REALLY CAN SURPRISE Y--
PAY ATTENTION, CULPEPPER!

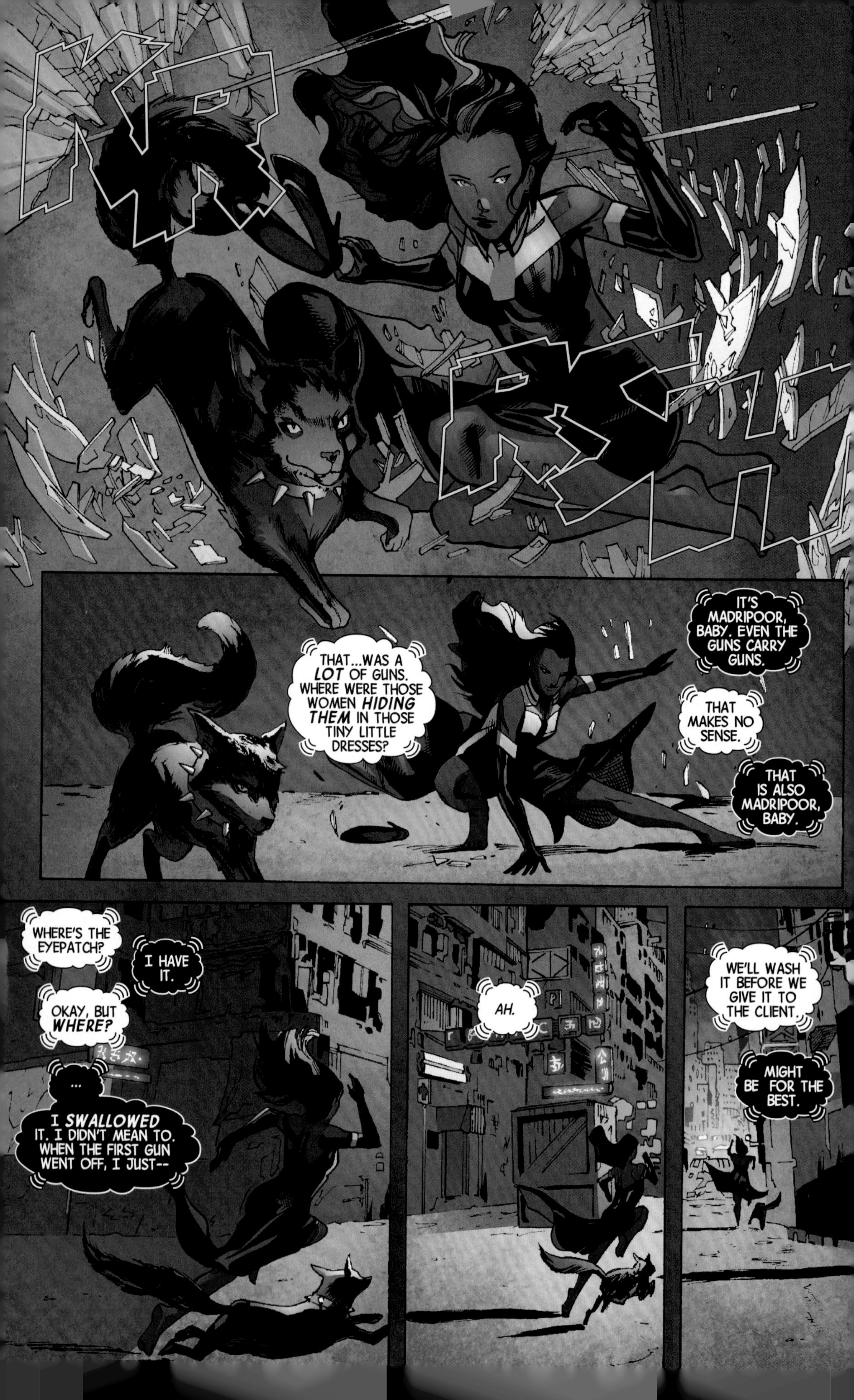
THAT...WAS A LOT OF GUNS. WHERE WERE THOSE WOMEN HIDING THEM IN THOSE TINY LITTLE DRESSES?
IT'S MADRIPOOR, BABY. EVEN THE GUNS CARRY GUNS.
THAT MAKES NO SENSE.
THAT IS ALSO MADRIPOOR, BABY.
WHERE'S THE EYEPATCH?
I HAVE IT.
OKAY, BUT WHERE?
...
I SWALLOWED IT. I DIDN'T MEAN TO. WHEN THE FIRST GUN WENT OFF, I JUST--
AH.
WE'LL WASH IT BEFORE WE GIVE IT TO THE CLIENT.
MIGHT BE FOR THE BEST.

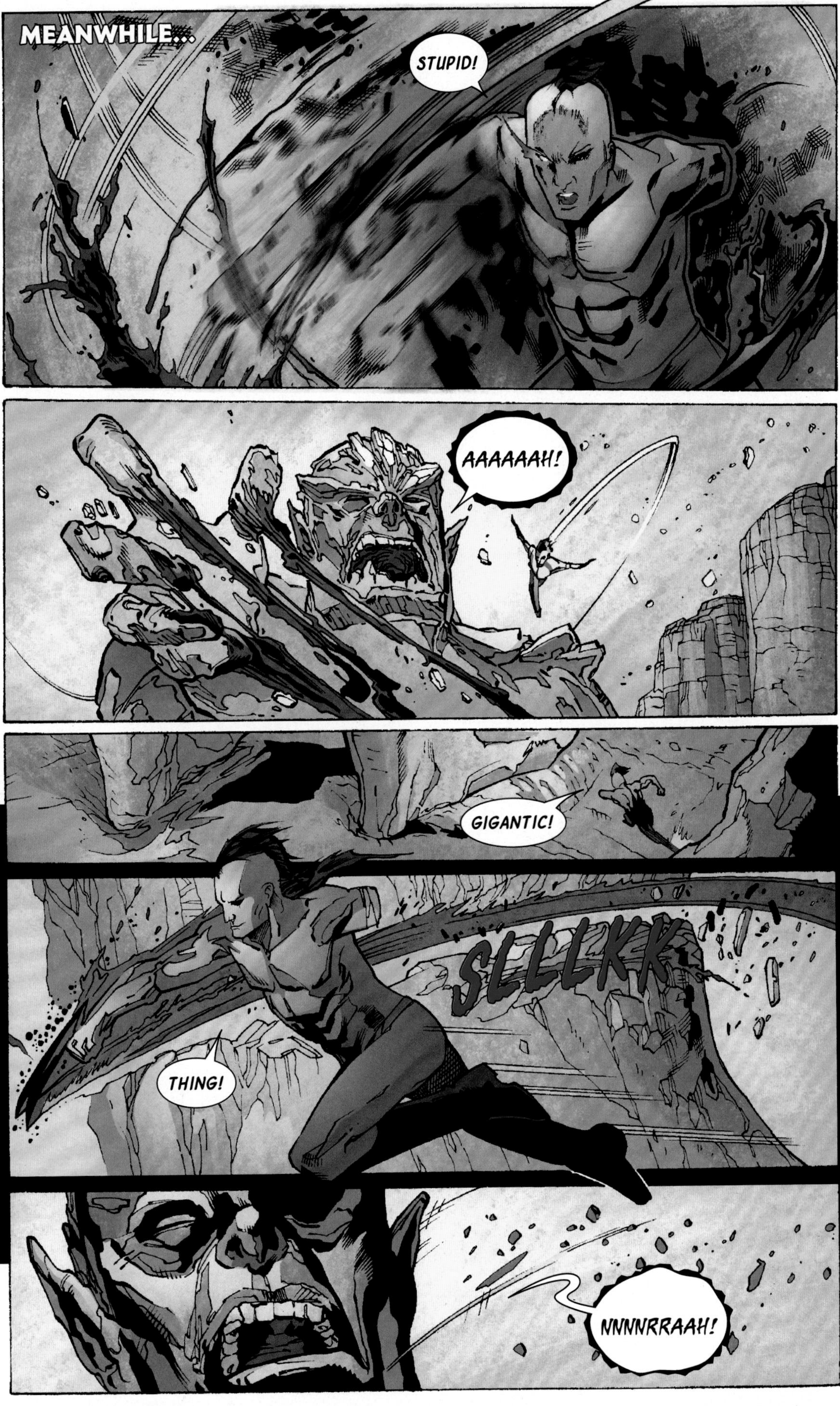
MEANWHILE...
STUPID!
AAAAAAH!
GIGANTIC!
SLLLKK
THING!
NNNNRRAAH!

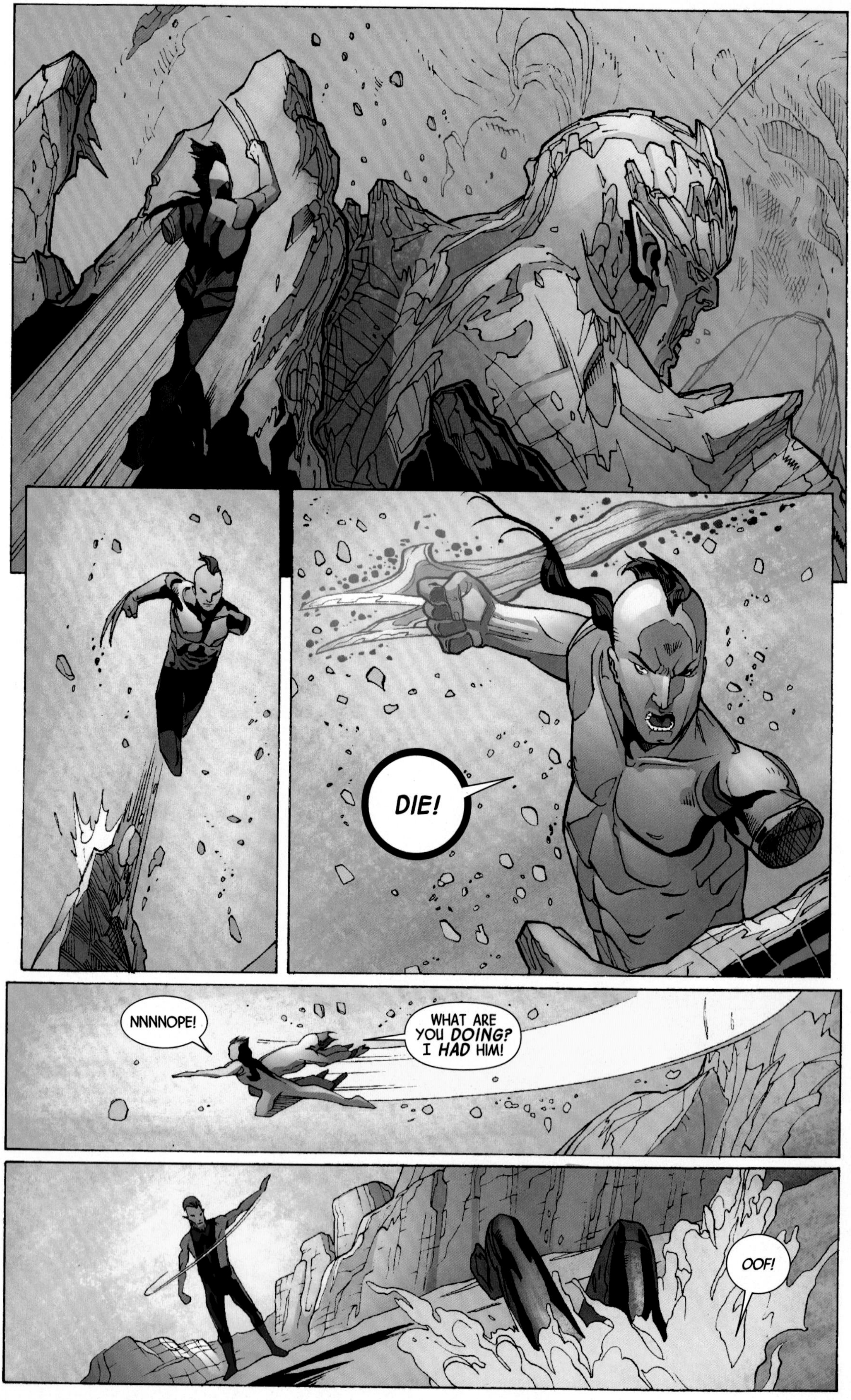
DIE!
NNNNOPE!
WHAT ARE YOU DOING? I HAD HIM!
OOF!

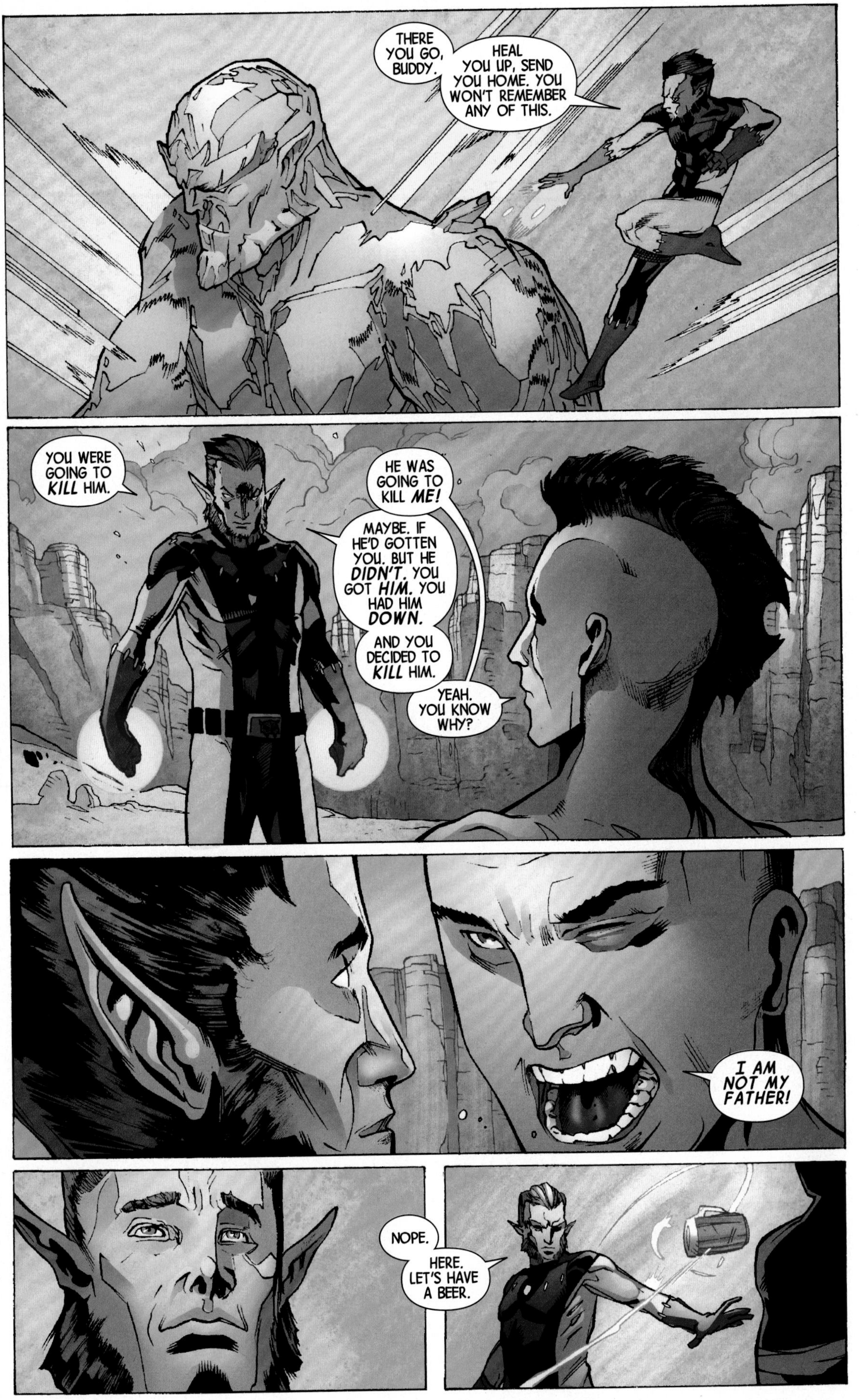
THERE YOU GO, BUDDY.
HEAL YOU UP, SEND YOU HOME. YOU WON'T REMEMBER ANY OF THIS.
YOU WERE GOING TO KILL HIM.
HE WAS GOING TO KILL ME!
MAYBE. IF HE'D GOTTEN YOU. BUT HE DIDN'T. YOU GOT HIM. YOU HAD HIM DOWN.
AND YOU DECIDED TO KILL HIM.
YEAH. YOU KNOW WHY?
I AM NOT MY FATHER!
NOPE.
HERE. LET'S HAVE A BEER.

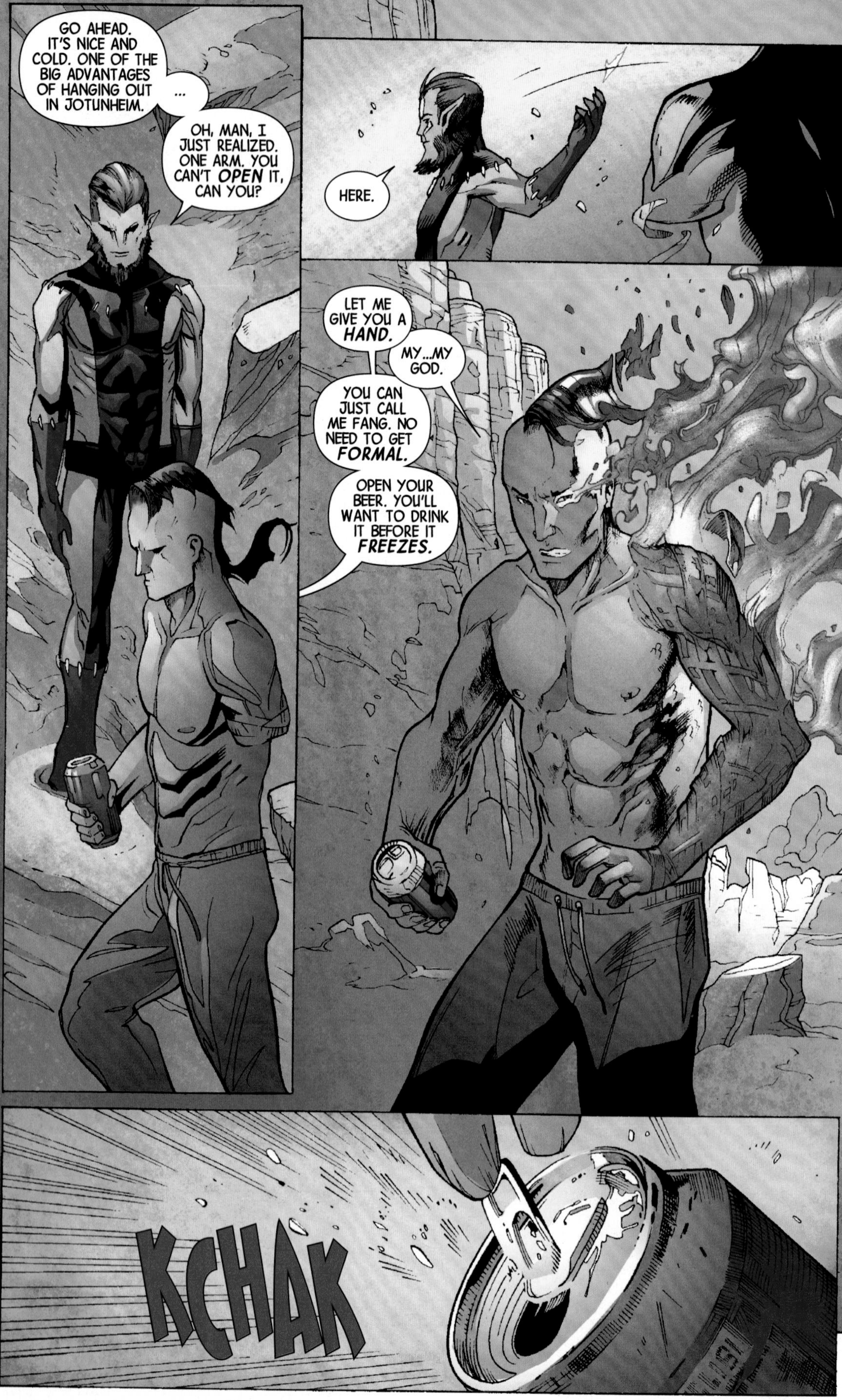
GO AHEAD. IT'S NICE AND COLD. ONE OF THE BIG ADVANTAGES OF HANGING OUT IN JOTUNHEIM.
...
OH, MAN, I JUST REALIZED. ONE ARM. YOU CAN'T OPEN IT, CAN YOU?
HERE.
LET ME GIVE YOU A HAND.
MY...MY GOD.
YOU CAN JUST CALL ME FANG. NO NEED TO GET FORMAL.
OPEN YOUR BEER. YOU'LL WANT TO DRINK IT BEFORE IT FREEZES.
KCHAK

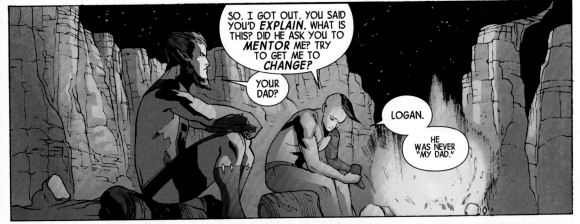

SO. I GOT OUT. YOU SAID YOU'D *EXPLAIN.* WHAT IS THIS? DID HE ASK YOU TO *MENTOR* ME? TRY TO GET ME TO *CHANGE*?

YOUR DAD?

LOGAN.

HE WAS NEVER "MY DAD."

HE *DID* LIKE TO MENTOR... TO *GUIDE* YOUNG PEOPLE. HE DID IT A LOT. KITTY PRYDE, JUBILEE, HISAKO...

...BUT, NO. HE DIDN'T WANT ME TO DO THAT WITH YOU.

GOOD. I AM NOT A *CHILD,* FANG. I WAS BORN IN 1946. THERE IS NOTHING LEFT TO *GUIDE.*

OH, HE KNEW THAT. ALL TOO WELL. MOST OF THE TIME, LOGAN TALKED ABOUT YOU LIKE YOU WERE A MONSTER. SOME UGLY *THING.*

HE SAW ME NOT LONG AFTER HE THOUGHT HE'D DROWNED YOU IN HAMMER BAY. YOU KNOW WHAT HE FELT? GUILT, SURE. REGRET. BUT MOSTLY...?

*RELIEF.* IMAGINE THAT. A FATHER, FEELING NOTHING BUT *RELIEF* AFTER KILLING HIS CHILD.

DOES *THAT* SOUND MORE LIKE THE FATHER YOU KNEW?

YES.

YES, IT DOES.

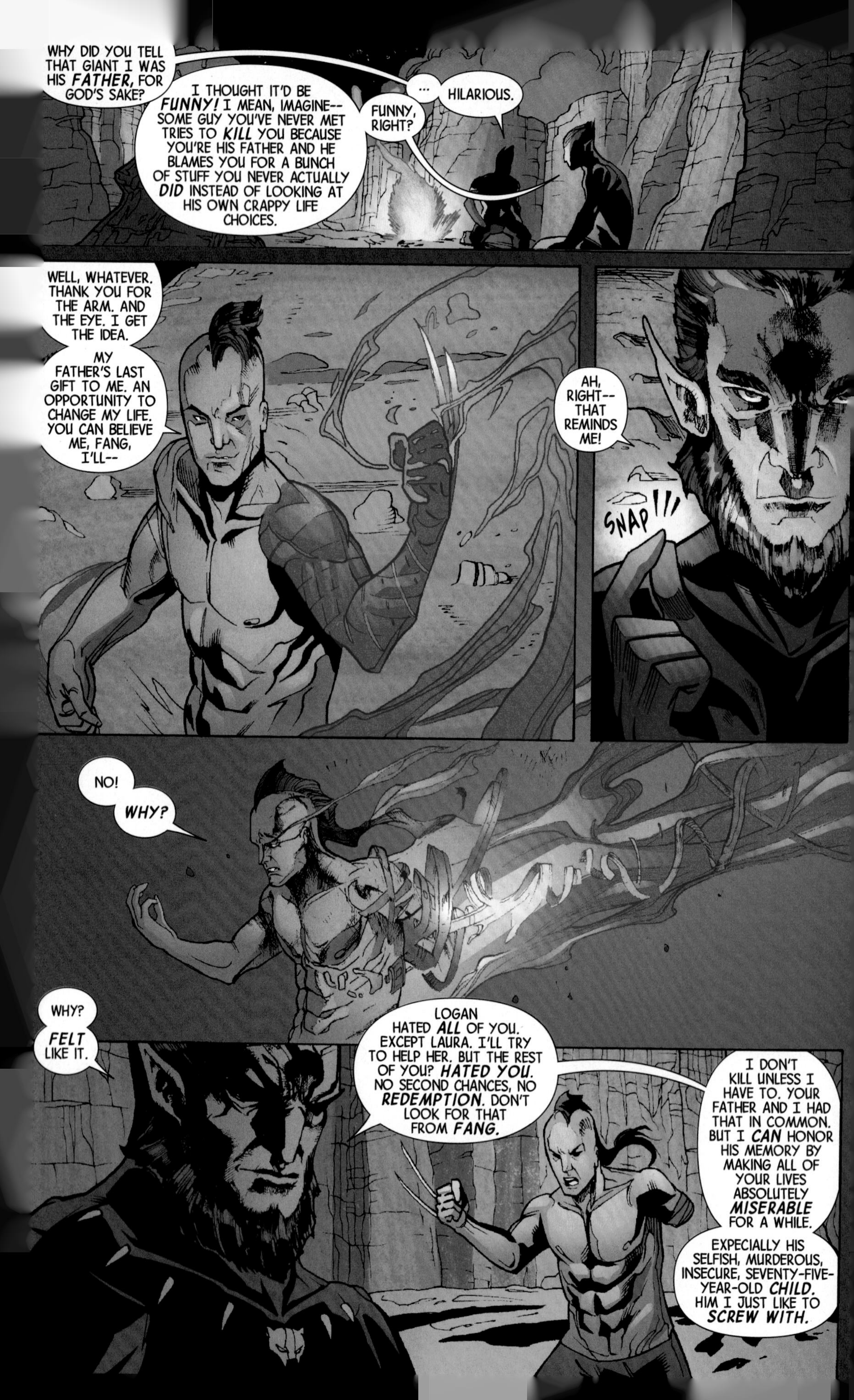
WHY DID YOU TELL THAT GIANT I WAS HIS FATHER, FOR GOD'S SAKE?
I THOUGHT IT'D BE FUNNY! I MEAN, IMAGINE-- SOME GUY YOU'VE NEVER MET TRIES TO KILL YOU BECAUSE YOU'RE HIS FATHER AND HE BLAMES YOU FOR A BUNCH OF STUFF YOU NEVER ACTUALLY DID INSTEAD OF LOOKING AT HIS OWN CRAPPY LIFE CHOICES.
FUNNY, RIGHT?
...
HILARIOUS.
WELL, WHATEVER. THANK YOU FOR THE ARM. AND THE EYE. I GET THE IDEA.
MY FATHER'S LAST GIFT TO ME. AN OPPORTUNITY TO CHANGE MY LIFE. YOU CAN BELIEVE ME, FANG, I'LL--
AH, RIGHT-- THAT REMINDS ME!
SNAP!!!
NO!
WHY?
WHY?
FELT LIKE IT.
LOGAN HATED ALL OF YOU. EXCEPT LAURA. I'LL TRY TO HELP HER. BUT THE REST OF YOU? HATED YOU. NO SECOND CHANCES, NO REDEMPTION. DON'T LOOK FOR THAT FROM FANG.
I DON'T KILL UNLESS I HAVE TO. YOUR FATHER AND I HAD THAT IN COMMON. BUT I CAN HONOR HIS MEMORY BY MAKING ALL OF YOUR LIVES ABSOLUTELY MISERABLE FOR A WHILE.
EXPECIALLY HIS SELFISH, MURDEROUS, INSECURE, SEVENTY-FIVE-YEAR-OLD CHILD. HIM I JUST LIKE TO SCREW WITH.

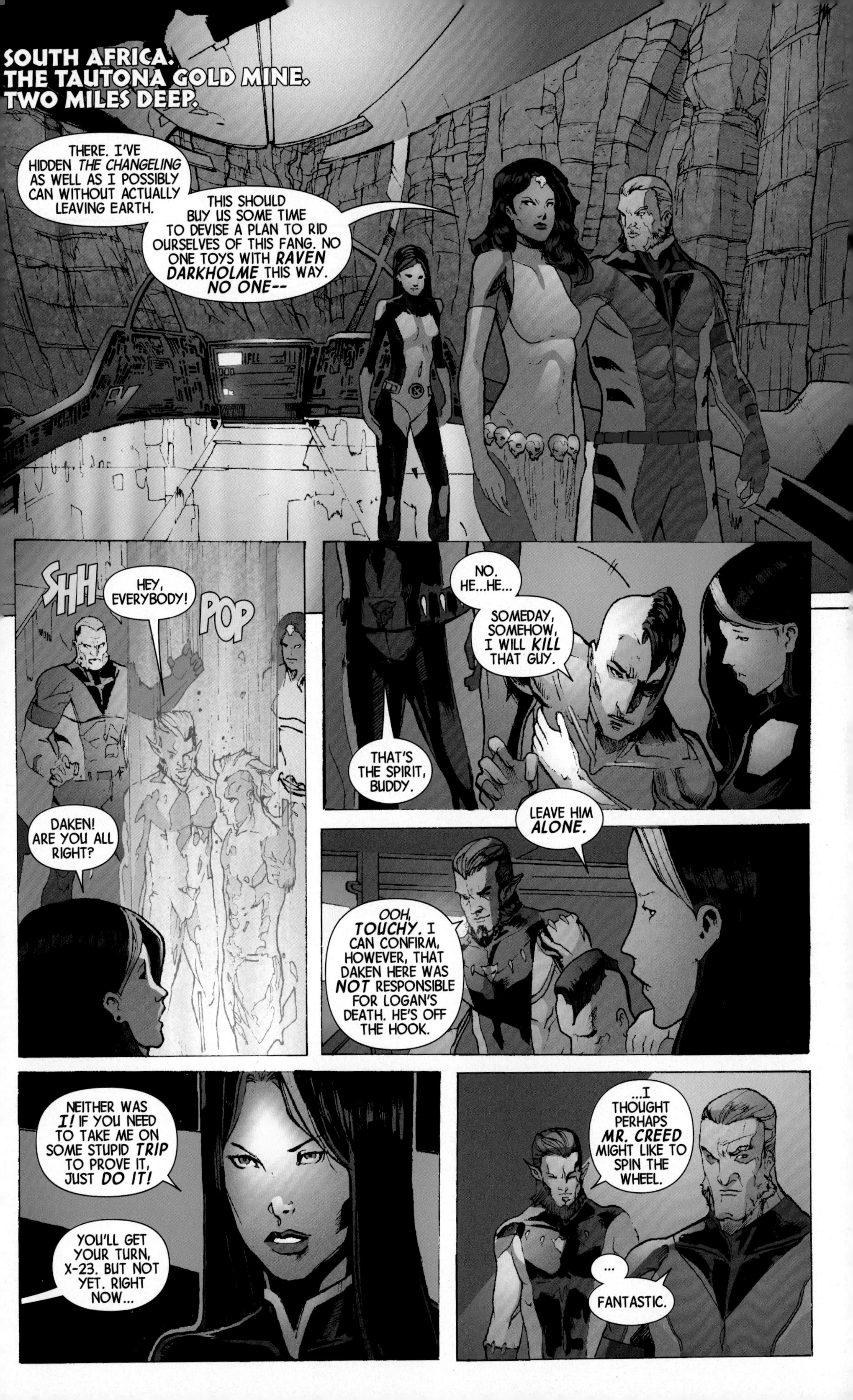
SOUTH AFRICA. THE TAUTONA GOLD MINE. TWO MILES DEEP.
THERE. I'VE HIDDEN THE CHANGELING AS WELL AS I POSSIBLY CAN WITHOUT ACTUALLY LEAVING EARTH.
THIS SHOULD BUY US SOME TIME TO DEVISE A PLAN TO RID OURSELVES OF THIS FANG. NO ONE TOYS WITH RAVEN DARKHOLME THIS WAY. NO ONE--
SHH
HEY, EVERYBODY!
POP
DAKEN! ARE YOU ALL RIGHT?
NO. HE...HE...
SOMEDAY, SOMEHOW, I WILL KILL THAT GUY.
THAT'S THE SPIRIT, BUDDY.
LEAVE HIM ALONE.
OOH, TOUCHY. I CAN CONFIRM, HOWEVER, THAT DAKEN HERE WAS NOT RESPONSIBLE FOR LOGAN'S DEATH. HE'S OFF THE HOOK.
NEITHER WAS I! IF YOU NEED TO TAKE ME ON SOME STUPID TRIP TO PROVE IT, JUST DO IT!
YOU'LL GET YOUR TURN, X-23. BUT NOT YET. RIGHT NOW...
...I THOUGHT PERHAPS MR. CREED MIGHT LIKE TO SPIN THE WHEEL.
...
FANTASTIC.

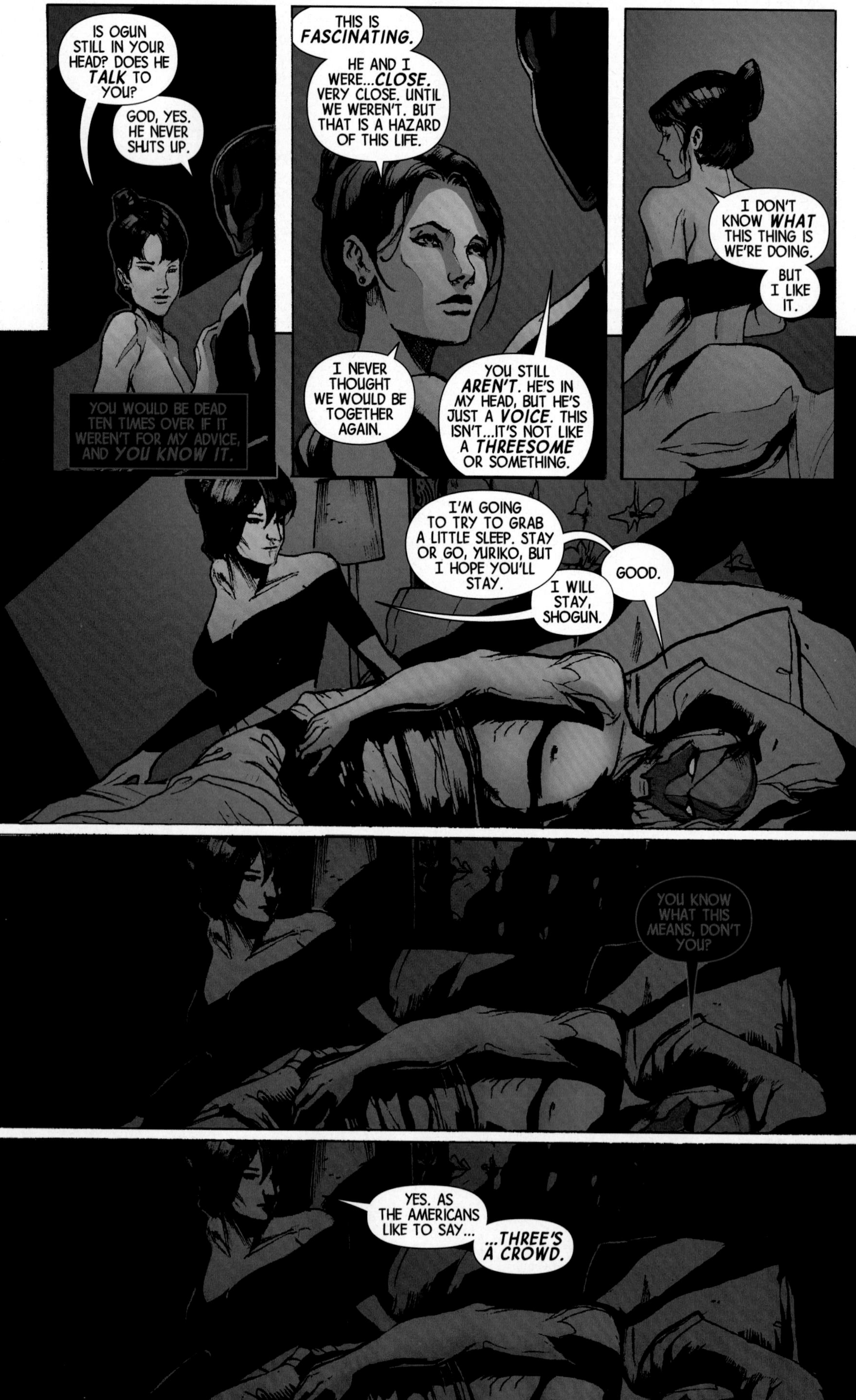

IS OGUN STILL IN YOUR HEAD? DOES HE TALK TO YOU?
GOD, YES. HE NEVER SHUTS UP.
YOU WOULD BE DEAD TEN TIMES OVER IF IT WEREN'T FOR MY ADVICE, AND YOU KNOW IT.
THIS IS FASCINATING.
HE AND I WERE...CLOSE. VERY CLOSE. UNTIL WE WEREN'T. BUT THAT IS A HAZARD OF THIS LIFE.
I NEVER THOUGHT WE WOULD BE TOGETHER AGAIN.
YOU STILL AREN'T. HE'S IN MY HEAD, BUT HE'S JUST A VOICE. THIS ISN'T...IT'S NOT LIKE A THREESOME OR SOMETHING.
I DON'T KNOW WHAT THIS THING IS WE'RE DOING.
BUT I LIKE IT.
I'M GOING TO TRY TO GRAB A LITTLE SLEEP. STAY OR GO, YURIKO, BUT I HOPE YOU'LL STAY.
I WILL STAY, SHOGUN.
GOOD.
YOU KNOW WHAT THIS MEANS, DON'T YOU?
YES. AS THE AMERICANS LIKE TO SAY...
...THREE'S A CROWD.

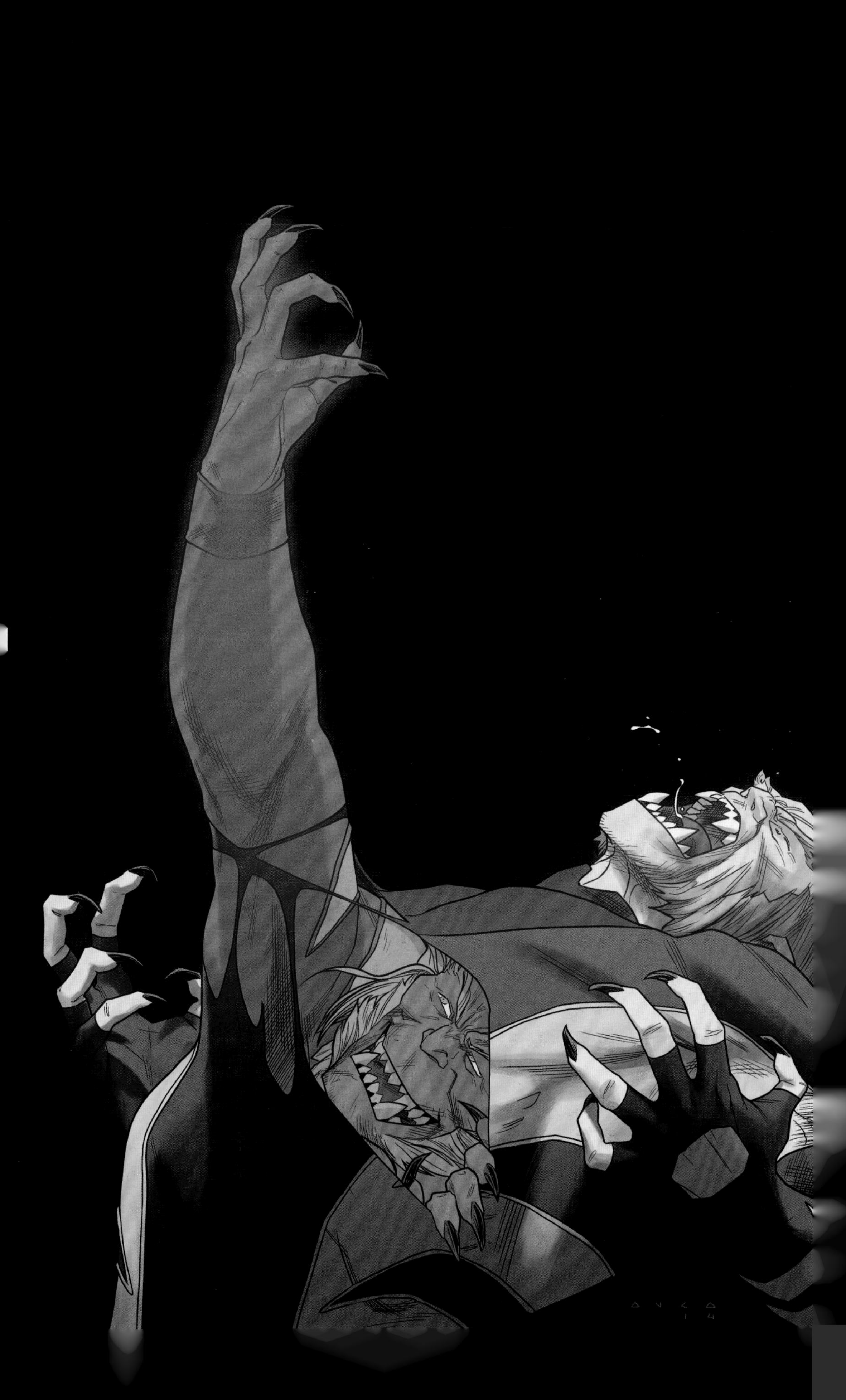

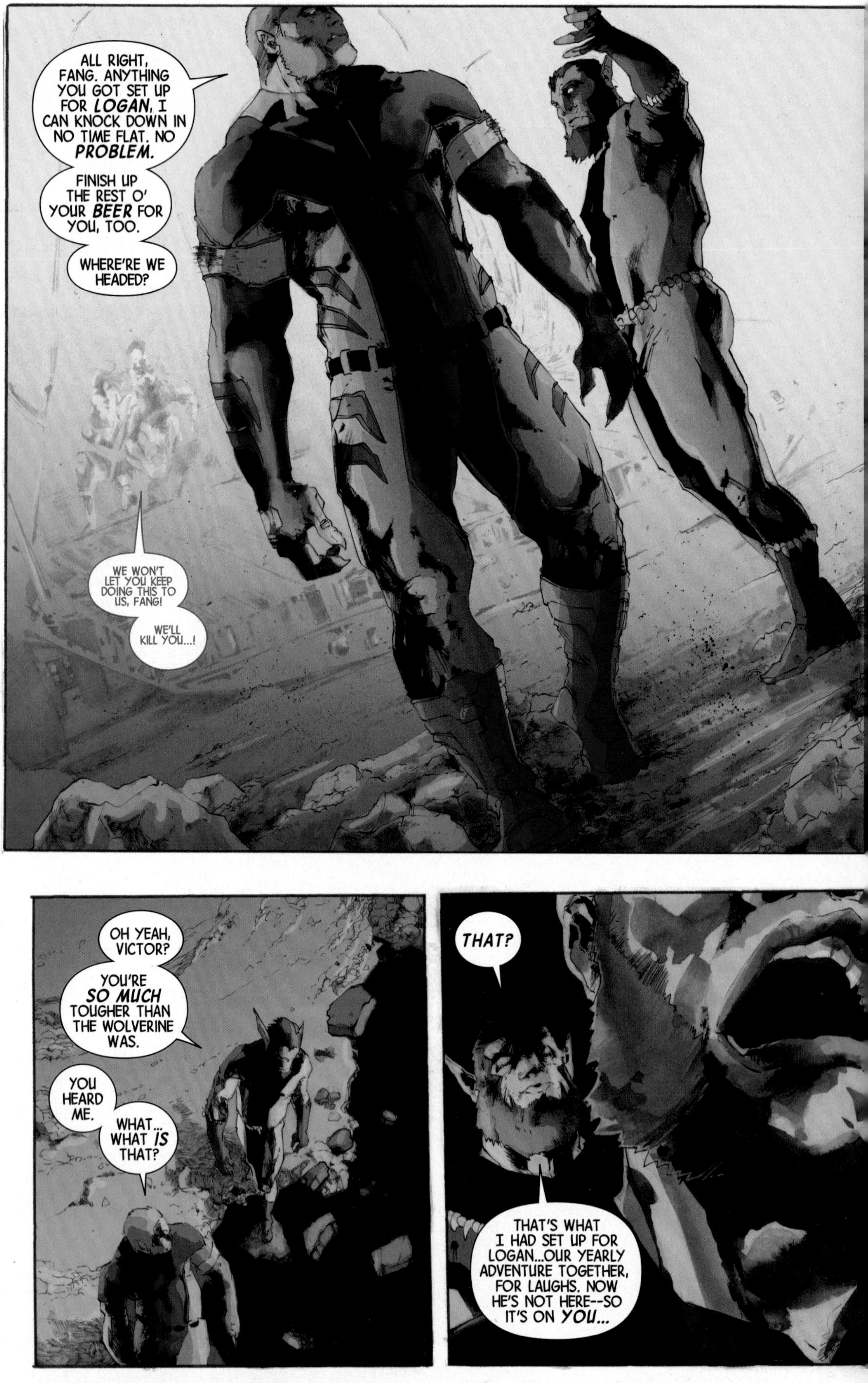
ALL RIGHT, FANG. ANYTHING YOU GOT SET UP FOR LOGAN, I CAN KNOCK DOWN IN NO TIME FLAT. NO PROBLEM.
FINISH UP THE REST O' YOUR BEER FOR YOU, TOO.
WHERE'RE WE HEADED?
WE WON'T LET YOU KEEP DOING THIS TO US, FANG!
WE'LL KILL YOU...!
OH YEAH, VICTOR?
YOU'RE SO MUCH TOUGHER THAN THE WOLVERINE WAS.
YOU HEARD ME.
WHAT... WHAT IS THAT?
THAT?
THAT'S WHAT I HAD SET UP FOR LOGAN...OUR YEARLY ADVENTURE TOGETHER, FOR LAUGHS. NOW HE'S NOT HERE--SO IT'S ON YOU...

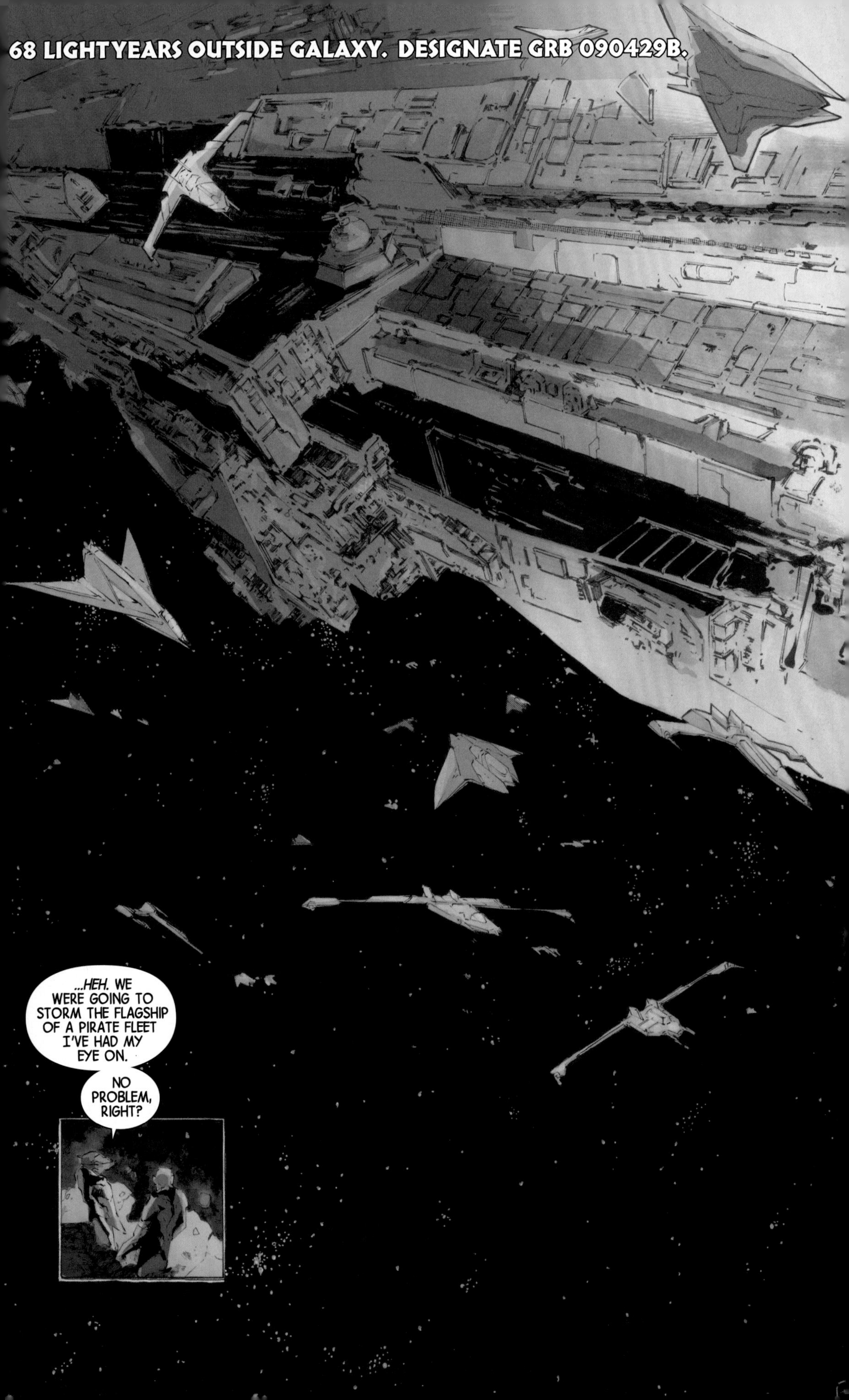
68 LIGHTYEARS OUTSIDE GALAXY. DESIGNATE GRB 090429B.
...HEH. WE WERE GOING TO STORM THE FLAGSHIP OF A PIRATE FLEET I'VE HAD MY EYE ON.
NO PROBLEM, RIGHT?

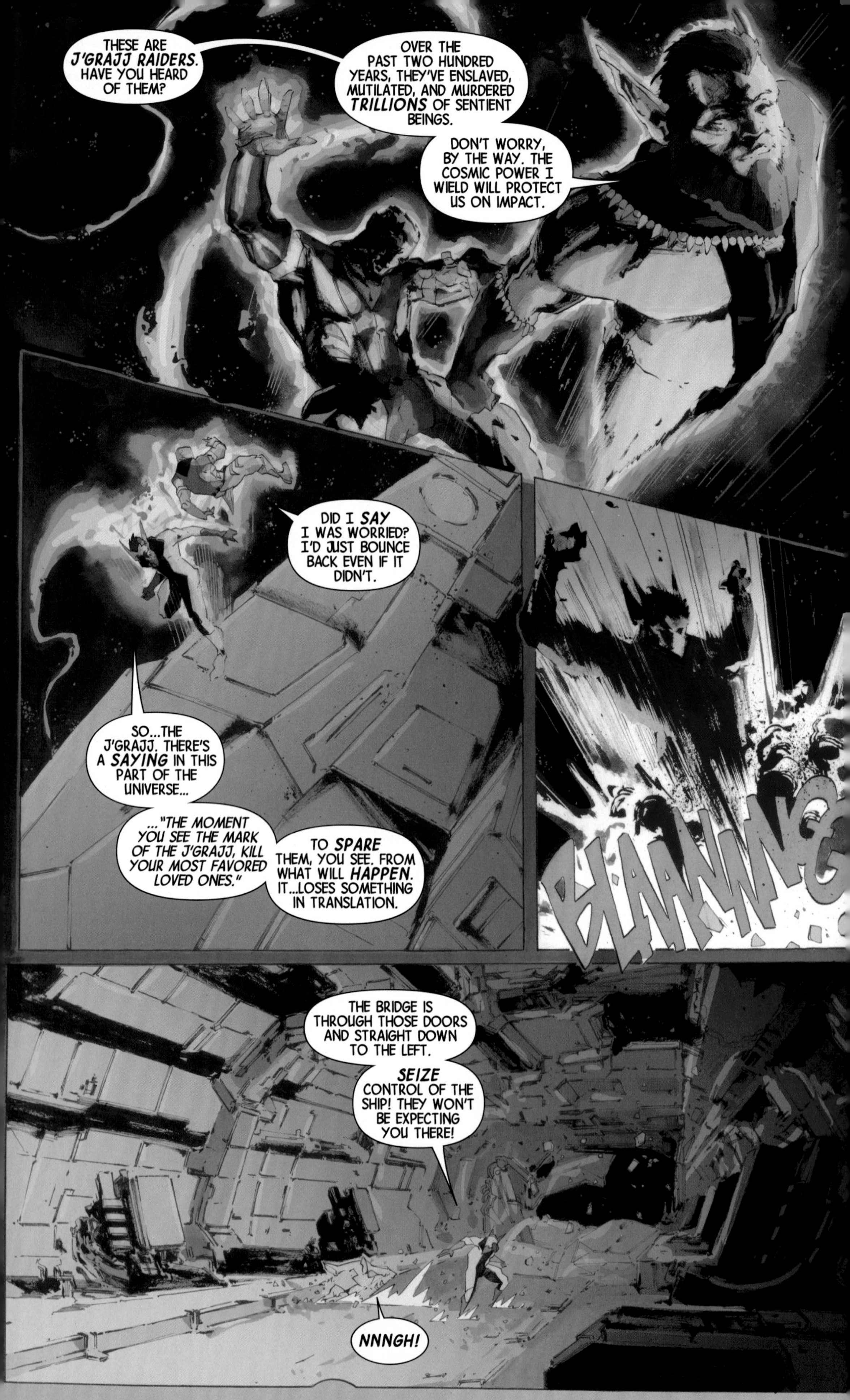
THESE ARE J'GRAJJ RAIDERS. HAVE YOU HEARD OF THEM?
OVER THE PAST TWO HUNDRED YEARS, THEY'VE ENSLAVED, MUTILATED, AND MURDERED TRILLIONS OF SENTIENT BEINGS.
DON'T WORRY, BY THE WAY. THE COSMIC POWER I WIELD WILL PROTECT US ON IMPACT.
DID I SAY I WAS WORRIED? I'D JUST BOUNCE BACK EVEN IF IT DIDN'T.
SO...THE J'GRAJJ. THERE'S A SAYING IN THIS PART OF THE UNIVERSE...
..."THE MOMENT YOU SEE THE MARK OF THE J'GRAJJ, KILL YOUR MOST FAVORED LOVED ONES."
TO SPARE THEM, YOU SEE. FROM WHAT WILL HAPPEN. IT...LOSES SOMETHING IN TRANSLATION.
BLAMMMG
THE BRIDGE IS THROUGH THOSE DOORS AND STRAIGHT DOWN TO THE LEFT.
SEIZE CONTROL OF THE SHIP! THEY WON'T BE EXPECTING YOU THERE!
NNNGH!

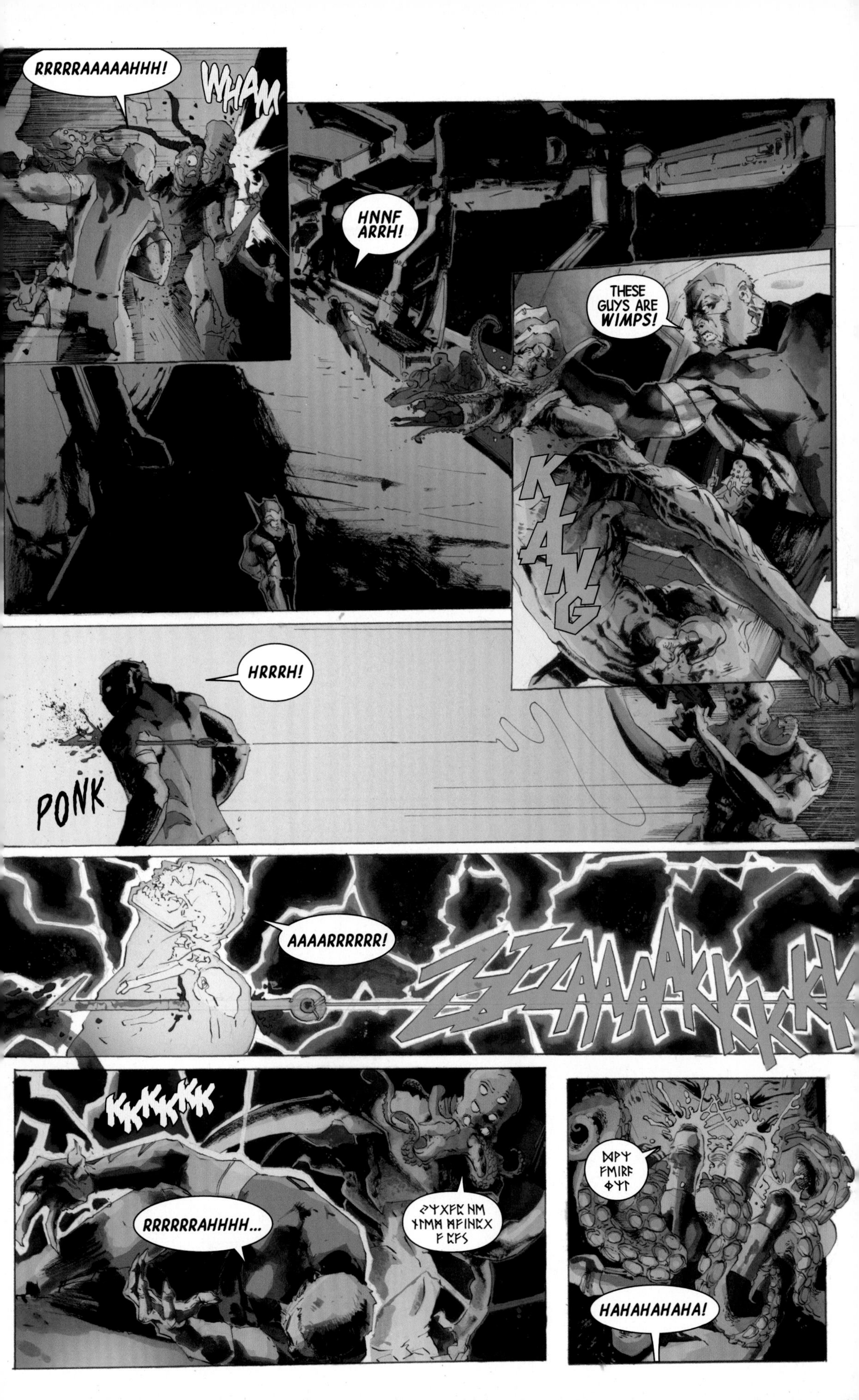
RRRRRAAAAAHHH!
WHAM
HNNF ARRH!
THESE GUYS ARE WIMPS!
KLANG
HRRRH!
PONK
AAAARRRRRR!
ZZZAAAKKKKK
KKKKKK
RRRRRRAHHHH...
HAHAHAHAHA!

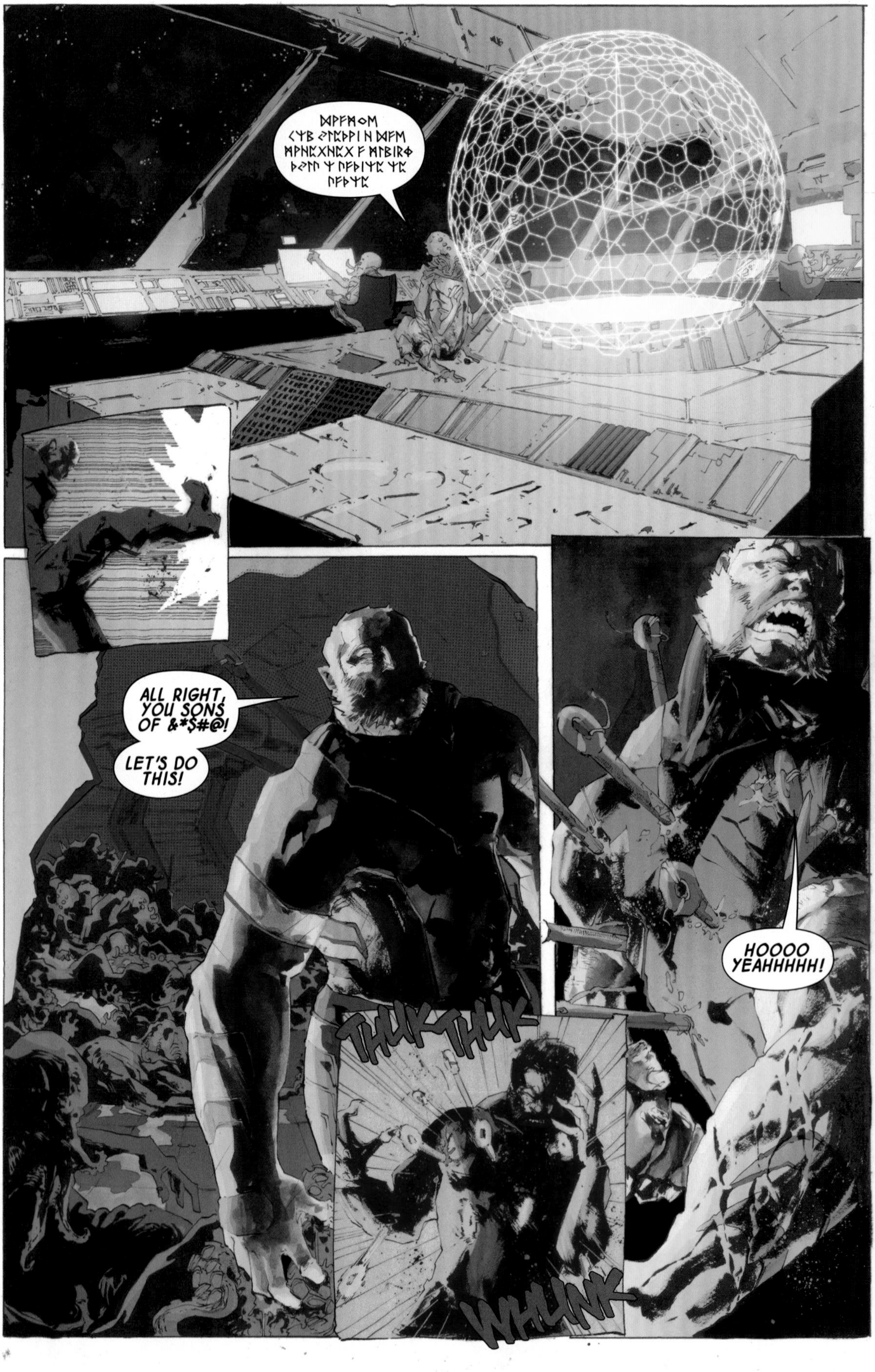
ALL RIGHT, YOU SONS OF &*$#@!
LET'S DO THIS!
HOOOO YEAHHHHH!
THUK THUK
WHUNK

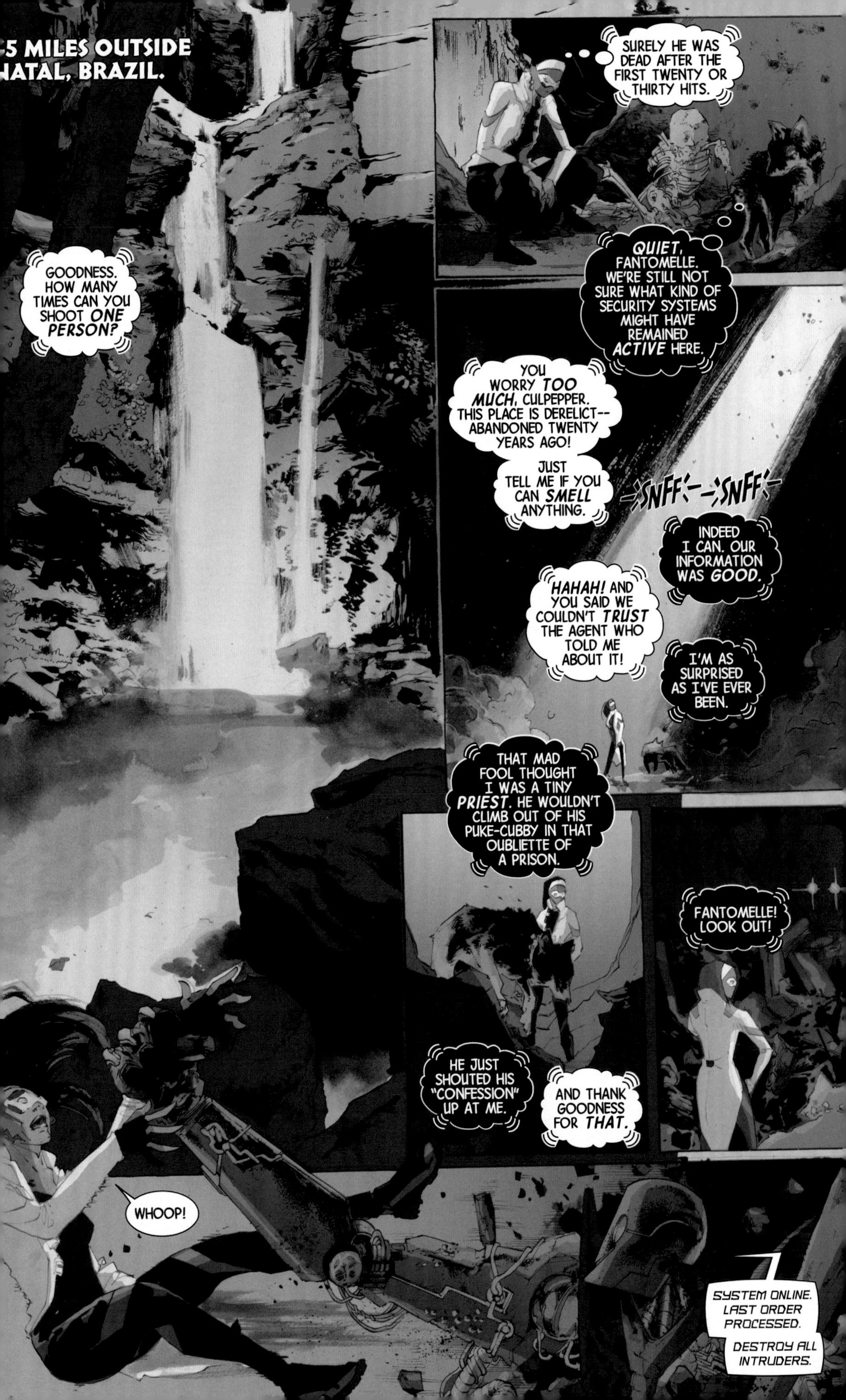

5 MILES OUTSIDE NATAL, BRAZIL.
GOODNESS. HOW MANY TIMES CAN YOU SHOOT ONE PERSON?
SURELY HE WAS DEAD AFTER THE FIRST TWENTY OR THIRTY HITS.
QUIET, FANTOMELLE. WE'RE STILL NOT SURE WHAT KIND OF SECURITY SYSTEMS MIGHT HAVE REMAINED ACTIVE HERE.
YOU WORRY TOO MUCH, CULPEPPER. THIS PLACE IS DERELICT-- ABANDONED TWENTY YEARS AGO!
JUST TELL ME IF YOU CAN SMELL ANYTHING.
SNFF SNFF
INDEED I CAN. OUR INFORMATION WAS GOOD.
HAHAH! AND YOU SAID WE COULDN'T TRUST THE AGENT WHO TOLD ME ABOUT IT!
I'M AS SURPRISED AS I'VE EVER BEEN.
THAT MAD FOOL THOUGHT I WAS A TINY PRIEST. HE WOULDN'T CLIMB OUT OF HIS PUKE-CUBBY IN THAT OUBLIETTE OF A PRISON.
HE JUST SHOUTED HIS "CONFESSION" UP AT ME.
AND THANK GOODNESS FOR THAT.
FANTOMELLE! LOOK OUT!
WHOOP!
SYSTEM ONLINE. LAST ORDER PROCESSED.
DESTROY ALL INTRUDERS.

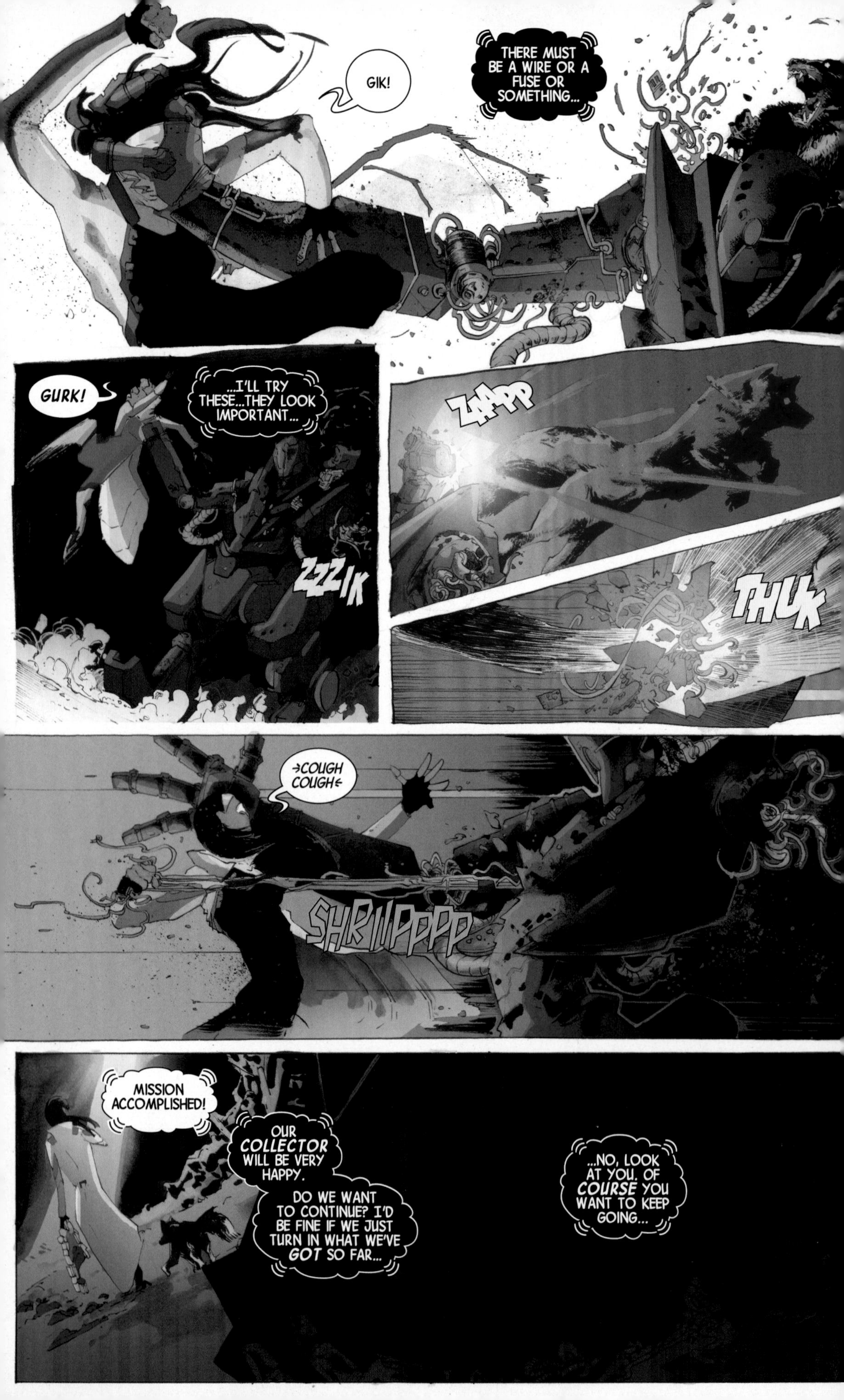

GIK!
THERE MUST BE A WIRE OR A FUSE OR SOMETHING...
GURK!
...I'LL TRY THESE...THEY LOOK IMPORTANT...
ZZZIK
ZAPP
THUK
COUGH COUGH
SHRIIPPPP
MISSION ACCOMPLISHED!
OUR COLLECTOR WILL BE VERY HAPPY.
DO WE WANT TO CONTINUE? I'D BE FINE IF WE JUST TURN IN WHAT WE'VE GOT SO FAR...
...NO, LOOK AT YOU, OF COURSE YOU WANT TO KEEP GOING...

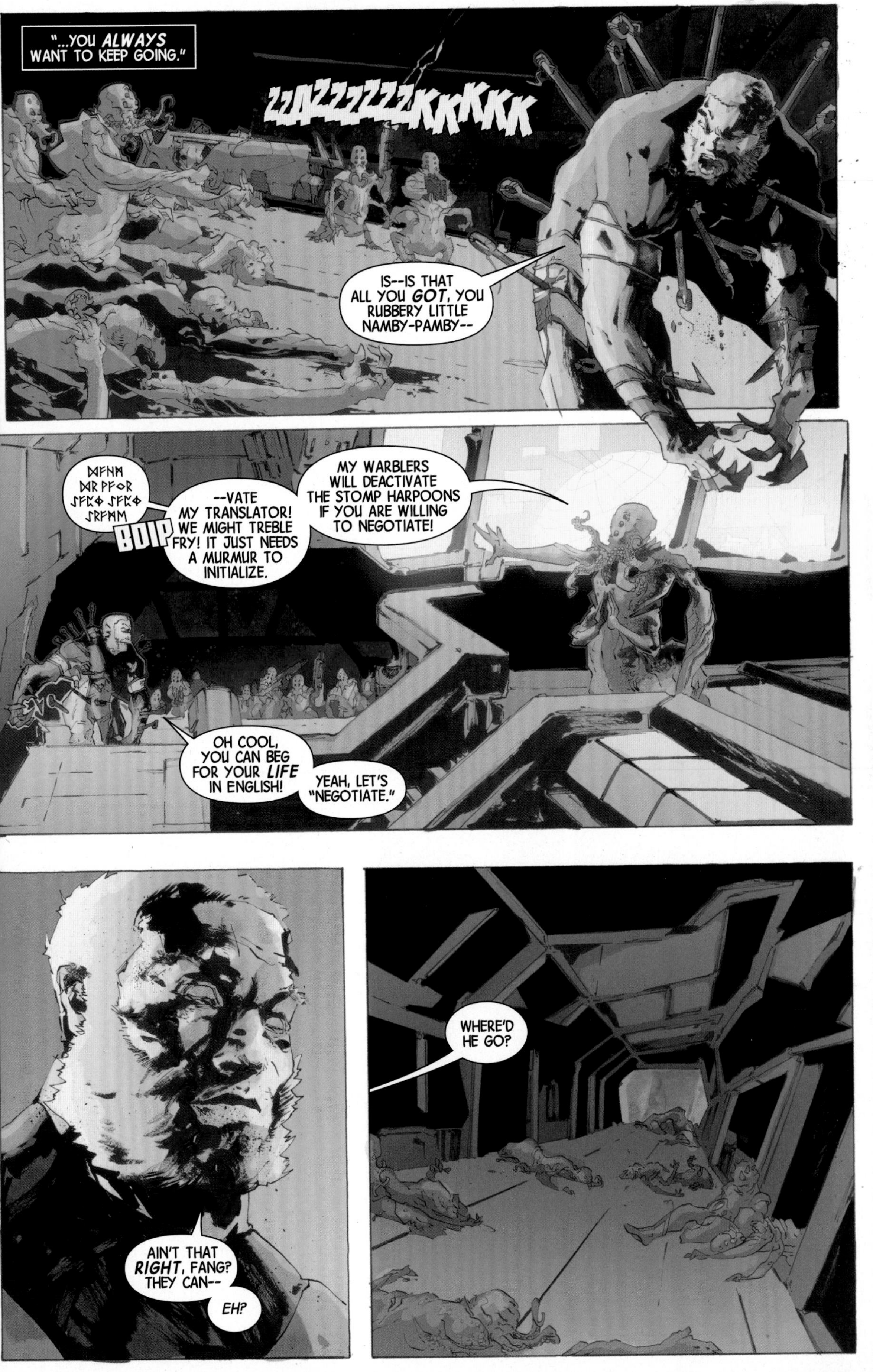
"...YOU ALWAYS WANT TO KEEP GOING."
ZZAZZZZZZZKKKKK
IS--IS THAT ALL YOU GOT, YOU RUBBERY LITTLE NAMBY-PAMBY--
BOIP
--VATE MY TRANSLATOR! WE MIGHT TREBLE FRY! IT JUST NEEDS A MURMUR TO INITIALIZE.
MY WARBLERS WILL DEACTIVATE THE STOMP HARPOONS IF YOU ARE WILLING TO NEGOTIATE!
OH COOL, YOU CAN BEG FOR YOUR LIFE IN ENGLISH!
YEAH, LET'S "NEGOTIATE."
AIN'T THAT RIGHT, FANG? THEY CAN--
EH?
WHERE'D HE GO?

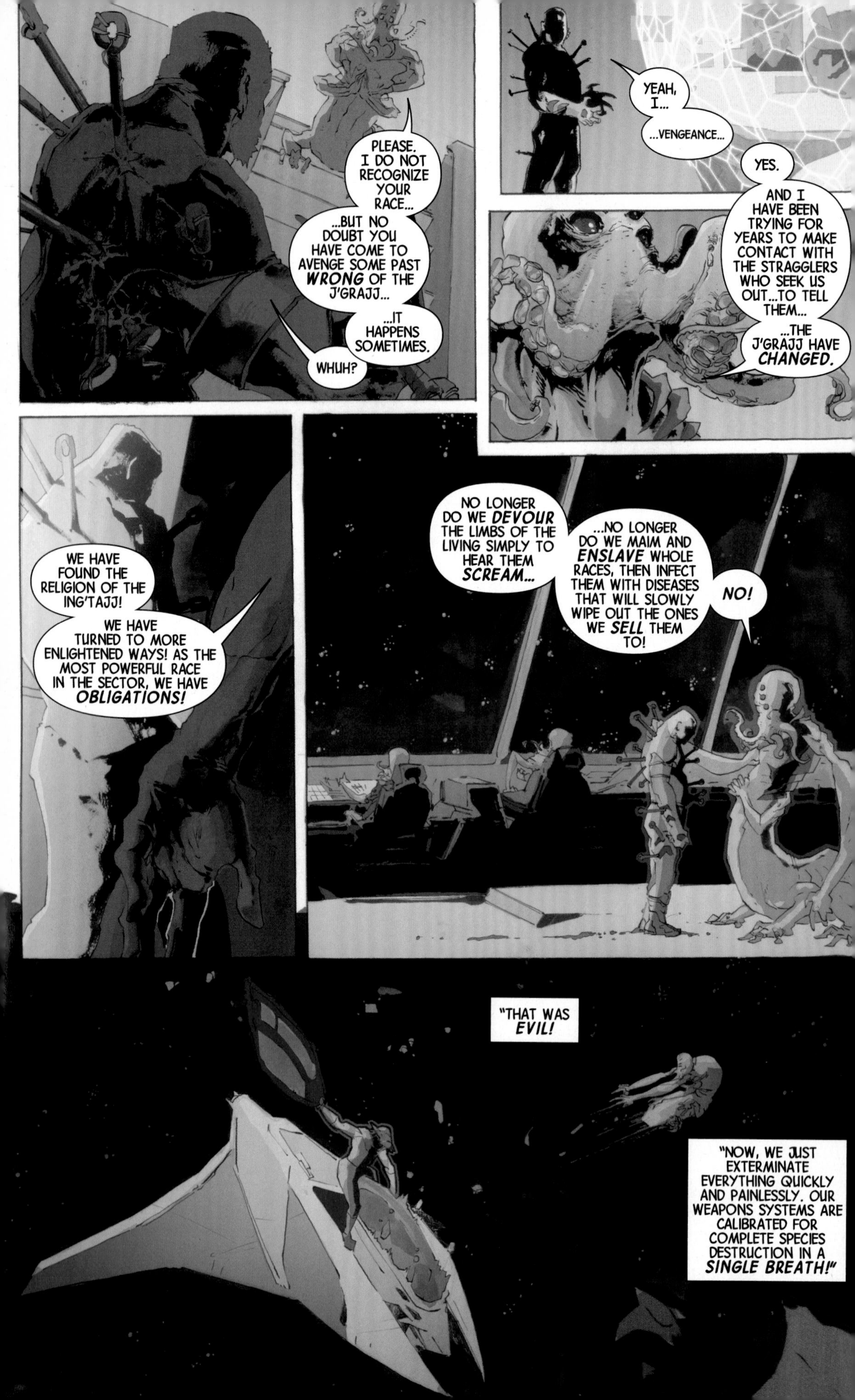
PLEASE. I DO NOT RECOGNIZE YOUR RACE...
...BUT NO DOUBT YOU HAVE COME TO AVENGE SOME PAST **WRONG** OF THE J'GRAJJ...
...IT HAPPENS SOMETIMES.
WHUH?
YEAH, I...
...VENGEANCE...
YES.
AND I HAVE BEEN TRYING FOR YEARS TO MAKE CONTACT WITH THE STRAGGLERS WHO SEEK US OUT...TO TELL THEM...
...THE J'GRAJJ HAVE **CHANGED.**
WE HAVE FOUND THE RELIGION OF THE ING'TAJJ!
WE HAVE TURNED TO MORE ENLIGHTENED WAYS! AS THE MOST POWERFUL RACE IN THE SECTOR, WE HAVE **OBLIGATIONS!**
NO LONGER DO WE **DEVOUR** THE LIMBS OF THE LIVING SIMPLY TO HEAR THEM **SCREAM...**
...NO LONGER DO WE MAIM AND **ENSLAVE** WHOLE RACES, THEN INFECT THEM WITH DISEASES THAT WILL SLOWLY WIPE OUT THE ONES WE **SELL** THEM TO!
**NO!**
"THAT WAS **EVIL!**
"NOW, WE JUST EXTERMINATE EVERYTHING QUICKLY AND PAINLESSLY. OUR WEAPONS SYSTEMS ARE CALIBRATED FOR COMPLETE SPECIES DESTRUCTION IN A **SINGLE BREATH!**"

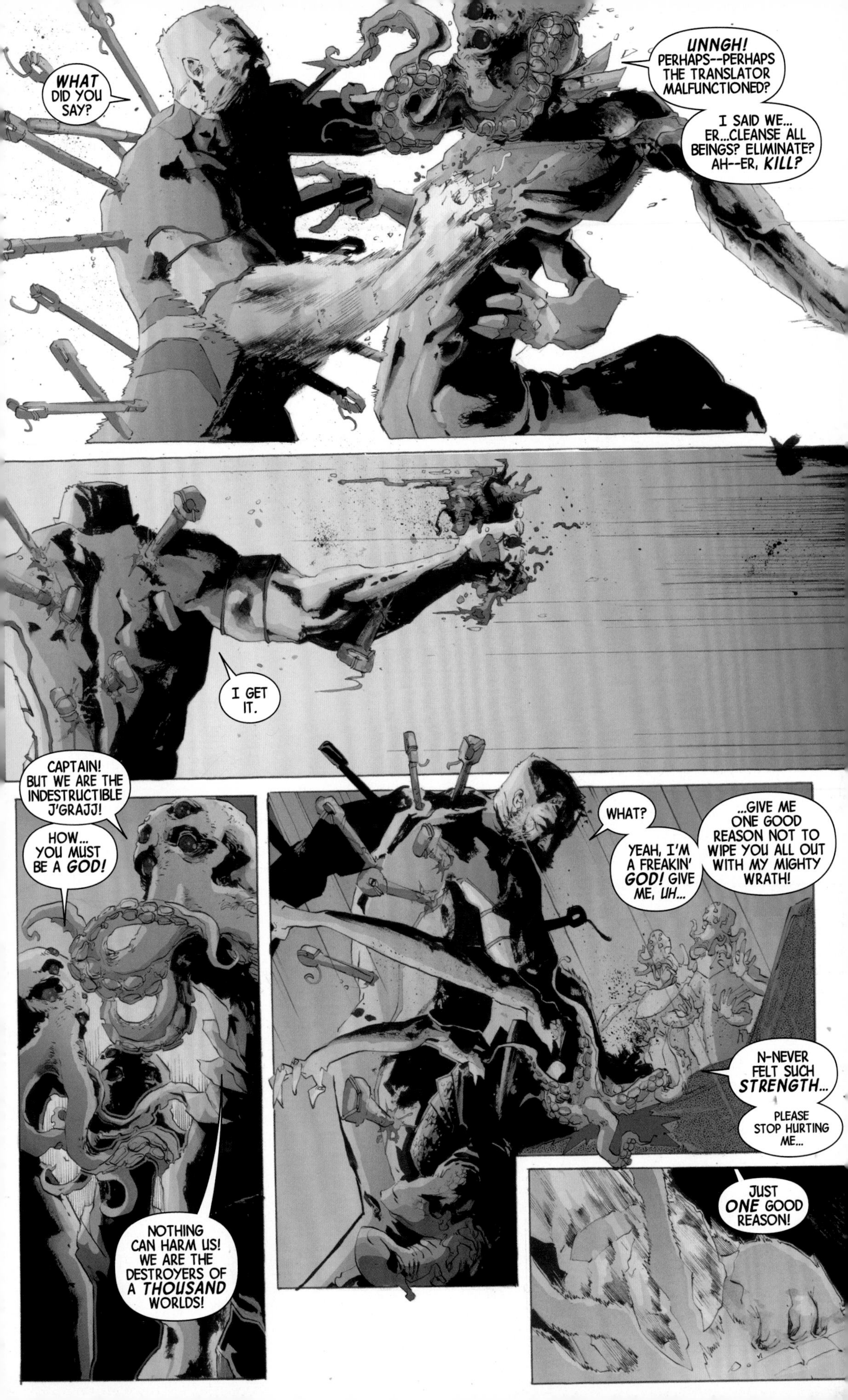
WHAT DID YOU SAY?
UNNGH! PERHAPS--PERHAPS THE TRANSLATOR MALFUNCTIONED?
I SAID WE... ER...CLEANSE ALL BEINGS? ELIMINATE? AH--ER, KILL?
I GET IT.
CAPTAIN! BUT WE ARE THE INDESTRUCTIBLE J'GRAJJ!
HOW... YOU MUST BE A GOD!
NOTHING CAN HARM US! WE ARE THE DESTROYERS OF A THOUSAND WORLDS!
WHAT?
YEAH, I'M A FREAKIN' GOD! GIVE ME, UH...
...GIVE ME ONE GOOD REASON NOT TO WIPE YOU ALL OUT WITH MY MIGHTY WRATH!
N-NEVER FELT SUCH STRENGTH...
PLEASE STOP HURTING ME...
JUST ONE GOOD REASON!

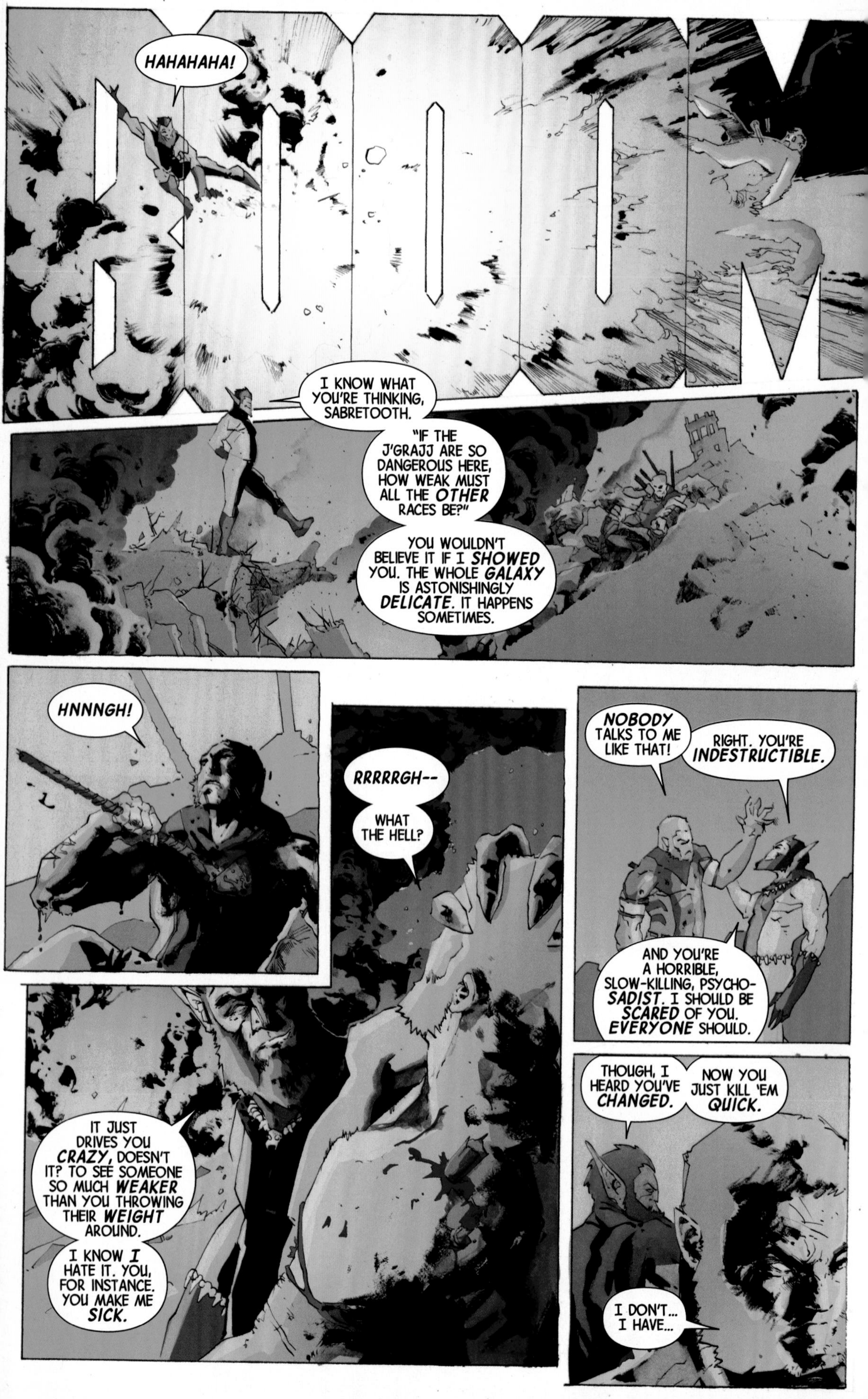
HAHAHAHA!
BOOOOOM
I KNOW WHAT YOU'RE THINKING, SABRETOOTH.
"IF THE J'GRAJJ ARE SO DANGEROUS HERE, HOW WEAK MUST ALL THE OTHER RACES BE?"
YOU WOULDN'T BELIEVE IT IF I SHOWED YOU. THE WHOLE GALAXY IS ASTONISHINGLY DELICATE. IT HAPPENS SOMETIMES.
HNNNGH!
RRRRRGH--
WHAT THE HELL?
IT JUST DRIVES YOU CRAZY, DOESN'T IT? TO SEE SOMEONE SO MUCH WEAKER THAN YOU THROWING THEIR WEIGHT AROUND.
I KNOW I HATE IT. YOU, FOR INSTANCE. YOU MAKE ME SICK.
NOBODY TALKS TO ME LIKE THAT!
RIGHT. YOU'RE INDESTRUCTIBLE.
AND YOU'RE A HORRIBLE, SLOW-KILLING, PSYCHO-SADIST. I SHOULD BE SCARED OF YOU. EVERYONE SHOULD.
THOUGH, I HEARD YOU'VE CHANGED.
NOW YOU JUST KILL 'EM QUICK.
I DON'T... I HAVE...

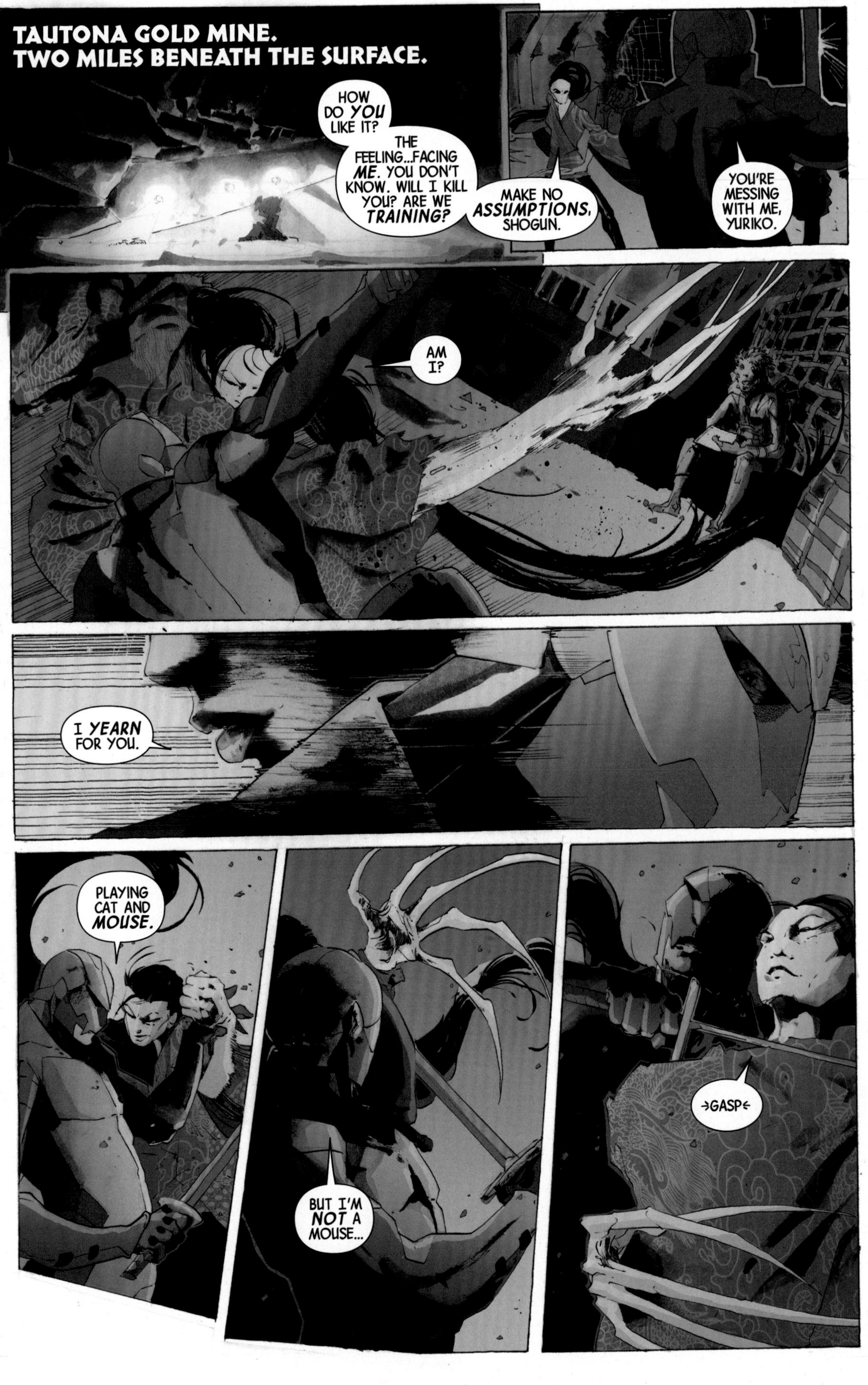
TAUTONA GOLD MINE.
TWO MILES BENEATH THE SURFACE.
HOW DO YOU LIKE IT?
THE FEELING...FACING ME. YOU DON'T KNOW. WILL I KILL YOU? ARE WE TRAINING?
MAKE NO ASSUMPTIONS, SHOGUN.
YOU'RE MESSING WITH ME, YURIKO.
AM I?
I YEARN FOR YOU.
PLAYING CAT AND MOUSE.
BUT I'M NOT A MOUSE...
GASP

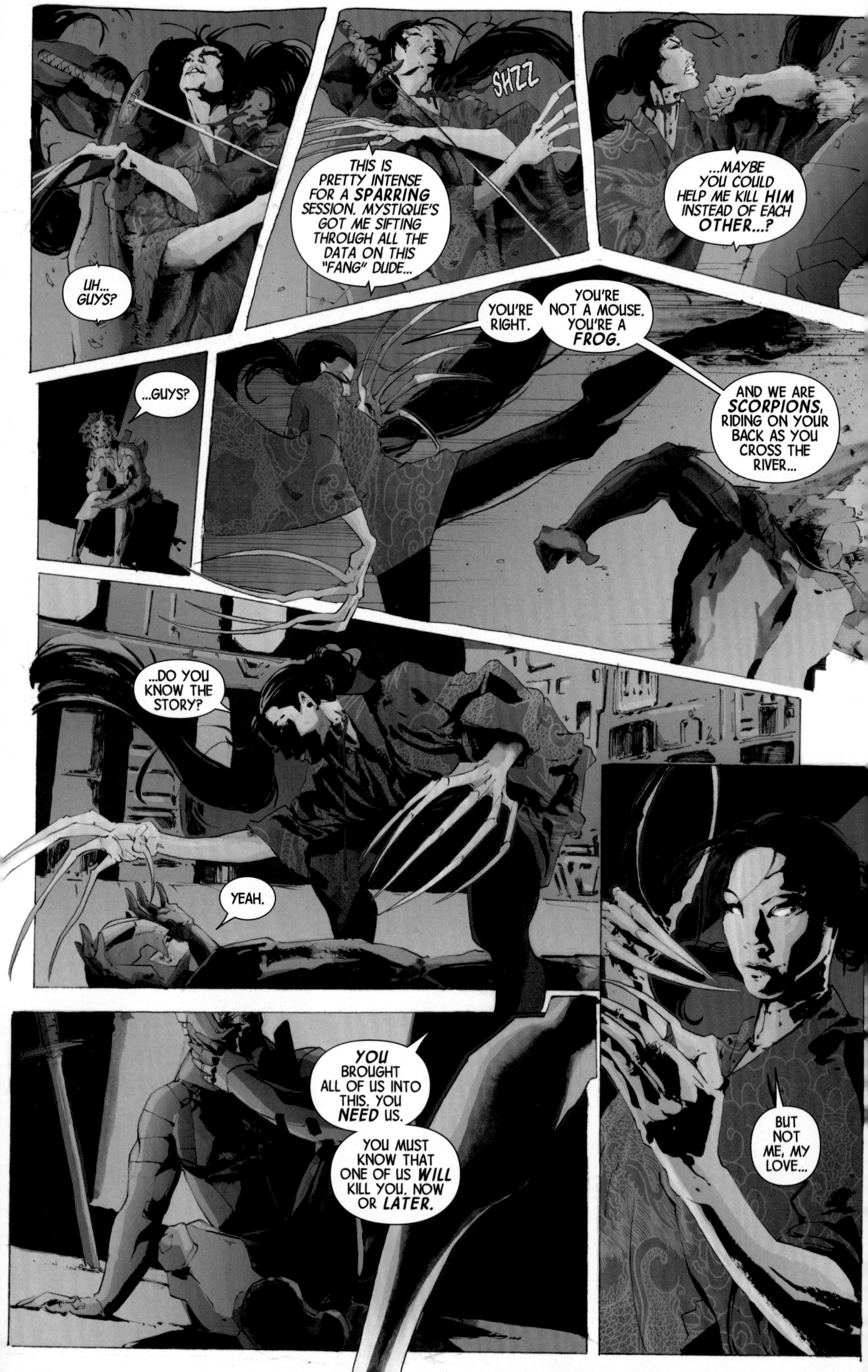
UH... GUYS?
SHZZ
THIS IS PRETTY INTENSE FOR A SPARRING SESSION. MYSTIQUE'S GOT ME SIFTING THROUGH ALL THE DATA ON THIS "FANG" DUDE...
...MAYBE YOU COULD HELP ME KILL HIM INSTEAD OF EACH OTHER...?
...GUYS?
YOU'RE RIGHT.
YOU'RE NOT A MOUSE. YOU'RE A FROG.
AND WE ARE SCORPIONS, RIDING ON YOUR BACK AS YOU CROSS THE RIVER...
...DO YOU KNOW THE STORY?
YEAH.
YOU BROUGHT ALL OF US INTO THIS. YOU NEED US.
YOU MUST KNOW THAT ONE OF US WILL KILL YOU. NOW OR LATER.
BUT NOT ME, MY LOVE...

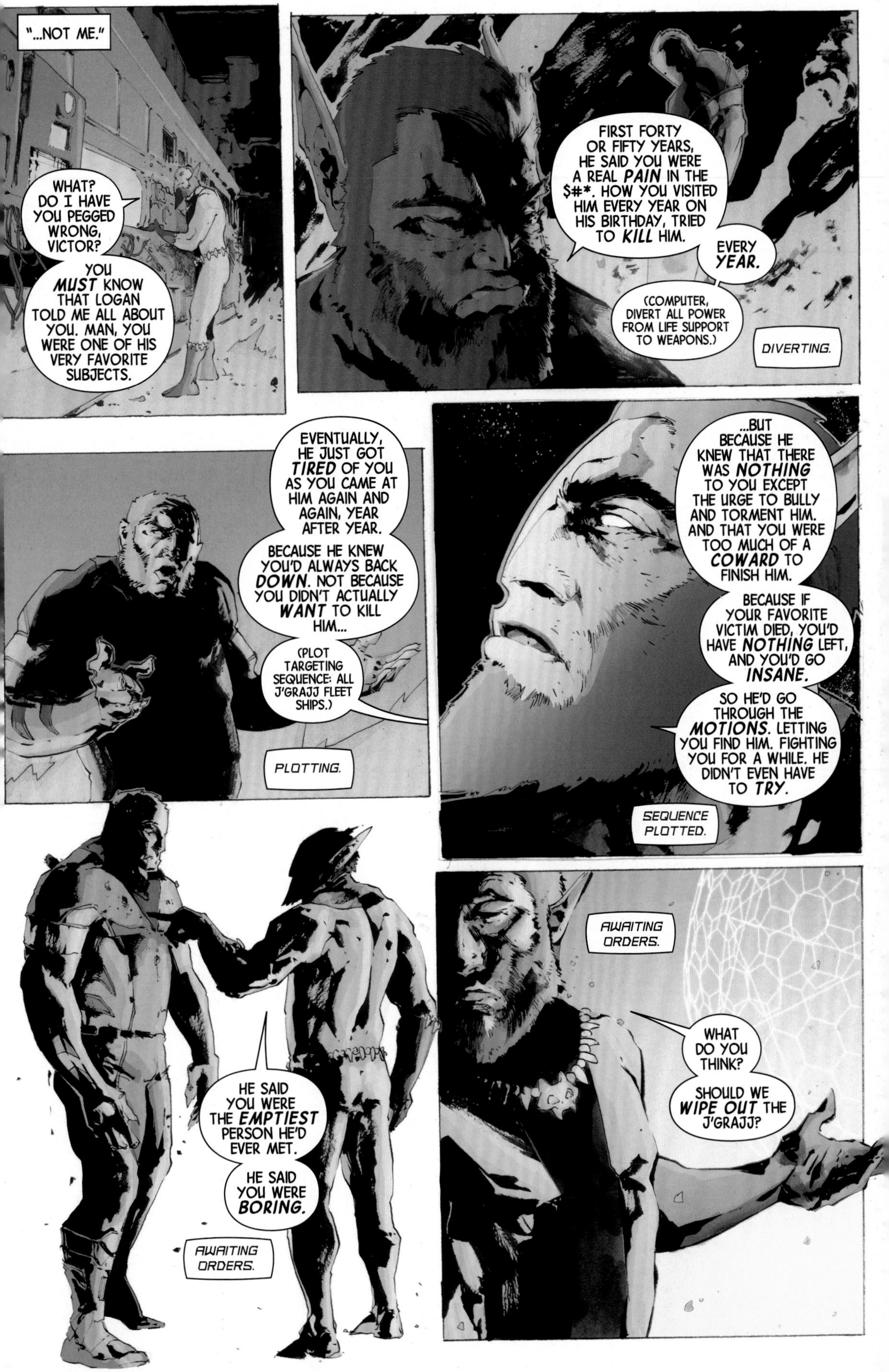
"...NOT ME."
WHAT? DO I HAVE YOU PEGGED WRONG, VICTOR?
YOU MUST KNOW THAT LOGAN TOLD ME ALL ABOUT YOU. MAN, YOU WERE ONE OF HIS VERY FAVORITE SUBJECTS.
FIRST FORTY OR FIFTY YEARS, HE SAID YOU WERE A REAL PAIN IN THE $#*. HOW YOU VISITED HIM EVERY YEAR ON HIS BIRTHDAY, TRIED TO KILL HIM.
EVERY YEAR.
(COMPUTER, DIVERT ALL POWER FROM LIFE SUPPORT TO WEAPONS.)
DIVERTING.
EVENTUALLY, HE JUST GOT TIRED OF YOU AS YOU CAME AT HIM AGAIN AND AGAIN, YEAR AFTER YEAR.
BECAUSE HE KNEW YOU'D ALWAYS BACK DOWN. NOT BECAUSE YOU DIDN'T ACTUALLY WANT TO KILL HIM...
(PLOT TARGETING SEQUENCE: ALL J'GRAJJ FLEET SHIPS.)
PLOTTING.
...BUT BECAUSE HE KNEW THAT THERE WAS NOTHING TO YOU EXCEPT THE URGE TO BULLY AND TORMENT HIM. AND THAT YOU WERE TOO MUCH OF A COWARD TO FINISH HIM.
BECAUSE IF YOUR FAVORITE VICTIM DIED, YOU'D HAVE NOTHING LEFT, AND YOU'D GO INSANE.
SO HE'D GO THROUGH THE MOTIONS. LETTING YOU FIND HIM. FIGHTING YOU FOR A WHILE. HE DIDN'T EVEN HAVE TO TRY.
SEQUENCE PLOTTED.
HE SAID YOU WERE THE EMPTIEST PERSON HE'D EVER MET.
HE SAID YOU WERE BORING.
AWAITING ORDERS.
AWAITING ORDERS.
WHAT DO YOU THINK?
SHOULD WE WIPE OUT THE J'GRAJJ?

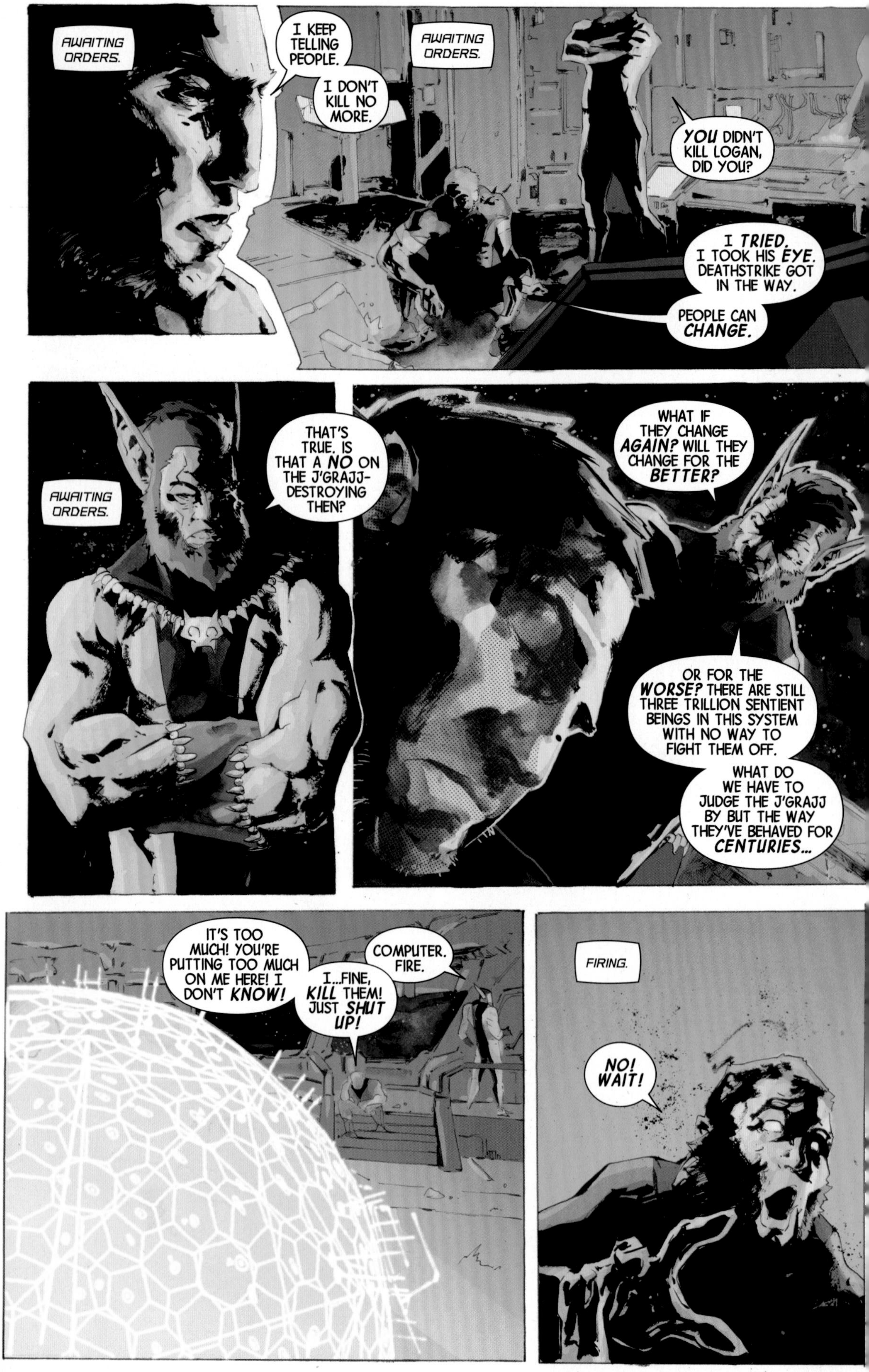
AWAITING ORDERS.
I KEEP TELLING PEOPLE.
I DON'T KILL NO MORE.
AWAITING ORDERS.
YOU DIDN'T KILL LOGAN, DID YOU?
I TRIED. I TOOK HIS EYE. DEATHSTRIKE GOT IN THE WAY.
PEOPLE CAN CHANGE.
AWAITING ORDERS.
THAT'S TRUE. IS THAT A NO ON THE J'GRAJJ-DESTROYING THEN?
WHAT IF THEY CHANGE AGAIN? WILL THEY CHANGE FOR THE BETTER?
OR FOR THE WORSE? THERE ARE STILL THREE TRILLION SENTIENT BEINGS IN THIS SYSTEM WITH NO WAY TO FIGHT THEM OFF.
WHAT DO WE HAVE TO JUDGE THE J'GRAJJ BY BUT THE WAY THEY'VE BEHAVED FOR CENTURIES...
IT'S TOO MUCH! YOU'RE PUTTING TOO MUCH ON ME HERE! I DON'T KNOW!
COMPUTER. FIRE.
I...FINE, KILL THEM! JUST SHUT UP!
FIRING.
NO! WAIT!

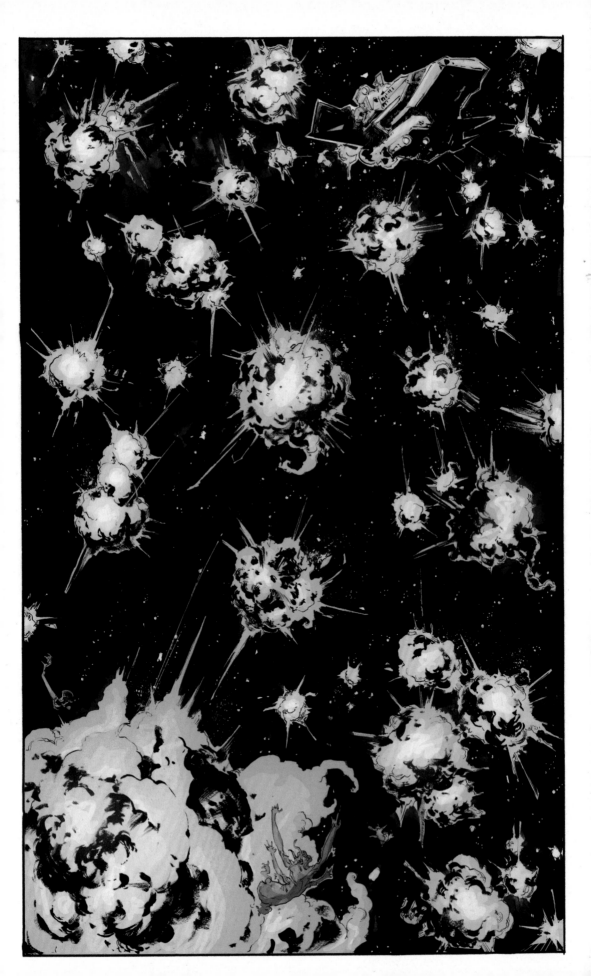

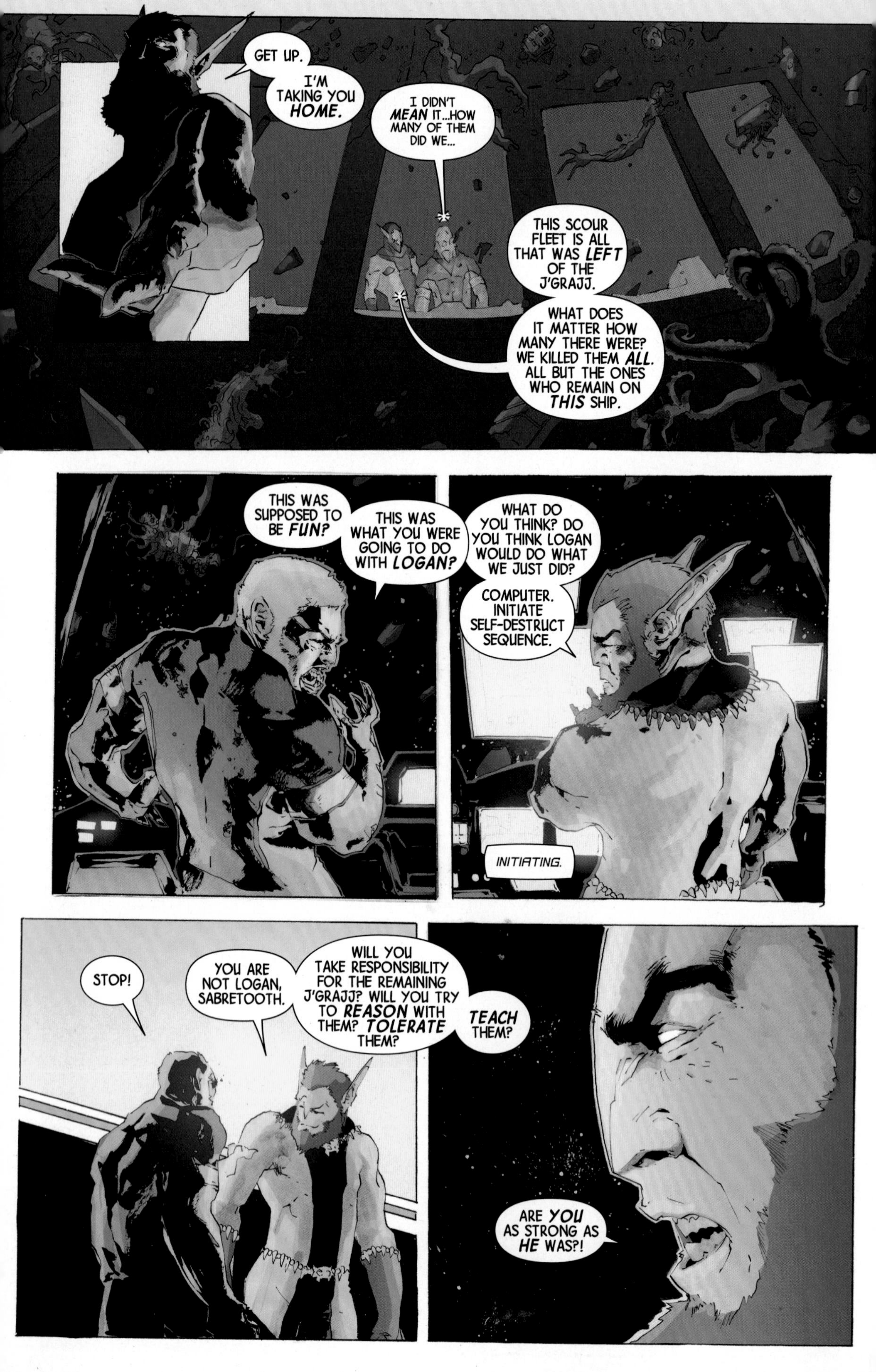

GET UP.
I'M TAKING YOU HOME.
I DIDN'T MEAN IT...HOW MANY OF THEM DID WE...
THIS SCOUR FLEET IS ALL THAT WAS LEFT OF THE J'GRAJJ.
WHAT DOES IT MATTER HOW MANY THERE WERE? WE KILLED THEM ALL. ALL BUT THE ONES WHO REMAIN ON THIS SHIP.
THIS WAS SUPPOSED TO BE FUN?
THIS WAS WHAT YOU WERE GOING TO DO WITH LOGAN?
WHAT DO YOU THINK? DO YOU THINK LOGAN WOULD DO WHAT WE JUST DID?
COMPUTER. INITIATE SELF-DESTRUCT SEQUENCE.
INITIATING.
STOP!
YOU ARE NOT LOGAN, SABRETOOTH.
WILL YOU TAKE RESPONSIBILITY FOR THE REMAINING J'GRAJJ? WILL YOU TRY TO REASON WITH THEM? TOLERATE THEM?
TEACH THEM?
ARE YOU AS STRONG AS HE WAS?!

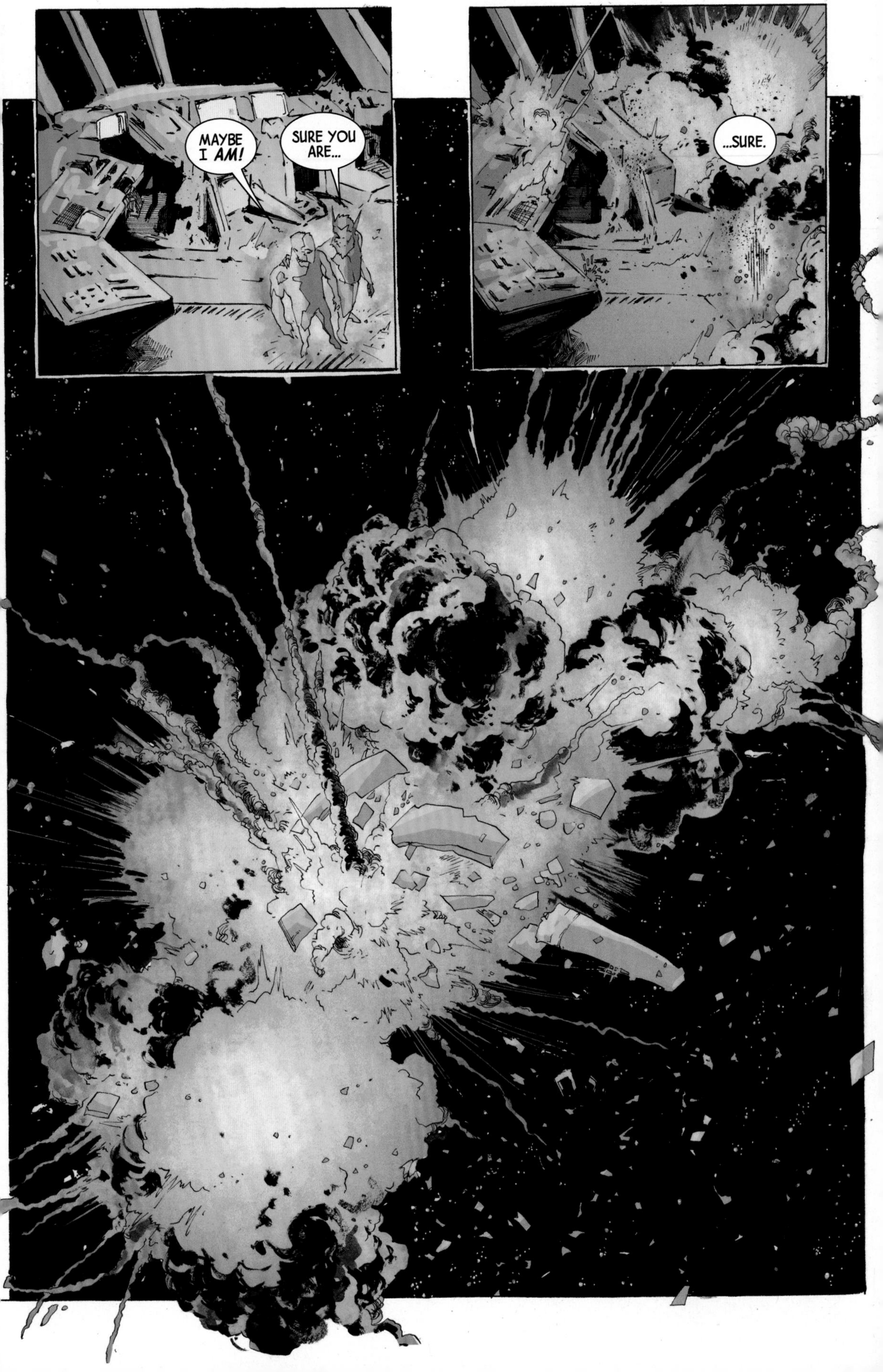
MAYBE I AM!
SURE YOU ARE...
...SURE.

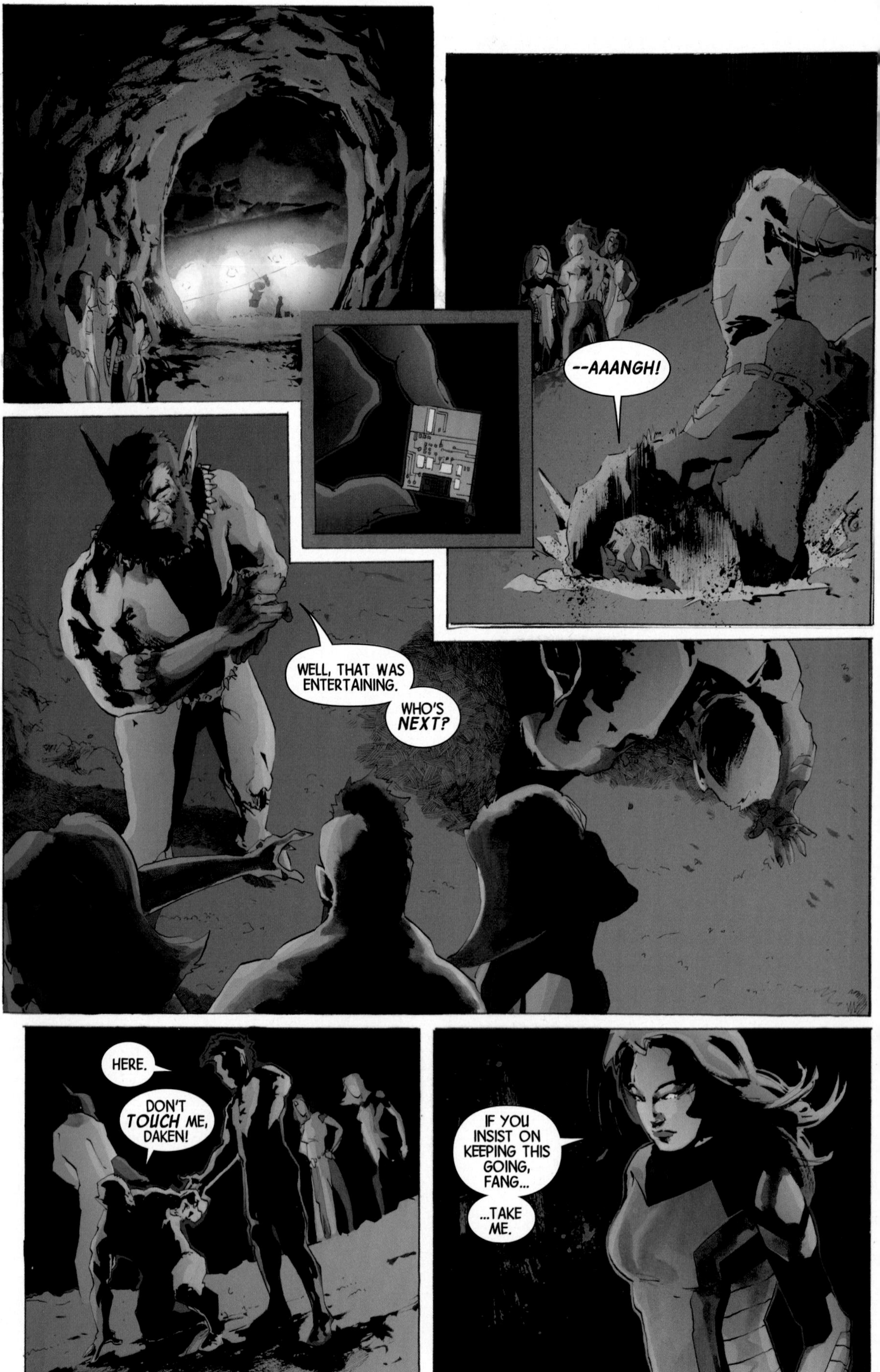
--AAANGH!
WELL, THAT WAS ENTERTAINING.
WHO'S NEXT?
HERE.
DON'T TOUCH ME, DAKEN!
IF YOU INSIST ON KEEPING THIS GOING, FANG...
...TAKE ME.

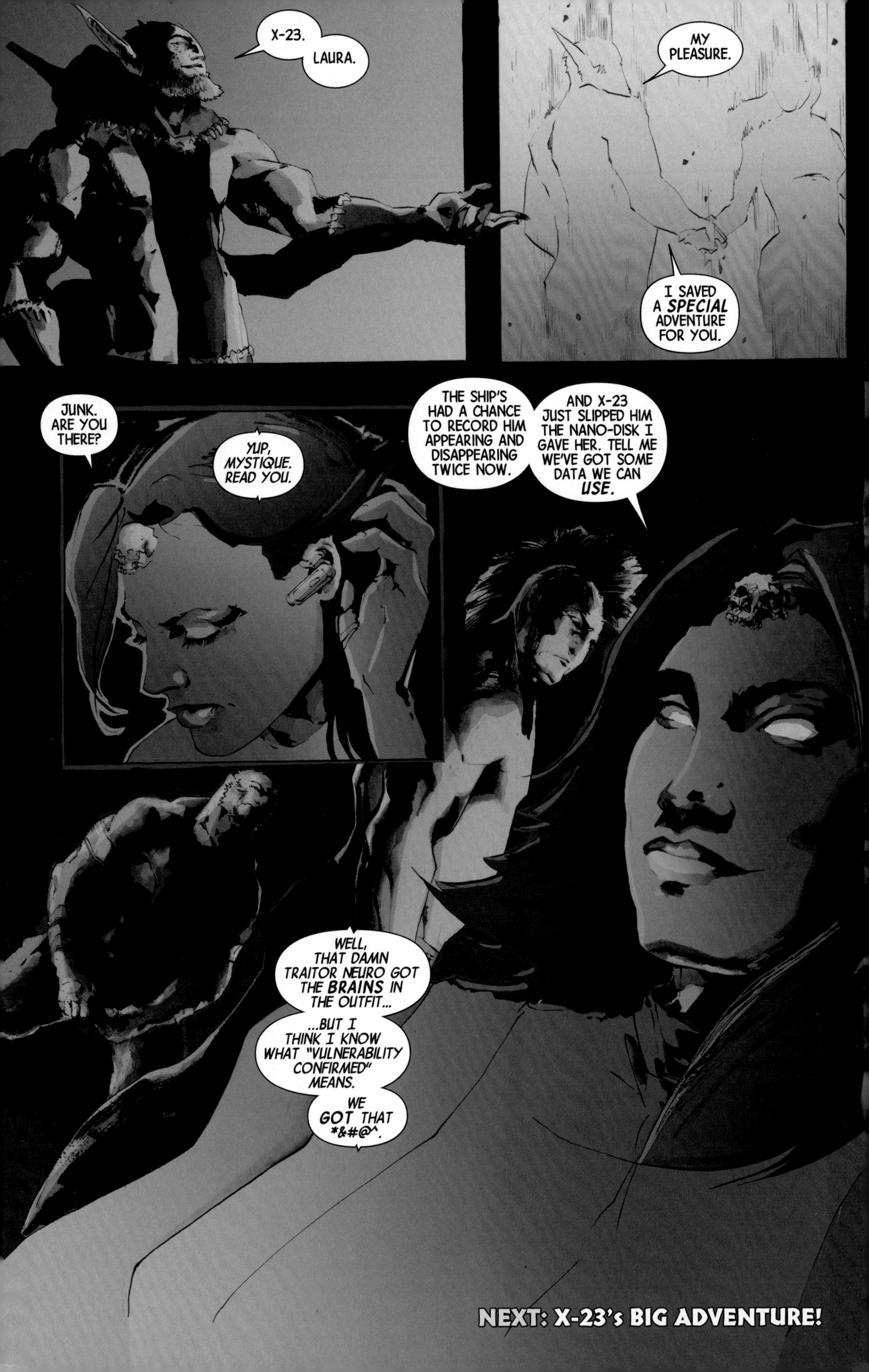
X-23.
LAURA.
MY PLEASURE.
I SAVED A SPECIAL ADVENTURE FOR YOU.
JUNK. ARE YOU THERE?
YUP, MYSTIQUE. READ YOU.
THE SHIP'S HAD A CHANCE TO RECORD HIM APPEARING AND DISAPPEARING TWICE NOW.
AND X-23 JUST SLIPPED HIM THE NANO-DISK I GAVE HER. TELL ME WE'VE GOT SOME DATA WE CAN USE.
WELL, THAT DAMN TRAITOR NEURO GOT THE BRAINS IN THE OUTFIT...
...BUT I THINK I KNOW WHAT "VULNERABILITY CONFIRMED" MEANS.
WE GOT THAT *&#@^.
NEXT: X-23's BIG ADVENTURE!

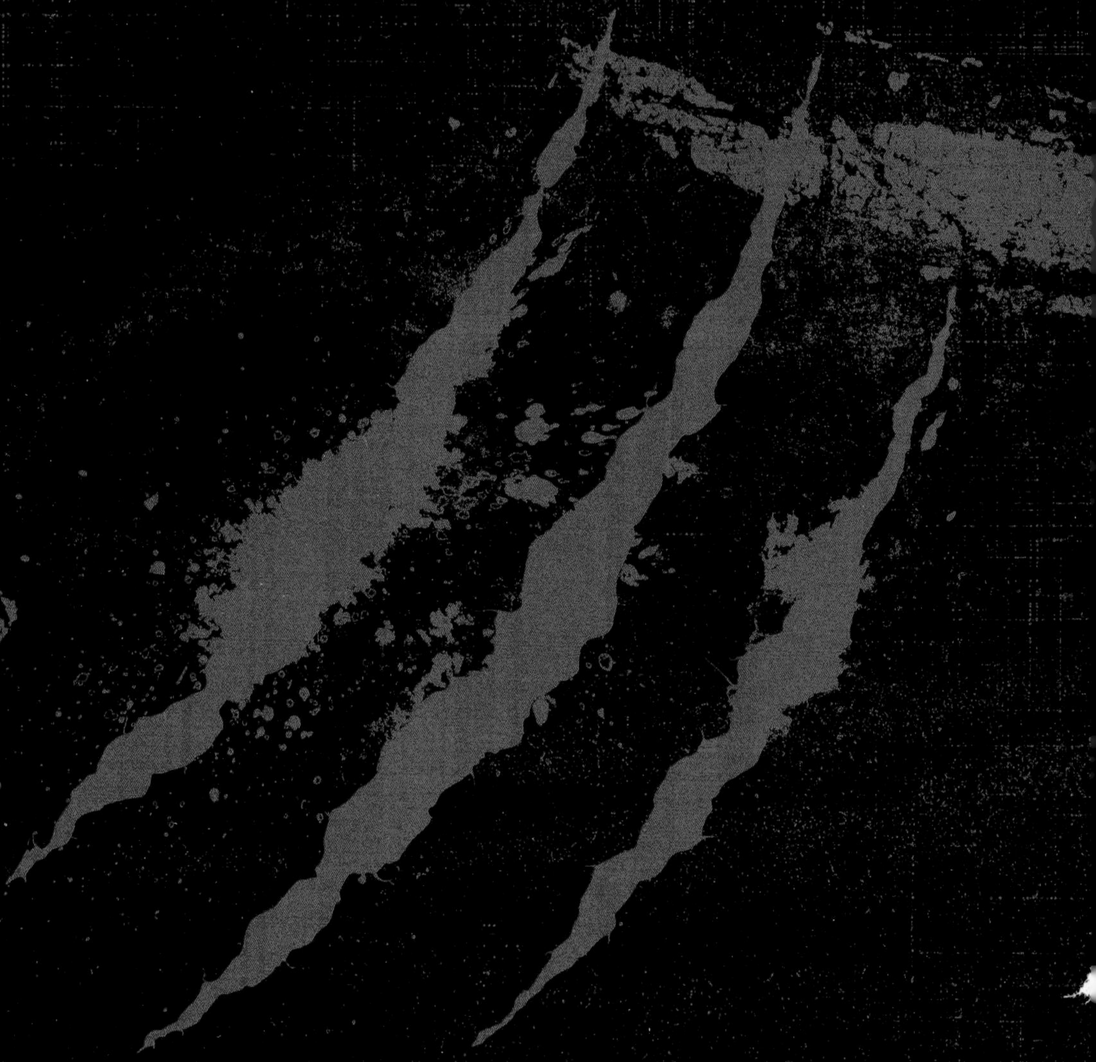